Social Decision Making/Social Problem Solving for Middle School Students

Skills and Activities for Academic, Social, and Emotional Success

Maurice J. Elias

Linda Bruene Butler

GRADES 6-8

Research Press • 2612 North Mattis Avenue, Champaign, Illinois 61822
(800) 519-2707 • www.researchpress.com

Copies of this book may be ordered from Research Press at the address given on the title page.

Composition by Jeff Helgesen
Cover design by Linda Brown, Positive I.D. Graphic Design, Inc.
Printed by McNaughton & Gunn, Inc.

ISBN 0-87822-514-5

Library of Congress Control Number 2004115931

Contents

Worksheets and Exhibits

WORKSHEETS

EXHIBITS

Acknowledgments

As our work enters its third decade, we look back with amazement and gratitude at the hundreds of colleagues who have been instrumental in the development of our work. We cannot possibly mention them all, but we hold them all in our hearts with tremendous gratitude and admiration. Those whose role in getting the SDM/SPS work started deserve special mention. These are Myrna Shure, George Spivack, and Steve Larcen, who generously shared their initial work with Interpersonal Cognitive Problem Solving, and Tom Schuyler, John Clabby, and Charlotte Hett, whose collaboration, vision, commitment, and enthusiasm in the first decade of the work helped it flourish despite many obstacles.

In subsequent years, we have been blessed with being able to work with many talented colleagues who have taught us so much and lent their expertise to our work. Again, there are too many to name, but we want to note several whose ongoing work with us has gone above and beyond any reasonable expectation and whose ideas have come to mesh with our own in ways very hard to disentangle. These include Jacqueline Norris, Phil Brown, Vicki Poedubicky, Judy Lerner, Lois Brown, Frank Fehn, Karen Welland, Bruce Ettinger, Larry Leverett, Joseph Sperlazza, and Robin Stern. Linda would like to give special acknowledgment to Bruce Stout of University of Medicine and Dentistry of New Jersey–University Behavioral Health Care for his continuing mentorship and tangible and logistical support, and Maurice would like to extend the same to Lew Gantwerk of Graduate School of Applied and Professional Psychology–Center for Applied Psychology.

We also mention with deep appreciation and awe Erin Bruno, Maureen Papke, and Teresa Shapiro, who tangibly assisted us in compiling this volume and who carry the legacy of SDM/SPS work so brilliantly every day. They, along with other long-time SDM/SPS staff members Jeff Kress, Carl Preto, Lisa Blum, Margo Hunter, Mary Ellen Taylor, Ronda Jones, and Deborah Mosley, as well as Steven Tobias and Brian Friedlander, have developed the ideas that appear in our curriculum in the spirit of continuous improvement.

Finally, we thank the remarkable team at Research Press, who believe in our work so deeply and care so much about how it is presented to the world. Ann Wendel, Russ Pence, Karen Steiner, Dennis Wizeicki, Hilary Powers (our capable freelance copyeditor), and an incredibly talented production staff have made it possible to put our best work forward and provide materials to our colleagues in schools about which we are very, very proud. The effort represented in this curriculum will have the ultimate effect of helping children, and that is the point of all of our work.

A personal note from Maurice: I am filled with gratitude for so many people, immediate and extended family, friends, close colleagues, and amazing students, past and present, who have been so supportive of my work. Your contributions, tangible and intangible, have made the best of this work better and have helped keep me refreshed, enthused, and ready to persist and create in the service of improving kids' lives. A special thank you to cherished friend, source of mirth and chocolate, and collaborator Ed Dunkelblau; the incredible team at the Collaborative for Academic, Social, and Emotional Learning; my parents, Agnes and Sol; my in-laws, Myra and Lou Rosen; and last, and most of all, my wife, Ellen, and daughters Sara Elizabeth and Samara Alexandra—all three of whom are my best sources of feedback, support, and kvelling.

A personal note from Linda: I would like to thank Dr. John Gottman for his mentoring and making me so aware at an early and foundational stage of my career of the critical importance of a child's social and emotional competency. I also want to thank my amazing circle of family and friends for all of their love and support and for so richly filling the much too little time I have to play. My inner-circle family support group includes my mothers, Joan and Edna; my Aunt Marcy; Kay; Joannetta and Mern; my twin sister, Laura, and sisters Diane, Carrie, Linda Bruene II, Jane, Pat, Jeannie, Jennifer, and Amy; my brothers, John and Bob, and my uncles, Mike and Bud. I could not work or survive without my amazing circle of friends, which includes Nancy, Andrew, Annette, Val, Lois, Lizzie, Howard, Freddie, Donna, Sandra, Riki, Vicky, and Teff. Last of all, thanks to my loving husband, Chris, who continues to capture my respect for his emotional intelligence, and to my most adoring buddy/golden retriever, Josh.

Introduction

Do you remember when you were in middle school yourself? Can you picture what you were like? What your friends were like? Can you get an image of your school? What was a typical day like? What were the teachers like? Equally important, what can you recall about your neighborhood and home situation, about your before- and after-school worlds? Some people believe that we have been given mercifully little accurate recall of what our days were like as early adolescents. It is an awkward, confusing time. The world is opening up to young adolescents in so many ways—and so are their bodies, their minds, and their responsibilities. Into this volatile mix, we are placing unprecedented demands for academic learning. Of course, this is important, but try to recall what academics meant to you when you were of middle school age. Academics had to fit into a larger context of figuring out who you were, who you wanted to be, and what your friends, teachers, parents, and other relatives wanted you to be.

You probably can remember some adults, perhaps teachers or counselors, who seemed to understand you and what you were going through. They made demands on you to learn and grow, but somehow their demands felt different. They were worthwhile, sometimes fun, and they usually seemed to make sense to you. Plus, these adults always seemed to care about you as a person, not just as a student. They could listen to your stories, your woes with your friends, your emerging issues with boys or girls, and your concern with style, fashion, what's "in" and "cool" and what's not, and they could deal with your energy or lack of it.

This curriculum guide is grounded in activities developed by educators and other school-based professionals who share vivid, realistic memories and present-day perspectives on what it is like to be a child in middle school. Their awareness, combined with deep concern over the before- and after-school life of early adolescents today, has motivated them to work to build middle school students' social-emotional skills, social decision making and social problem solving skills, life skills, and character. Unless opportunities are provided, through both the school and the home, too many young adolescents will wind up as social casualties and never fulfill their potential.

Like the preschool period, which should prepare children for a good start in their schooling, the middle school period is a crucial point in children's life trajectories. For many, young adolescence is a time to move their identities in positive and hopeful directions—or to enter negative, downward spirals. The primary dynamics of dropping out of school, for example, seem to be set during the middle school years. It is a time when the skills necessary for adult citizenship and for productive involvement in community, family, and economic life are being developed.

EVIDENCE-BASED APPLICATIONS OF SOCIAL DECISION MAKING/SOCIAL PROBLEM SOLVING

Individuals working with middle school students already devote time and concern to the issues of social-emotional skills, how everyday decisions are made and problems are solved, and the many other skills young adolescents need in their school and home lives. There is a shared concern with preventing violence, drug and alcohol use, smoking, inappropriate sexual behavior, delinquency, school failure and dropout, and, of course, acquired immune deficiency syndrome (AIDS) and other sexually transmitted diseases. This curriculum presents applications of the award-winning social decision making approach that has been approved by the National Goals Panel and the Expert Panel on Safe, Drug Free Schools of the U.S. Department of Education; the National Association of School Psychologists; the Collaborative for Academic, Social, and Emotional Learning (www.CASEL.org); and the Character Education Partnership. The social decision making/social problem solving (SDM/SPS) approach is featured because of its exceptional promise, its link to academic and social areas, its emphasis on critical thinking, and the ease with which it can be infused into already ongoing middle school activities, curricula, and programs. Indeed, it is aligned well with national and state standards in the areas of health, social studies and civics, school and classroom climate and safety, bullying and violence or victimization prevention, substance abuse prevention, and literacy promotion in all its various forms (print, media, and interpersonal and social cues).

HOW TO USE THE MATERIALS IN THIS MANUAL

The materials in this book are designed to complement and blend with the programs and practices already in place in middle schools. Think of them as a vitamin supplement, or a fuel additive for your car. They are designed to boost performance by providing the latest in the pedagogy of successful practice in SDM/SPS, social-emotional learning

(SEL), and character education. While they are based on the principles of SDM/SPS, the activities and lessons included here are compatible with any high-quality SEL or character education program. Above all, they help make links to literacy and academic performance and increase engagement in school by reaching a broad spectrum of learners, including those with the special education classifications of emotional disturbance, social maladjustment, behavior disorder, and related conditions.

In the Classroom

Middle school teachers realize the unique concerns of contemporary early adolescents. This group is not the same as its predecessors in earlier generations. Its members are media-fed and come from households that are under great stress. The sources of this stress can vary immensely, from the deprivations of poverty to the pressures and distractions of great wealth and everywhere in between. Today's middle schoolers can be affected by such demands as two-income families, economic uncertainty, and, for tens of thousands of children, the uprootedness that can accompany parental calls to military service or reserve duty.

Among the most important skills students need are strategies for responsible decision making and problem solving. Any child without these skills will be left behind, regardless of intellectual gifts. Lesson formats for building these skills in classrooms are provided in Part 1. Something else the literature makes clear is that many children have a difficult time adjusting to middle school. Its logistics and procedures can seem daunting, and the nature of academic demands is often qualitatively as well as quantitatively different from previous schooling for many students. Part 1 also provides teachers with procedures to give students essential middle school survival skills, including locker management, notebook organization, and study skills.

Shouldn't students have these abilities prior to entry into middle school? Absolutely. Can't they learn them quickly once they enter middle school? Certainly. But the reality is that many children don't have the skills and don't learn them well. Estimates from the research suggest that 25 percent of students start a negative trajectory in middle school, even after having no problems in the elementary years, for lack of organizational and study skills. And it is likely that at least another 25 percent have inadequacies in these skills that hold them back significantly from reaching their academic potential. Even more students are simply hampered and distracted by deficiencies in knowing how to study, prepare for projects, and manage time well (Blythe, Simmons, & Carlton-Ford, 1983; Dryfoos, 1998).

In a Counseling and Group Context

Perhaps more than students of any other age group, middle schoolers are sensitive to stigma. And few things are more stigmatizing than going to counseling or therapy groups in school.

The approaches in this volume provide a way around this problem that is empowering, fun, and effective. By creating groups in which students can be valued contributors and do something useful, interesting, and productive, school professionals will find themselves better able to teach the skills that students need. Whether the focus is anger management, assertiveness, group interaction, emotional self-control, or nonverbal cue recognition, skills can be taught in ways that maximally preserve the students' dignity. Various activities prepare them to be citizens inside and outside school, to develop video documentaries and public-service announcements to share with others, and to engage in cross-disciplinary projects to look into current environmental, political, or moral-ethical questions. These activities inspire students to want to learn the skills so that they can participate in accomplishing the task or taking advantage of the opportunity laid out before them. Thus the various activities in Parts 1 and 2 can be transformed into structures for group counseling or classroom-based advisory or guidance activities.

OVERVIEW OF CONTENTS

Part 1 gives background that is common to the whole program and all the instructional procedures in this volume. Chapter 1 begins with an overview of developmental issues in middle school children, taking into account the changes occurring in our fast-paced, increasingly technological and information-oriented society. Chapter 2 presents an overview of the social decision making pedagogy. Here readers can learn about key social and life skills required for middle school students' positive development in academic and interpersonal areas as well as about strategies used to instruct children in everyday critical thinking and problem solving.

Part 2 begins, in Chapter 3, with materials that allow students to learn basic skills for SDM/SPS, including a strategy to use when making decisions and solving problems in both interpersonal and academic areas. The term *FIG TESPN* is used as an acronym for this strategy, and it has been found to be appealing to all children—and especially so to at-risk students. The acronym stands for the following steps:

F — Feelings cue me to problem solve.

I — Identify the problem.

G — Goals give me a guide.

T — Think of many possible solutions.

E — Envision outcomes.

S — Select the best solution.

P — Plan the procedure, anticipate pitfalls, and practice.

N — Notice what happened and remember it for next time.

The materials show how to get a middle school group or class ready for social decision making and social problem solving activities, how to use FIG TESPN to solve a problem or make a decision, and how to apply FIG TESPN to diverse social situations and academic areas.

Chapter 4 provides activities designed to help students entering middle school learn basic survival skills. As noted earlier, researchers in the United States and other countries have found that up to 25 percent of students entering middle school encounter serious difficulty, largely because they are not prepared for the differences between elementary and middle school. These difficulties are responsible for thousands of discipline referrals each year, creating a major drain on and disruption of education at the middle school and also making negative contributions to students' emerging identities. This chapter presents self-organization and study skills activities for use with students during their first year in middle school. The practical, enjoyable materials include ways of helping students organize their lockers and manage their mass of papers, keep track of assignments, study in appropriate places and in reasonable ways, and integrate and apply their skills through cooperative small-group activities.

Part 3 contains specific materials designed for use by those who wish to focus on infusion of social decision making and social skills development into academic instruction. And, in reality, that needs to be everyone, including those in counseling roles. Counseling broadly focused on social-emotional, interpersonal, academic, and media literacy will find itself much better accepted and supported in schools than counseling limited to purely psychological issues. Specific application areas focus on history, current events, civics, and democracy education (Chapter 5), language arts literacy (Chapter 6), media literacy (Chapter 7), and projects related to the environment, other disciplinary issues, and current issues and problems facing schools and communities (Chapter 8). The units on media literacy provide activities that guide students to work with the revolution in media, communication, and video technologies and harness the power of television to improve students' social decision making and its application to media and other areas. This approach, which has shown particular success with students who have behavioral and emotional disturbances and learning disabilities, transforms students into active consumers and shapers of the media. It helps them exercise critical thinking muscles instead of passively accepting media messages at face value. This application of SDM/SPS pedagogy represents genuine empowerment of students at all levels.

In Part 4, supports for instruction and the overall quality and effectiveness of programs are addressed. Activities are presented in three focal areas: genuine engagement of parents in education (Chapter 9), and creating multicultural awareness so students are ready to make decisions and solve problems in the sophisticated, diverse world that awaits them (Chapter 10).

All professionals have a moral, ethical, and practical obligation to understand the impact of what they are doing and to work to improve their effectiveness. In Chapter 11, we provide practical, easy-to-use tools to monitor and evaluate a range of middle school programs in the social decision making and life skills areas. The emphasis is on consumer satisfaction—for students, teachers, and administrators—and on taking information about the impact of the activities and using that information to improve the activities and refine their use to reach more students more effectively.

RESOURCES

The area of SDM/SPS and its related fields, social-emotional learning, emotional intelligence, character education, and service learning, are in a constant state of growth, and new materials and resources are becoming available all the time. The most reliable sources of information on these materials and resources can be found at the following Web sites. At these sites or their links, you will find not only ideas but downloadable materials to support your instructional and counseling work based in SDM/SPS.

- www.CASEL.org: Collaborative for Academic, Social, and Emotional Learning
- www.Character.org: Character Education Partnership
- www.nprinc.com: National Professional Resources, Incorporated
- www.ESRNational.org: Educators for Social Responsibility/Resolving Conflicts Creatively
- www.tolerance.org: Teaching Tolerance Resource Center
- www.Communitiesofhope.org: HOPE Foundation for Harnessing Optimism, Potential, and Excellence
- www.GLEF.org: George Lucas Educational Foundation
- www.6Seconds.org: 6 Seconds and Nexus Emotional Intelligence Services and Conferences

- <u>www.CSEE.net</u>: Center for Social and Emotional Education, focusing on special education
- <u>www.EIConsortium.org</u>: Consortium for Research on Emotional Intelligence in Organizations

Part 1

Development and Pedagogy of Early Adolescents

1 Developmental Issues and Key Skills for Social and Academic Growth

- A high school diploma is a dead end that won't get me anywhere anyway.
- I can't afford to stay in school because I have to earn money (or help take care of my family).
- I feel lousy when I am in school: Nobody cares for me, I'm not important, everyone's better than me in what counts, and they won't miss me if I go.
- The school people don't really want me there; they suspend me for everything and they keep asking when I am going to be sixteen and wouldn't I like to get a job and earn some money.
- I can't stay at school and take care of my baby at the same time.

The troubled voices of many students of middle and high school age around the country indicate that forceful action is needed to ensure that current and future generations possess the skills they will require to be healthy, productive, and satisfied members of adult society. These situations, drawn from the work of Michelle Fine (1986), represent different routes traveled by students on the way toward dropping out of school. Middle school is a critical stage in students' journey toward success in school and life. It is the time when they develop an identity about themselves and their future. By the time they get ready to leave middle school, many students have a strong sense of their own level of competence and what the future may or may not hold for them. They also have a clear sense of how, if at all, school fits into their future.

Students must be prepared for the tests of life—not just a life of tests. Academic and social-emotional development are intertwined and interrelated. Teachers cannot expect to develop academic skills without also developing students' skills for getting along with others in different contexts as well as for understanding themselves (Elias, 2003). Some recognition of these issues has been part of the impetus for educational reform and school restructuring efforts in recent years. These are most clearly reflected in health and social studies standards, initiatives in character education and bullying and violence prevention, and the continued growth of evidence-based programs in social-emotional learning.

Attempts at educational reform must have goals. Yet these goals must not increase the distance between students within and among our schools and communities, a distance that is more than just intellectual (Crabbe, 1989; Eisner, 2003; London, 1987). There seems to be consensus that middle school is an optimal time to reach out to students before the distance between them and the social mainstream becomes irrevocable, and disaffected or disruptive students turn into dropouts. But this is not a matter for leisurely attention; patterns of disaffection or disruption in grades five through eight are widespread and suggestive of a high level of risk for disengagement with the learning process. This is an outcome just as devastating as formally dropping out of school, and actually can be more insidious because of its relatively low visibility (Carnegie Council on Adolescent Development, 1989).

ALL IS NOT WELL WITH STUDENTS' WELL-BEING

Indeed, evidence is abundant that—despite increases in material possessions and improvements on many indicators of health and safety, the mental health and well-being of adolescents is not showing corresponding improvement. The Centers for Disease Control and Prevention survey in 1999 showed that 64 percent of American high school students had smoked at least once, 28.5 percent were current smokers, and 29.1 percent smoked six cigarettes on the days that they smoked (CDC, 2000). In the United States, the majority of high school students have tried alcohol, 81 percent having had at least one drink in their lifetime. Even more alarming, 13 percent have driven a vehicle one or more times after drinking alcohol, and 32 percent reported episodic heavy drinking during the past month. Among U.S. adolescents, 27 percent used marijuana during the past month and 10 percent had used cocaine at least once (Kahn et al., 2000). And in 1997, approximately one in five arrests made by U.S. law enforcement agencies involved a person under the age of eighteen. Juveniles accounted for 37 percent of burglary arrests, 30 percent of robbery arrests, 24 percent of weapons arrests, 14 percent of drug arrests, and 5 percent of violent crimes (Snyder & Sickmund, 1999). What makes these statistics especially important is the recognition that the trajectory for problems in adolescence begins in middle school (Haggerty, Sherrod, Garmezy, & Rutter, 1994).

Thus the Carnegie Council on Adolescent Development (1989) has labeled the middle school years as a turning point for good reason. Students are reaching a series of developmental crossroads that make this a critical period for their future life courses. Among the points of intersection are the following:

- Transition to middle school marks a time of increased referral to mental health services.

- Events of puberty combine with cognitive and social development changes to make middle school transition quite complex. Lots of things are happening at once, more than during any other general school-related transition.

- The change from elementary to middle school is mainly a qualitative change; the change from middle to high school is mostly a quantitative change.

- Rates of smoking, alcohol, drug, and violence problems that appear to peak in the high school really have their start in the middle school. The same is true with school dropout rates and disaffection.

- Girls suffer particular damage to self-esteem and seem to lose interest and confidence in math- and science-related subject areas and careers, largely due to social pressures they experience during middle school years.

As we look at the national educational debate, there is a distressing absence of discussion of the unique needs of middle school students. Rather, the talk seems to center on students' academic achievement, as if this somehow is of primary concern to all students at all times and, more centrally, as if all that matters about adolescents is their role as students and future employees. Thus amid all of the emphasis on what kinds of "world-class" students our nation's schools should turn out, we run the risk of losing a more encompassing focus: encouraging the development of *world-class people.*

The Consortium on the School-Based Promotion of Social Competence (1991) offers one vision of the kinds of skills that can help middle schoolers become world-class people—and students. They should:

- Possess a positive sense of self-worth.

- Feel capable as they interact with others and take on new developmental tasks and challenges.

- Behave ethically and act responsibly toward others.

- Develop sound work habits, motivation, and values.

- Have a perspective on the future that provides a source of positive direction and energy.

- Appreciate the benefits of a multiracial society and respect the values of others.

- Be skilled in interpersonal encounters and communication, get along with others, and develop long-term interpersonal relationships.

- Engage in health-enhancing and health-protective behaviors.

- Be motivated to become productive citizens by serving as positive, contributing members of their peer group, family, school, and community.

- Avoid engaging in behavior that may lead to negative consequences such as substance abuse, unwanted teen pregnancy, AIDS, social isolation, serious physical injury, school dropout, depression, suicide, unemployment, or criminal prosecution.

How young adolescents cope with what happens to them during the middle school years is determined in large part by the skills they bring into problematic situations, their ability to use available resources, and the outreach of those resources to them (Masten, Best, & Garmezy, 1990). Taking this broad vision and then taking a closer look at early adolescence can lead to a refocusing on educational issues for this pivotal age group. Moreover, it can serve to redirect our attention away from an overemphasis on academics that is likely to result in poorer overall achievement and greater problems among our students than is currently the case (Wynne & Walberg, 1986).

DEVELOPMENTAL TASKS OF EARLY ADOLESCENCE

Early adolescence—the middle school years, ages ten to fourteen or thereabouts—is most obviously a time of intense physical change. This includes a growth spurt, a reduction in "baby fat," and the appearance of secondary sex characteristics related to the onset of puberty. Perhaps most significant are the varying rates at which all of these changes occur, both for a given child and across students. This means that the middle school child can look like an elementary school child, a high school child, or anywhere in between. As students see their schoolmates reach various milestones at different times, they inevitably make comparisons and, all too often, see themselves as deficient. As a result, middle school students can seem moody, unpredictable, and a bit illogical. (In other words, they seem a lot like the adults most of us deal with on a day-to-day basis!)

Dorman and Lipsitz (1984) declare that it is a myth that adolescence should be defined as a period of stress, turmoil, and rebellion, and the evidence certainly bears them out. Nevertheless, early adolescents must work through certain developmental tasks on their path toward adulthood, and these certainly can be sources of both exhilaration and consternation (Dorman & Lipsitz, 1984; Elias, Tobias, & Friedlander, 2002; Lipsitz, 1980).

Cognitive Factors

Early adolescence is a time of cognitive awakening. Students awaken to the world of possibility and potential, of abstract thinking, and going from the specific to the general. They retain a certain egocentrism, which leads them to believe they are unique, special, even invulnerable to harm. At the same time, these students worry about the great anonymous "they" and what "they" think. To help them deal with the vast cognitive awakening they are experiencing, early adolescents often see things in black and white or "good-bad" terms. This leads to the possibilities of catastrophizing, denial, and overgeneralization. Nevertheless, it is marvelous to see their increased social concern, the very beginnings of their realization that what they do in the present will make a difference in what they will be able to do in the future, and the innocent exuberance they bring to so many of life's issues and challenges.

Personality Factors

Early adolescence represents a time during which there is still a good deal of experimentation with possible identities, without a real sense that the activity fits into a future plan. That means, of course, that many students do not view school as systematically related to their future life goals or options. Erik Erikson (1954) noted that a sense of "industriousness" characteristic of early adolescence can be seen both in a strong orientation to certain tasks and in a faddish commitment to certain things for relatively short periods of time. This partly explains why middle school students can be such avid collectors. It is important during the middle school years for students to achieve some sense of mastery in one or more activities in which they are displaying their industriousness. Of course, that does not automatically translate into motivation relating to school achievement. Having the best baseball card or DVD collection may be more than sufficient for some students.

Relationship Factors

There is no doubt that peer relationships begin to increase in their importance and influence during the early adolescent years. Yet teachers, as well as parents and other adults, must not be lulled into thinking that their influence as role models and sources of advice is in any way diminished. What often tends to occur is that students may be less likely to admit or acknowledge this influence during the middle school years than they might have been in prior years. This means that the role of being a source of support will often be quite thankless or even downright frustrating. However, it can be a lifeline for youth who otherwise would derive most of their views from their peers. Part of the emerging emphasis on relationships is differential tendencies toward sexual relationships. Some middle schoolers are dating; others view members of the opposite sex as entities from different and often inferior biological strata.

As most parents can attest, the telephone, e-mail, and instant messaging, which paradoxically allow both distance and closeness, become major relationship tools during early adolescence. Without the added pressure and salience of visual contact, middle school students can share thoughts and feelings that they would be less likely to share in person. These ways of communicating become part of what enables the development of more sustained, sharing, personal, and responsive friendships than most students will have had in the past. Yet there still will be short-term shifts in peer relationships, as the cognitive tendencies noted earlier allow someone to be a friend today, an enemy tomorrow, and a friend the day after. Overall, it is fair to say that middle school represents a time when peer relationships gain great influence, and everyone involved—students, educators, and family members—must be prepared to deal with this realignment of relationships.

AN INTEGRATIVE PERSPECTIVE: DEVELOPMENTAL TASKS AND EMERGING IDENTITIES

Increasingly, child development experts are turning their attention toward the developmental needs that accompany young adolescents' attempts at establishing a personal identity and coping with the middle school and then the high school (Damon, 1988; Dorman, 1984; Dorman & Lipsitz, 1984; Elias et al., 2002; Gullotta, Adams, & Montemayor, 1990; Kessler, 2000). These needs can be looked at as features that should be nurtured by school and home settings. The nine features listed in this section appear most important. To the extent that they are absent, a child can be considered at risk for school failure and dropout; to the extent to which a child does not appear to be motivated to engage in or benefit from opportunities in these areas, that child may be viewed as disaffected. Engaging in negative forms of the features numbered 3, 5, 6, and 8 indicates that a child is likely to be a disruptive force in the school.

1. *Self-exploration.* Young adolescents are engaged in the task of figuring out how they can, should, and want to relate to their family, friends, and school. They explore by trying on different roles and patterns of behavior, often those that they see modeled by their peers. This can lead to some behaviors that adults, both parents and teachers, find upsetting. However, these explorations are often short-lived; they can be likened to trying on clothes in a fitting room.

2. *Diversity.* Since adolescents are really just trying on roles as part of their self-exploration, it is important to offer them routines, instruction, curriculum, and topics that reflect some diversity.

3. *Structure and clear limits.* In schools and families, the act of exploration is aided by having the security of clear limits and boundaries. What the Center for Early Adolescence finds, though, is that things go more smoothly when students feel some involvement in how the structure and limits are set up—something that is not always acceptable to educators and parents.

4. *A sense of competence.* Schools have the job of selling academic (and other) competencies. This task should be approached in a way that helps students emerge from the middle school with some improved skills but, above all, with a sense of competence about learning and about themselves that is strong enough to provide vital momentum as they enter high school.

5. *Meaningful participation and a clear sense of belonging.* Alongside young adolescents' know-it-all and independent ways of behaving is a realization that they are not adults and need some guidance in how to carry out adult roles and responsibilities. Much of this comes from being able to feel that they genuinely belong to and are valued by school and family. This occurs in a number of ways, but most often by being able to be true participants in ongoing tasks, long-range projects, or other engaging activities that include adults either directly or as visible leaders. Teens need groups to belong to. That's what motivates some to join gangs. They are looking for places where they:

   - Have a role

   - Feel a sense of purpose

   - Discover positive peer relationships

   - Join others who have similar interests or abilities

   - Learn things

   - Experience inspiring leadership

   - Find a safe, comfortable, accepting place to be

6. *Positive social interaction.* During young adolescence, students begin to go through puberty. Too many adults have forgotten how

involved they were with their social appearance and social status during these years. Some of the situations we put ourselves into were uncomfortable then and even embarrassing to recall now; faulty memory of them can become a merciful convenience. Schools cannot ignore the importance of helping students become socially skilled in their dealings with peers and with adults (with whom they will have to negotiate extensively to get permission, transportation, funding, and so on to do what they want to with peers). If students are preoccupied with their social difficulties, they will not be available mentally or emotionally to absorb, retain, and creatively use the learning opportunities they receive at school and at home.

7. *Appreciation.* What is the most cherished talent of each of your students? Maybe you see it in their hobbies. Maybe you don't see it because it happens in the privacy of their rooms or only with trusted friends. Be alert to what it is your students really like to do and seem good at. It might be math, science, languages, writing, computers, creating media, art, music, getting along with other people, sports, dance, outdoor activities, sailing, selling—the list is endless. Howard Gardner refers to the "multiple intelligences" as the range of talents that students have; their future identities are strengthened when they have positive outlets to express and develop these talents (Blythe & Gardner, 1990). Giving your teens a chance to discover and develop their talents is a bit tricky and sometimes leads to a dead end, but these efforts can make a life-changing difference. Regardless of their success, your appreciation of the efforts matters more than you might think.

8. *A commitment to good health.* There is little that we can pass along to students that is more important to their sense of competence and to their ability to learn, to perform tasks, and to develop positive relationships than a commitment to good health. This involves, in the middle school years, positively channeling their needs for frequent physical activity, their enjoyment of competition, and their developing physical skills and coordination. It also includes addressing middle schoolers' questions about trying on roles that involve health-compromising and high-risk behaviors such as smoking, drinking, taking drugs, engaging in premature sexual intercourse, delinquency and vandalism, and living in the real world with only limited education.

9. *Contribution.* Teens may appear to be self-centered, but that is really because the teen years are so much about self-discovery, not really about selfishness—unless we allow it to go in that direction. Teens actually thrive on helping, on making contributions to causes, saving the environment, helping senior citizens, teaching what they know to younger, needier kids, working in soup

kitchens, helping in political campaigns, raising funds for people who are suffering, helping their religious institutions reach their charitable goals. Contributions are part of what helps teens—and adults—feel a sense of fulfillment. And this sense of fulfillment and importance actually is strong enough to compete with the thrill of far more antisocial influences.

A PSYCHOLOGY OF ADOLESCENCE FOR A GLOBALLY INTERDEPENDENT WORLD

It is important to take a visionary look at adolescence in the twenty-first century. Educators and other developmentalists are rethinking the pathway that students take to arrive at adolescence, as well as the nature of the destination. Traditional views of the psychology of adolescence and the attainment of identity are being rethought. In American culture, it has been traditional to place movement toward greater autonomy and independence, particularly as relates to one's parents, as a desirable aspect of establishing identity. However, Carol Gilligan (1987) and others have expressed a view of identity that seems compatible with current social realities and still puts many of the high-risk and health-compromising behaviors in which adolescents engage in a new perspective. Identity does not incorporate autonomy as much as it involves self-regulation; further, adolescents need to incorporate into their identities values and behaviors consistent with interdependence and commitment. The latter notions are highly consistent with Erikson's view of the postadolescent stages of intimacy and generativity, as well as with a perspective on the future that emphasizes global interdependence and cultural diversity. It does not mesh well with the view that adolescence is about independence.

Kolbe (1985) has astutely pointed out that independent health decisions are in fact mediated through social relationships and therefore can in no real sense be viewed as autonomous. If a teenager smokes, it affects others. If a middle school student goes off alone and drinks beer in the park, or does so with a few friends, there are clear ramifications for parent-child and other familial relationships. Eating habits may lead to distractible or lethargic, inattentive behaviors, with an impact on peer and teacher relationships in school. The results of these health decisions and behaviors illustrate that interdependence, rather than independence, should be a focus in adolescence. It is likely that negative feedback will come to the child from peers, parents, and teachers. While directed at the distressing health behavior, such feedback is not differentiated by the young adolescent from disapproval or rejection of the child *as a person*. The resulting dynamic serves to energize what Adler (1927) called a "vicious cycle," characterized by withdrawal, further negative behavior, derivation of support from a similarly distressed peer group, and a deepening sense of alienation and low self-worth.

This perspective is highly consistent with empirical findings. Research on students during the middle school period provides no compelling evidence to suggest that independence promotes positive health and school adjustment (Gullotta et al., 1990; Irwin, 1987). Indeed, as developmentalists consider the pathway toward adolescence, there is increasing reconsideration being given to a view of Piaget's (1984) that has been lost in recent years: affect, cognition, and social relationships are inextricably linked, reflecting what Piaget refers to as "dissociability." This reassessment carries with it significant implications. Sound development requires the coordinated growth of caring, attachment, commitment, discernment, reasoning, decision making, and other related attributes.

MIDDLE SCHOOLS: SETTING SAIL TOWARD ADULTHOOD WITH MINIMAL SOCIAL CASUALTIES

Hamburg (1990) has written eloquently that the social foundation necessary to provide guidance to many students in their attempts to develop social and academic competence and to carve out an interdependent identity can no longer be presumed to exist in the normal course of childhood experiences. Relationships between adults and students have changed as adults' relationships to the workplace, their communities, and each other have changed. The skills needed to cope effectively with everyday life challenges must be taught and explicitly nurtured, if we are to avoid turning too many students into social casualties.

Thus, on the voyage to academic excellence, we must not lose the child as a person. The middle school years represent a particularly tricky set of currents and choppy seas during which many students can get thrown overboard. Unlike students in the elementary school years, middle schoolers are not being watched so vigilantly that their departures are always noticed immediately. Unlike high school students, they often lack the wherewithal to get the attention of the captain and crew, or to somehow clamber back onto the boat. We must equip all middle schools with handholds throughout and lifelines around the ship, extending far into the sea for those who do fall overboard. Among the most important handholds and lifelines are social decision making skills.

The social decision making and social problem solving approaches that are provided in this book are directed at meeting the needs of young adolescents as they have just been described. These children's capacity to respond to situations they find themselves in with peers, teachers, and parents, and their ability to think clearly and make decisions under stress, affects their ability to handle the problematic areas, both small and large, that they will inevitably face. Their ability to handle these problems—not in isolation but in partnership with classmates and adults in their lives—exercises considerable influence on their identity as capable, confident, interdependent, worthwhile, and perhaps even world-class people.

2   The Pedagogy for Building Lasting Skills

If students are to experience healthy relationships and occupy meaningful and productive roles in society as adults, they must be competent at communicating and working cooperatively with others. They need to be able to express their own opinions and beliefs, to understand and appreciate the perspectives of others who differ from them in background, needs, or experiences, and to become skilled at reasoned disagreement, negotiation, and compromise as methods of solving problems when their own needs or interests conflict with those of others. Indeed, in the face of decreasing resources and increasing global interdependence, it can be argued that such qualities are essential to human survival. The question, then, is not *whether* we must enhance students' social competencies but rather *how* to accomplish this goal (Battistich, Elias, & Branden-Muller, 1992, p. 231).

SOCIAL DECISION MAKING, SOCIAL SKILLS, AND LIFE SKILLS DEVELOPMENT

The Social Decision Making/Social Problem Solving (SDM/SPS) program is an evidence-based approach to building the skills students need if they are to attend school mentally alert, ready to learn, and ready to contribute to their classrooms, families, and communities. It has been recognized as a Promising Program by the U.S. Department of Education's Expert Panel on Safe and Drug Free Schools and by the Character Education Partnership, as a Model Program by the National Education Goals Panel and the National Association of School Psychologists, and as a "Select SEL" program by the Collaborative for Academic, Social, and Emotional Learning (www.CASEL.org). SDM/SPS is considered a social-emotional learning program—that is, one of a grouping of programs designed to build students' emotional intelligence skills as a way of maximizing their academic potential and chances for success in school and life (Elias, Zins et al., 1997). Such programs are characterized by strong empirical support and a highly effective, social learning based pedagogy to ensure successful use in classroom or group contexts (Bruene-Butler, Hampson, Elias, Clabby,

& Schuyler, 1997; Elias, Gara, Schuyler, Branden-Muller, & Sayette, 1991; Elias, Rothbaum, & Gara, 1986; Elias & Tobias, 1996). SDM/SPS approaches are being used by educators (and parents) throughout the United States and in countries around the world.

In the middle school, SDM/SPS does not take the form of a formal, yearlong series of lessons. Instead, we have found it best to use modules that fit flexibly into existing curricula and instruction and school routines and practices. Under the No Child Left Behind legislation and given the increased movement toward character education and social-emotional learning, many schools have programs or program elements in place. *One great strength of SDM/SPS in the middle school is how smoothly it fits into current academic and counseling activities.* It presents "FIG TESPN," an acronym for a problem-solving strategy that middle school students remember and enjoy. They are also taught an essential readiness skill: emotional self-control that enables them to stop and think before acting impulsively and makes it possible for them to allow themselves to use their SDM/SPS skills. Gradually, students deepen and extend these skills and their applications, beginning to learn how to manage difficult choices when they are under peer pressure and other kinds of stress. So fortified, students are able to be effective learners and citizens in the many communities of which they are a part. They learn both social-emotional skills and life skills, and they learn how to use them when no adults are around to prompt or assist them.

WHAT ARE SOCIAL DECISION MAKING/SOCIAL PROBLEM SOLVING SKILLS?

Competence in SDM/SPS is consistent with what many have defined as essential skills for students' development (Collaborative for Academic, Social, and Emotional Learning, 2003; Dodge, Pettit, McClaskey, & Brown, 1986; National Mental Health Association, 1986; Rutter, 1987; Spivack & Shure, 1974). Entering a third decade of work with many dozens of schools, hundreds of educators and parents, and thousands and thousands of students, as of the time of this writing, we have identified a core set of skills that truly matter for students' social and academic growth and success. We have divided these skills into three key areas:

- *Self-Control Skills.* These are skills necessary for accurate processing of social information, for delay of behavior long enough to engage in thoughtful accessing of social decision making abilities, and for being able to approach others in a way that avoids provoking anger or annoyance. They include the ability to listen carefully and accurately, follow directions, calm down when under stress, and talk to others in a socially appropriate manner.

- *Social Awareness and Group Participation Skills.* These are skills that underlie the exercise of social responsibility and positive interactions in groups. They include learning how to recognize and elicit trust, help, and praise from others; how to recognize others' perspectives; how to choose friends wisely; how to share, wait, and participate in groups; and how to give and receive help and criticism.

- *Decision-Making and Problem-Solving Skills.* This is a set of skills that combine to form a strategy to guide students in thoughtful decision making when facing choices or problematic situations, particularly when under stress. It includes skills in understanding signs of feelings, both personal and in others, deciding on personal goals, thinking of many alternate ways to solve a problem (especially when planning a solution and making a final check for obstacles), and envisioning long- and short-term consequences both for oneself and for others.

The strategy presented in the table on the following page consists of a set of social decision making skills that are taught to students from elementary school through high school, as well as to the parents and educators who work with them. This creates a common language and shared perspective on competence that reinforces and solidifies learning over time. Table 2.1 also provides an outline of the basic structure of the social decision making approach. It is grounded in everyday circumstances so that the skills for competence can be developed and reinforced frequently and over a period of years.

In schools, social decision making is carried out as part of the curriculum by teachers of regular and special education students, and in groups run by other school professionals such as school psychologists, guidance counselors, school social workers, health educators, and learning consultants. In the home, social decision making is carried out by parents as part of their everyday parenting responsibilities, particularly during routines such as getting ready in the morning, mealtimes, homework time, and in discipline situations (Elias et al., 2002).

For students, knowing that there is a strategy of SDM/SPS is very important. They can look around and begin to understand the importance of being aware of their own feelings and those of others, of having clear goals, of understanding short- and long-term consequences and consequences both for themselves and for others, of planning and anticipating obstacles, and of using past experiences as a guide to future action. Note also how these skills (and their effective use) are based on being able to listen carefully and accurately, to act with self-control and not impulsively, and to function effectively in group and social situations.

Social Decision Making and Social Problem Solving Skills: Phases of Instruction and Target Skill Areas

Preparation for Sound Decision Making and Problem Solving

	Self-Control	*Social Awareness*
Readiness Phase (skill training and establishing prompts and cues)	Listening Paying attention Following directions Keep Calm BEST (assertive communication) Resisting provocation Sharing ways to cope with hassles	Sharing ideas and feelings with a group Asking for, giving, and receiving help (cooperation) Giving and receiving praise Perspective taking Conversation skills Giving criticism Choosing friends

FIG TESPN: An Eight-Step Strategy for Decision Making and Problem Solving

Instructional Phase (overlearning of thinking steps)	**F** —Feelings cue me to problem solve. **I** —Identify the problem. **G**—Goals give me a guide. **T** —Think of many possible solutions. **E** —Envision outcomes. **S** —Select the best solution. **P** —Plan the procedure, anticipate pitfalls, and practice. **N** —Notice what happened and remember it for next time.

Interpersonal and Academic Practice

Application Phase	Repeated practice in applying problem-solving skills to a wide variety of interpersonal and academic situations

Perhaps most significantly for middle school students, social decision making skills play a role in their coming to an understanding of the fact that there are decisions that offer no healthy alternatives, such as those dealing with drug and alcohol use and smoking, and that must therefore be avoided. Students also benefit from having a strategy to use when weighing the risks and benefits of resisting pressures to engage in high-risk and unlawful behaviors, and for deriving constructive, responsible means of coping with those pressures.

This may seem like a sophisticated set of skills. However, SDM/SPS is as basic to students trying to negotiate kindergarten circle time, middle school hallways, or high school classrooms as it is to those who are trying to negotiate the business of the board of education, the home-school association, or the teachers' union. The key is to make a commitment to the importance of these skills to students and to take the time to build the skills systematically. This requires more than an occasional social skills unit or a few scattered life skills modules. It requires the use of an acknowledged, pedagogically sound instructional approach across as much of the students' day as possible.

THE INSTRUCTIONAL APPROACH

Gathering

The basic step is the *gathering.* Whether one calls it a sharing circle (the name used in Social Decision Making/Social Problem Solving activities—see Supplemental Activity in Chapter 4 for an example of how to run a sharing circle), morning meeting, sharing time, advisory group, circle time, or any of a number of related titles, the reality is that middle school students welcome the chance to come together informally to address issues of emotional concern. Students benefit from a buffer between socially challenging parts of their day and the academically challenging parts. The social challenge is especially great during the preparation for and trip to school, lunch and recess, and dismissal. For this reason, schools find it useful to have meetings to start the school day, after lunch and after recess, and at the end of the day. It is equally useful to begin group meetings with a convening activity. Such activities recognize and help to implement the following three essential SEL principles (National Center for Innovation and Education, 1999).

Caring Relationships Form the Foundation of All Lasting Learning

Gatherings bring everyone together and make a statement that while agendas are important, relationships come first. They also set a climate in which learning is most likely to be internalized and lasting.

Emotions Affect How and What We Learn

Academic work can't proceed when students' emotions are churned up or when students are anxious, fearful, or angry. The group focus during start-of-day gatherings is on providing an opportunity for some expression of concern, or at least using a ritual beginning to give students a chance to get their own emotions regulated a bit. By so doing, they are better prepared for the academic tasks ahead of them. At the end of the day, addressing students' emotions makes it more likely that the day's learnings and good intentions with regard to homework and projects and such will be followed through.

Goal Setting and Problem Solving Provide Direction and Energy to Learning

Gatherings provide a chance to reaffirm common goals, set personal goals, problem solve issues of general concern, or transition into the SDM/SPS activity about to be undertaken. Gatherings also reinforce goals by providing opportunities for testimonials about progress on projects, attempts to use new skills, and requests for feedback on aspects of SDM/SPS that are proving difficult.

It is this flexible use of gatherings that led the activities in the various modules to be described as "Topics," rather than "Lessons." There are times when the immediate needs of the group, including the need to review what went on in the prior meeting, will lead to less progress on the day's planned activities. However, because the emphasis on SDM/SPS is on long-term, generalizable skill development, when a choice exists between deep learning and coverage of more topics, the former is preferred.

Caveats: Taking Care with Student Disclosure and Student Hurt

In sharing circles or other gatherings, as well as in problem-solving discussions, there is the possibility that students will share family or other personal home circumstances with peers. It is important to set up ground rules, from the very beginning, that family matters should not be topics of general discussion. Further, many groups establish a rule that they will not talk about people who are not in the room at the time. With adolescents, it is also important to let them know that if information is revealed that can be of harm to any student (for example, suicidal thoughts, child abuse, or drug abuse by a parent), you are required by law to report it to appropriate authorities or agencies. There is no confidentiality in cases of potential serious harm. That being said, you also want to be sure to convey to students that they can and should individually approach you, a counselor, school psychologist or social worker, or other school professional whenever they are facing difficult personal or interpersonal problems or circumstances.

These considerations are especially powerful when students are coming to class with a great deal of emotional hurt. Often they are in need of opportunities to express their strong feelings. And they may try to do so despite warnings that such personal disclosures are not appropriate for the group. Try to be aware of what is happening in the lives of students and offer those who are dealing with difficulties chances to meet with you or another member of the school staff on an individual basis. Your alertness to both quiet and overt signs of distress can make a large difference in the lives of students. The work of the PassageWays Institute is a valuable resource to teachers in addressing these concerns (www.passageways.org).

The Facilitative Approach of Open-Ended Questioning

The leader of SDM/SPS groups (whether in classroom or counseling contexts) is not there to solve students' problems or to make students' decisions for them. Instead, the leader is there to facilitate problem solving and decision making on the part of the students themselves. Facilitators are not experts, whose job is to impart information, nor are they counselors,whose job is to provide potential solutions. The approach they need to take involves asking questions rather than telling—and not all questions are equally useful. Consider four types of questions:

- Closed ("Did you hit him?")
- Interrogative ("Why did you hit him?")
- Multiple choice ("Did you hit him because he was teasing you or because of something else?")
- Open-ended ("What happened?")

Closed questions require a yes or no or other one-word response from students and do not elicit much reflection. "Are you angry?" will elicit much less information than an open-ended question such as "What feelings are you having?" Middle school students have a particular dislike of "why" questions because their own insecurity often leads them to feel defensive and blamed. Middle school students are also not the most reflective and are not usually aware of, or able to artic- ulate, the deep reasons behind their actions; this is especially true of students with behavioral and emotional difficulties.

An honest response to "Why did you hit him?" is something very few students will be able to provide. No one will say, "Because I lack self-control and have an inconsistent social learning history with regard to getting negative consequences as a result of my violent actions" or "I think it comes from a chaotic home, some poor parental modeling, and an overexposure to movies, TV, and video games that glorify aggression, with no adult supervision." Open-ended questions won't get those responses either, of course, but they will tend to maximize a student's own thinking about the problem. Further, getting students more invested in the problem-solving process leads them to feel more ownership of and responsibility for the solution. Multiple choice questions are useful with students who need to be brought along as problem solvers, who are immature or have cognitive limitations, or who are initially resistive or draw blanks to open-ended questions.

Two Question Rule

The Two Question Rule is a powerful, simple way to stimulate students' thinking. In leading a group of students, the rule is "Follow up a question with another question." It reminds the leader to stay in a questioning mode. Follow-up questioning serves notice to students that the leader is genuinely interested in hearing details. For example, "How are you feeling?" can be followed up by "What other feelings are you aware of?" And "What are you going to say when you go up to the lunch aide?" can be followed up by "How exactly are you going to say it?" An example in an academic context would be following a question like "What are the ways that the body regulates temperature?" with "How do you know that is true?" Indeed, as a follow-up probe, "How do you know that is true?" is especially useful, given the array of misinformation and partial information that characterizes adolescence. Overall, the more that students elaborate on a problem or issue under consideration, the better understanding both the adults and students involved will have. Follow-up questioning helps students clarify their own thoughts, feelings, goals, and plans.

Paraphrasing

Especially after asking students questions, it is important to reflect back to them what you heard them say. This kind of paraphrase helps any speaker feel listened to, understood, and validated, and recognize that the listener takes them seriously—all of which reinforce them for speaking. Another useful aspect of paraphrasing is that the listener can gently rephrase students' statements into more accurate or appropriate language. Students often have difficulty stating their feelings. For example, in response to "How are you feeling?" a student might reply, "He's an idiot." This can be paraphrased with a statement like this: "It sounds to me like you are really angry with him." Translating students' rough expressions helps them clarify thoughts and also develop a better problem-solving vocabulary.

Modeling

Students all find that seeing adults use problem-solving skills is much more effective than hearing adults instruct them to problem solve. As students hear adults try to use SDM/SPS skills, they realize that it is normal to have negative feelings, that adults do not always have the perfect solution right at their fingertips, and that adults turn to problem solving when they face difficult situations or choices. Leaders need to find ways of modeling aspects of the program. When introducing a skill, leaders can discuss times they used the particular skill in their own lives. Or when a school-related decision is confronting leaders, they can use FIG TESPN to help them arrive at a plan.

Prompting and Cuing Skills Learned Previously

After skills have been taught, it is necessary to promote generalization. One way to get students to use skills more independently and spontaneously is to remind them. To do this, it is helpful to use a prompt or simple way of indicating to the student that now would be a good time to use the previously learned skills. The readiness skills covered in Chapter 3 have names such as "Keep Calm" or "Be Your BEST" and serve as cues to use a set of skills. For example, "Keep Calm" is a relaxation exercise that can be used when students need to settle down from an overstimulating experience or when they are anxious.

By using a simple prompt, the leader avoids having to stop the action and review the whole set of skills involved. In addition, others in the students' environment (such as teachers in various classes, school support personnel, parents) can be taught the prompt and when to use it without needing full training in how to facilitate social skills. The more pervasive the prompting of skills, the better the generalization will be. For example, school lunch aides can be taught to encourage students to use "YOUR Keep Calm" rather than yelling at them to sit down and shut up. This can be a more positive and effective intervention.

Review, Repetition, Reminders, Reinforcement, and Reflection: Pedagogy for Generalization of Skills

Generalization of skills comes from deep learning and guided practice. To accomplish this, SDM/SPS activities almost always begin with a review of prior activities, which is useful for the students who were present, those who were absent, and those who were present but not fully attentive. That is, skills are never presented just once with the assumption they will be learned for all time. Instead, the pedagogy of SDM/SPS involves repeated presentation of skills with numerous different examples. Through this repetition, students get the feel of how to apply the skill flexibly in many circumstances. For generalization of skills, students need as much experience as possible applying skills to a range of situations.

Part of generalization is to remember that middle school students have a lot on their minds. . . . They have DVDs to watch, MP3s to listen to, clothes to buy, sports to play, and Internet chats to plan. If adults want them to learn and use skills, they have to be willing to provide constant reminders to use the skills. SDM/SPS pedagogy assumes that students are amnesiacs. This is not true, of course, but if educators and counselors operate on the assumption that students will *not* remember and use what they learn in SDM/SPS activities, it will seem natural to stop and think about how to help students remember to use the skills. Here are some examples of useful reminders:

1. Anticipate a situation that will take place and remind students in advance that it will help them to use the skill (for example, to use "Keep Calm" before a class presentation).

2. Place posters, signs, and other tangible and visible reminders of SDM/SPS skills in classrooms, guidance offices, group rooms, the main office, and on bulletin boards.

3. Use some sharing circles as testimonials, where students can share examples of times they have used SDM/SPS skills—or could have used them to good advantage had they remembered to do so.

4. Develop verbal and nonverbal prompts to remind students to use various skills.

Reinforcement, or positive recognition, basically reflects social learning theory: When people receive benefit for doing something, they are likely to repeat it. This is not to say that a point system or intricate reward procedure is necessary, though it can be helpful, especially for students with behavior difficulties. Reinforcement means that adults in the school should not simply expect students to use their SDM/SPS skills and offer no special acknowledgment when they do so. Students of middle school age are especially attuned to appreciation, both from adults and from peers. A number of schools have instituted positive recognition systems, where students who see their peers using certain skills can let others know by filling out a card, giving a student something, telling an adult, or taking some similar action. When peers show appreciation to one another for using SDM/SPS skills, it can create momentum that significantly improves the climate of the school. Reflection is built into many SDM/SPS activities, in the form of sharing and self-disclosing during sharing circles and other aspects of group discussions. It is also fostered by self-rating sheets that students occasionally complete as a way of getting them to reflect on the nature of their SDM/SPS experiences and the meaning of these experiences in their everyday lives. Much of SDM/SPS is reflective, in that students are encouraged to think about what they are doing and learn from what happened for next time. Opportunities for reflection—via discussion, journaling, or other refreshers—build a habit of thoughtfulness in students that will stand them in good stead in many social and academic situations.

For those who want a more advanced look at the pedagogy of SDM/SPS, it can be instructive to look at exactly what it takes to develop a generalizable skill. There is a lot more to it than is typically acknowledged.

Steps in the Development of a Skill

The teaching of a skill can be broken down into a process of discrete steps. This process can be used regardless of the skill involved, and across a range of populations, and is not dependent on a specific content. It can guide the structure of social decision making activities. The steps in this process are as follows:

1. Determine the strengths and needs of the group (or individual) being addressed.
2. Select a skill focus.
3. Prepare the students by describing situations in which the skill can be used, explain the skill, and elicit a rationale from the group for the importance of the skill. (Note that a rationale must be provided before instruction can begin.)
4. Ask how the group has handled these situations before. What have they used or tried to help them cope?
5. Break the skill down into its component parts.
6. Teach a prompt or name for the skill to use when cuing the practice of the skill.
7. Ask the group to identify opportunities when the skill would be useful to them.
8. Teach the component parts through modeling.
9. Provide hypothetical situations (via stories, videos, role-playing vignettes) for guided practice and rehearsal with feedback.
10. Encourage use of the skill inside and outside the session and integrate with other skills when possible; assign homework.
11. Begin subsequent meetings with reviews and testimonials to monitor progress, reinforce skills, and determine the next area of focus (that is, cycle back to the beginning of the process).

The first contact with students is a discussion of the *rationale for the skill*. Students need to know why they are being asked or expected to do something, what the purpose is, how it fits into and is meaningful to their lives. The more obvious the connection between real life and the skill being taught, the more likely it is that the skill will be learned and used.

Knowing what the students have tried before in similar situations is diagnostic and sets the stage for new learning. This helps identify skills already mastered or areas of skill deficit. If the situation has been handled successfully, the skill use can be reinforced and generalized to other situations. If the outcome was unsatisfactory, motivation takes the form of recognizing the need for a new way of approaching the situation.

Dividing any complex instruction into *component parts* is sound teaching practice. Although common, social skills are often uncommonly complex. For example, "engaging in conversation" sounds simple enough, but it can be broken down into the following component parts:

1. Picking a person to talk to
2. Thinking of something to say or a topic to talk about
3. Approaching the person in a nonthreatening manner and at an appropriate time
4. Staying at a comfortable distance and making appropriate eye contact
5. Listening actively
6. Taking turns and timing your comments
7. Keeping the conversation going
8. Asking relevant questions
9. Assessing the other person's interest in what you are saying
10. Modifying your statements relative to the other person's responses
11. Ending the conversation
12. Assessing whether you want to talk to that person again
13. Planning future contact

Each of these subskills can be analyzed further. For example, ending a conversation may involve:

1. Being aware of time constraints
2. Bringing closure to the conversation
3. Being sensitive to the other person's perception of how you end the conversation
4. Terminating eye contact
5. Moving away from the other person

Too often, adults working with children assume that they already possess reasonable skill levels in these areas. A rule of thumb for working with students is to start from where they are and then progress to where you want them to be in small, success-based steps. Therefore, it is necessary to break down social skills into these discrete steps and teach them as a way to avoid social failure and rejection. This staged approach can also help avoid resistance. If students decide that talking to the other party is likely to get them to a solution of a problem but do not know how to do this, they will fail to reach their goals and will then be more resistant to trying something else in the future.

As noted earlier, prompts are a shorthand way to remind others to use a particular skill. It is often helpful to let the group come up with a name or to use an individual's words. For example, there are many ways to calm down in a crisis and many labels for those ways, such as "Breathing," "Staying Calm," "Keeping Calm," and "Concentrating." Groups personalize skills when they create the prompts, or names, by which they want the skills known.

It promotes generalization to ask the group to identify opportunities when the skill would be useful. Again, things need to be presented in a concrete manner. Students will not necessarily realize that, for example, the same self-calming technique can be used in a baseball game, before a test, when asking a girl on a date, and to help resist provocations by others. Also, having students say when they are planning to use a skill (or might have used it, in retrospect) creates a positive social climate for using the skill. No student wants to be the only one doing something. When students give public statements about when they are going to use a skill, it helps reduce inhibition in others.

As discussed earlier, modeling is an important way to teach any skill. Middle school students of any grade, and especially those with learning disabilities, benefit from tangible examples of a skill put into action. Modeling can be combined with posing hypothetical situations. When practicing, give students feedback and guide them through a refinement of the skill. One enjoyable way of modeling and using guided practice is to use a role-playing game. If the students are working on a skill such as "anger expression" (our way of making the point that one does not learn to control anger as much as to express it appropriately), you can arrange to have situations that make the students angry written on slips of paper and put into a hat or bowl. Humorous situations can be included, as well. Students take turns pulling a paper from the hat, reading the situation, and assigning roles to others, who then act it out. Those who do not have parts give feedback to the angry person, and the role-play is repeated, if necessary, until the person handles it acceptably well. From activities such as this, students see models of how to handle anger-inducing situations in different, nonviolent ways.

The purpose of SDM/SPS training is for students to use the skills outside the group. This must be planned for, rather than assumed. Have others (parents, lunch aides) involved in prompting students to use the skills. Give specific homework to use a skill. Worksheets or assignment and agenda books can be used to have parents check off whether they saw their child practicing the skill outside school.

Once skills have been artificially broken down into component parts, it is necessary to put them back together into the complex array of skills that make up life in the real world. That is, when teaching and practicing skills, they can be taught individually as discrete elements—but they then have to be used all together. Think of basketball. Although you can teach the rules of basketball along with techniques for dribbling, hook shots, jump shots, passing, and other facets of the game, no one really knows how to play until they know how all the skills fit together in the context of an actual game. Therefore, when encouraging use of skills outside the session, make sure to relate them to other skills that might be needed. The activities in this book place great emphasis on helping students put their skills together.

Beginning meetings with a review and testimonial will reinforce all of the components of skill building and also encourage students to self-evaluate. Repetition of all the facets of skill building is essential for ultimate success; review procedures also are diagnostic, used to determine what additional skills or subskills need to be worked on in future sessions.

ENCOURAGE STUDENTS TO BE THOUGHTFUL DECISION MAKERS AND PROBLEM SOLVERS

The entire SDM/SPS approach is built on promoting generalization and application, and for this, confidence building is essential. Foremost, teachers, counselors, other implementers, and parents are encouraged to communicate with students in a manner that stimulates students' own thinking. Through the use of open-ended questions and dialogue that facilitates students' higher order thinking skills ("What are all the ways that you can think of to handle that problem with Lee?"), adults keep the channels of communication open. They let students know that they *can* solve their own problems and that their ideas are worthwhile. Moreover, this approach lets students see adults around them listening to them and caring about and respecting what they say. This builds a sense of empowerment. In addition, they are learning skills they can use every day. They are prompted, coached, and guided to practice using the skills, and then given feedback aimed at helping them increase their effectiveness. Success is an important source of confidence, but so is giving students praise for effort and progress and *giving students the expectation that they are on a pathway to success.* This is an important message for self-doubting middle schoolers, who may be prone to see even a 90 percent full glass as half empty.

Because SDM/SPS is grounded in the social world of students—even when the applications are to academic areas—students who otherwise seem disaffected, unengaged, or at high risk do not feel excluded. Many teachers find that social decision making activities lead to increases in students' involvement in cooperative learning activities. Thus it is more than the content of social decision making that is important in skill building. The instructional principles built into every activity that follows from the social decision making tradition are designed to enhance a range of social and life skills and build self-confidence by helping students see that they are valued members of something worthwhile. Whether it is being used in a classroom, group, club, advisory, counseling, or clinical context—or in after-school programs—the SDM/SPS approach helps students (and adults) recognize that they are part of a cooperative problem-solving and decision-making team.

Part 2

Basic Skills for Sound Decision Making, Problem Solving, and Effective Studying

3 A Short Course or Time-Limited Group on Social Decision Making and Social Problem Solving

This chapter serves to operationalize many of the basic aspects of the program. Specific skills are the basis of Social Decision Making/Social Problem Solving. Although the activities described throughout this book build these skills inductively, it is often of greatest benefit to provide students with an opportunity to learn skills systematically. This chapter provides a time-limited course or group that gives middle school students the primary skills needed for SDM/SPS. It includes general principles of group and classroom development and structure that can be used along with activities throughout the book (such as group rules or dealing with put-downs) and as skill-building tips that can be used to supplement other activities in the book, as needed (such as the FIG TESPN decision-making and problem-solving strategy). Each of the eight topic sections begins with a general discussion of the background and standards relating to the topic, then proceeds with the details needed to present the topic to a class.

TOPICS IN THIS CHAPTER

1. Classroom Constitution and Group Rules
2. Putting Down Put-Downs: Help Students Talk to Each Other in More Civil Ways
3. Self-Control and Self-Calming Strategies
4. Confident and Effective Communication and Social Literacy: How to Be Your BEST in Many Situations

Thanks to Steven E. Tobias, Charlotte Hett, and Howard (Haim) M. Rubinstein for their contributions to this chapter.

5. Identifying Trigger Situations: How to Recognize Personal Sources of Stress

6. Tracking Troubles: Coping with Personal Sources of Stress

7. How to Be a Good Decision Maker and Problem Solver: FIG TESPN

8. Extra Practice in Recognizing Feelings

1 Classroom Constitution and Group Rules

The first task is to set up a system for classroom or group management and expectations for how students will relate to one another. If students do not feel a sense of order and safety, they will be reluctant to participate in SDM/SPS activities or to put the principles they learn to use in their lives. The class also will not be ready for optimal achievement of academic goals.

OBJECTIVES

- To engage students in a democratic and interactive rule-setting process
- To discuss and develop social norms for classroom and group behavior
- To establish a reference for reminding students of behavioral expectations and prompting appropriate social behavior

MATERIALS

Poster board and markers

LEADER'S GUIDE

1. Introduce the topic.

Discuss the Constitution in general. Review vocabulary and concepts related to the Constitution; laws, contracts, rights, and responsibilities are the most relevant concepts. The idea of a constitution with articles and possible amendments flows well from these.

Discuss why a constitution is important—that is, what would happen if there were no constitution or law. Students should be helped to understand the various ways and reasons this is of relevance and benefit to them.

Discuss ways in which a constitution would be helpful to the group. For example:

- Helps maintain order.
- Facilitates respect for one another.
- Establishes rules that both students and adults would need to abide by.
- Enables students to know what is expected of them.

2. Build a constitution for the class.

Generate a list of articles for appropriate classroom behavior. This list should be wide open and can encompass whatever the students and teacher believe to be important. Include both do's and don'ts. Teachers have found that including both rights and responsibilities is helpful (these would be for teachers and students). You may even wish to call the resulting list a bill of rights and responsibilities.

Write down all proposed articles in a brainstorming process and then review and edit them. As part of the review process, introduce a conversation about what happens when rules are broken. Here are some questions to ask:

- Why is it sometimes hard to follow rules?
- What are the hardest rules to follow? What makes them hard to follow?
- What are the easiest rules to follow?
- What is an example of a time you didn't follow the rules?
- How do you feel when you are not following the rules?
- How do you feel when you are following the rules?

Key points to make in the conversation:

- We are all working together to follow the rules.
- Following rules takes a lot of practice.
- Everyone makes mistakes. We all forget or choose not to follow rules from time to time.
- When students forget or choose not to follow a rule, it's the teacher's job to help them fix the problems that resulted and help them learn to do better next time.

Decide if this discussion should lead to any changes in the constitution and, if so, make them.

3. Accept and adopt the constitution.

Review the final constitution with the students and take a vote to adopt it. Indicate that this will now be the "law" of the classroom. Also indicate that the constitution can be amended if the need arises (in other words, if further clarification or additional rules are necessary). If you have students from one year to another, you can call a constitutional convention at the beginning of each year to review and revise the constitution. Have students sign a copy of the completed constitution.

Students can make individual copies of the constitution, using calligraphy or a computer. Encourage them to embellish the document with symbols such as eagles, school insignia, and the like. It is often useful for group building and morale to have the students create a classroom motto, pledge, and anthem.

4. Post the constitution.

Make a classroom poster of the constitution. This can be a group project.

IMPLEMENTATION TIPS

1. State rules in a positive, descriptive manner. For example, you may well begin with lots of rules in the brainstorming process that sound like "Don't interrupt." In the review and edit phase, these rules should be rephrased if at all possible to read like this: "Students have the right to speak and be listened to by others."

2. The initial generation of the rules should proceed without censorship or criticism. When editing them into a final version, try to reach a consensus. This process foreshadows the "Envision outcomes" step of FIG TESPN. If a student suggests an inappropriate rule, such as "We have the right to chew gum," ask what will happen if the group had this rule and point out some of the adverse consequences of this rule (it will get all over the desks, we might get in trouble at our next group, it might distract us from learning, and so on). The teacher can always bring these consequences up and if necessary state that the rules of the classroom cannot contradict the rules of the school, just as the laws of the states cannot contradict federal law. In addition, point out that the teacher acts as supreme court and has the responsibilities of (a) interpreting both federal law (school rules) and state law (the rules of the classroom), (b) adjudicating civil disputes, and (c) administering the appeals process in a fair manner.

3. State rules as specifically and behaviorally as possible. For example, "Be nice to others" can be defined as not talking out of turn, asking

permission to borrow something, or many other behaviors. Specifics can be generated by asking:

What would "nice" look like?

or

If you were being nice, what would or wouldn't you be doing?

4. When rules are violated after this topic is complete, remind students of the class constitution (sometimes just by pointing to it) and let them know that they generated the rules and agreed to abide by them. This can be done in a matter-of-fact manner:

Article 5 of our constitution states that students will refer to other students by their proper names or commonly accepted nicknames.

If you need to expand on this observation, you can point out that words like *stupid* or *jerk* do not qualify as accepted nicknames.

5. It will be necessary to review, revise, and reinforce the use of the constitution frequently.

6. If you choose to include both rights and responsibilities, see Exhibit 3.1 for a useful approach.*

7. You may wish to delineate your methods of discipline or punishment in the constitution. For example, you may state that one disruption in class gets a warning, the second disruption gets a detention, and the third disruption warrants being sent out of the classroom. It can also be useful to include rewards; for example, students who have no more than one disruption earn five minutes' free time at the end of class. Whatever your discipline policy is, it will be helpful to the students (and to you) to have it clearly and publicly stated.

8. Some students will reject the constitution or become disruptive during the process of developing it. You may explain to students that the alternative to a constitutional democracy is a dictatorship and that you will gladly serve as dictator in the absence of a constitution. This concept can be linked to issues in current events and social studies, including research and homework assignments on the effects of lack of democracy and of various forms of dictatorship. The concept of compromise can be introduced as well.

---

*This sample constitution was drafted by Lorraine Glynn and her sixth-grade students at the Benjamin Franklin Middle School, Ridgewood, New Jersey.

Exhibit 3.1   **Sample Classroom Constitution**

BILL OF RIGHTS AND RESPONSIBILITIES

STUDENTS

Article I

Right: Students may use the classroom properly.
Responsibility: Students must make sure whatever they use stays in good condition.

Article II

Right: Students may place their belongings at a specific desk.
Responsibility: Students must not touch another's belongings without asking.

Article III

Right: Students have a right to express themselves without interruption or name calling.
Responsibility: Students must listen and wait if they wish to share ideas.

Article IV

Right: Students have a right to sit at their desks to do work.
Responsibility: Students will not disturb others either physically (hitting, poking) or mentally (distracting by sounds or words).

Article V

Right: Students have a right to do both oral and silent reading.
Responsibility: Students must follow teacher's directions as to when each is needed.

Article VI

Right: Students have a right to chew gum at designated times.
Responsibility: Students will not chew gum at computers, blow bubbles, stick gum on school property, or chew gum outside of the classroom.

Article VII

Right: Students have a right to play computer games at designated times.
Responsibility: Students must be finished with assignments and check with the teacher before playing. Students must share computer time with other students.

FACULTY

Article I

Right: Faculty have the right to expect students not to go into the faculty members' desks or other belongings.
Responsibility: Faculty must let students know what they can use and when they can use it.

Exhibit 3.1 (continued)

Article II

Right: Faculty have the right to present the topics they are required to teach.

Responsibility: Faculty must allow enough time for students to complete topics and give whatever help is needed.

Article III

Right: Faculty have the right to be listened to during class without interruption and without insulting comments ("this is boring, stupid," etc.).

Responsibility: Faculty must allow students to express themselves equally, using appropriate behavior (speaking one at a time).

Throughout the school year, students and faculty members have the right to make changes in and additions to the bill of rights and responsibilities.

We inscribe our names.

Students: **Faculty:**

2 Putting Down Put-Downs: Help Students Talk to Each Other in More Civil Ways

Middle school students often live in a put-down culture. Some of this stems from their own search for identity and their attempts to reaffirm who they are by putting down others they perceive as different or threatening. Some stems from what they see in the media, and some comes from their tendency to form cliques. Regardless, put-downs are related to bullying and are toxic to creating a safe group and learning environment. A special focus is therefore needed to ensure that students have tools both to reduce their use of put-downs and to build their tolerance of put-downs from others.

OBJECTIVE

- To show students how to recognize put-downs and begin to discriminate levels of how these harmful words or actions can hurt another person.

MATERIALS AND PREPARATION

Chalkboard or easel pad

Copies or whole-class displays of the "Put-Down Tracker" (Worksheet 3.1) and "Put-Down Pain Scale" (Worksheet 3.2)

NOTE: During the week before presenting this topic, record an estimate of the number of put-downs that you hear being exchanged during the day or during a set period of time (such as during lunch, recess, or free period).

LEADER'S GUIDE

1. Review the preceding topic.

2. Introduce the concept of put-downs.

Write the word *put-down* on the chalkboard or easel pad. Tell the students that today they will be discussing put-downs—what they are and how they are harmful to others. Briefly mention your own personal definition of put-downs—for example, deliberately harmful words or actions toward another person. An example may help—but remember to direct your comments to an empty chair or some other object, rather than to a student who might wonder if you really mean it personally.

3. Motivate students.

Say:

> *Getting along with others is an important part of being successful as a member of a music group, athletic team, business, or classroom. When people start putting each other down, groups break up, teams tend to lose, people get fired from their jobs, and classrooms become unhappy places. So if you really want to learn to be part of a group, you need to recognize when you are giving or getting a put-down and eventually figure out a way to prevent it from ruining your group.*

4. Define the concept.

Elicit from the students their ideas of what a put-down is and write these ideas on the board. A full definition of a put-down can eventually include the concepts that are listed on the "Put-Down Tracker."

5. Present practice activities.

Look at current television programs or movies for examples of put-downs. Show students a short video clip that exemplifies put-downs. Ask the students to notice the put-downs so they can write them down within the appropriate category on the Put-Down Tracker. Alternatively, you or a student can be the official scribe for a whole-class display of this worksheet.

Discuss with students how put-downs feel to a person. For this, the Put-Down Pain Scale, used as a student worksheet or presented in a whole-class format, can help. Select several of the put-downs that were identified in the video, nominate some yourself, or, if the students are ready, ask them to volunteer some of their own feelings and then rate them on the pain scale.

Read comic strips that illustrate put-downs and the feelings they create in others and use these as sources for this topic's worksheets. You can also, as a part of an art class, have the students draw their own comic strip examples of put-downs and then analyze these in a similar fashion.

Present pictures from magazines or books, one at a time, and add an impromptu story line, such as "Hey, you're pretty strong for a girl." Ask students to decide whether the comment is a put-down or not. If it is, they can then categorize and note the severity of the put-down.

6. Report on current behavior.

Tell the students how many put-downs you counted in the week or other time period before this session and challenge them to reduce the total by a set number. For example, if you count an average of twenty put-downs in a day, challenge the students to reduce the number to fifteen or ten. Be mindful not to set an unrealistic goal—the students may give up if they see it as impossible to achieve. Keep daily records of the put-downs and report on progress each day. This can be done on a wall chart. Be sure to praise the students for their progress. Once the first goal is reached, it is possible to set a new goal to cut the number of put-downs even further.

7. Provide a summary.

Ask students to review their ideas about put-downs.

Establish a cue word or prompt: "Put-down." Encourage familiarity with this word and prepare students for what will happen during the next topic. Ask the students to look for put-downs between now and the next session. Tell them that you may stop the group to point out an interchange between two students that includes a put-down. In the following week, stop the group to point out any put-downs that occur in exchanges between students.

Student _____ Date _____

Put-downs are words or actions that deliberately hurt someone. Give examples of the following kinds of put-downs.

1. **Ignoring someone (deliberately not paying attention to someone) to make that person feel uncomfortable.**

   EXAMPLES _____

   _____

   _____

2. **Disrespecting or insulting someone (teasing a person by joking about their skills or appearance).**

   EXAMPLES _____

   _____

   _____

3. **Threatening someone (deliberately frightening someone by promising to do that person harm).**

   EXAMPLES _____

   _____

   _____

4. **Starting rough physical contact (different from self-defense, this refers to provoking a fight).**

   EXAMPLES _____

   _____

   _____

5. **Other categories**

   _____

   _____

Student _____ **Date** _____

Think about how someone might feel who received the put-down. Then rate the put-down by writing it next to the number that tells how painful the put-down was. Remember, each person may rate each put-down differently, and that's OK.

(REALLY PAINFUL)

10 _____

9 _____

8 _____

7 _____

6 _____

5 _____

4 _____

3 _____

2 _____

1 _____

(NOT SO PAINFUL)

3 Self-Control and Self-Calming Strategies

All students need to have a strategy for keeping calm, as well as a clear idea of what to do when upsetting things happen, especially put-downs, disappointments, rejections, and the like. Having self-control and being able to calm oneself down are essential in a variety of education-related areas (such as taking tests, participating in athletics and performing arts, and making verbal presentations and performances), as well as in the many interpersonal situations that arise in and out of school.

This topic teaches two self-calming strategies: "Keep Calm" and "YOUR Keep Calm." The first is a self-control procedure that involves stopping automatic responses to stressful situations by using self-talk and controlled breathing. Students who have participated in the SDM/SPS program in the elementary grades will have learned Keep Calm. These students will have the opportunity to review the skill.

All students will be introduced to the concept of YOUR Keep Calm— a personal strategy for self-calming and self-control. Many students already have ways of calming themselves down when they are in stressful situations. This topic gives them the opportunity to identify and formally acknowledge what is already working for them. Of course, not all students have these kinds of personal self-calming strategies. These students will have a chance to hear about the approaches that work for their classmates. They may choose to try out one or more of these approaches, if they wish. Anyone can choose to use the basic Keep Calm procedure at any time.

It is important to note that self-calming strategies should not be taught when students are already agitated; they need to be introduced when students are in a relatively quiet, receptive state. With enough practice, students can be prompted to use the skill of Keep Calm or YOUR Keep Calm when they are in—or about to be in—a stressful trigger situation.

OBJECTIVES

- To instruct students in the steps of a standard "Keep Calm" strategy

- To introduce students to the concept of "YOUR Keep Calm" as a label and prompt for their own self-calming strategy
- To encourage students to use a self-calming strategy when they find themselves in trigger situations, so as to prevent excessive stress

MATERIALS

Chalkboard or easel pad

Whole-class display of the "Keep Calm Procedure" (Worksheet 3.3)

LEADER'S GUIDE

1. Review the previous topic.

2. Introduce the skills covered in this topic.

Tell the group:

All people find themselves on the receiving end of put-downs or needing to deal with trigger situations from time to time. This is a natural part of life, especially in school, where there are many academic challenges and people challenges. Today we are going to talk about responding to put-downs and trigger situations.

Motivate students by saying:

When put-downs and trigger situations push us to fight or flee, our bodies can respond in several ways:

- With "awfulizing" thoughts
- With autonomic nervous system responses such as increased blood pressure, increased heart rate, sweaty palms, dry mouth, enlarged pupils, goose bumps, fast shallow breathing, or a sinking feeling
- With muscle tension in the face, neck, chest, back, arms, or legs

These experiences can result in our feeling that we are losing control and no longer in charge of our lives. Using a strategy to keep calm is one way to keep your self-control and stay in charge, especially of the automatic parts of your physical reactions, like heart rate, blood pressure, and breathing.

3. Present the Keep Calm strategy.

Tell the students that when they are experiencing a put-down or trigger situation, or when they notice their physical signs of stress, it is important to calm down before trying to solve the problem:

Today we are going to learn about ways to stay calm in these trigger situations. Some of you may already know how to do this first way, or you may have seen others do it.

Direct students' attention to the "Keep Calm Procedure" (Worksheet 3.3) and read through the steps with them:

1. Tell yourself to STOP.
2. Tell yourself to KEEP CALM.
3. Slow down your breathing with two long, deep breaths.
4. Praise yourself for a job well done.

Explain that this technique is very popular with sports stars, actors, actresses, and other performing artists, such as rock stars. Some of the students may have seen athletes taking slow, deep breaths to calm themselves down before pitching a baseball, serving in tennis, or shooting a foul shot.

Ask the group if anyone can think of times when they might be able to use Keep Calm to better handle trigger situations. Write these examples on the chalkboard or easel pad.

4. Have students practice Keep Calm.

Ask students to imagine being in one of these trigger situations, and then talk them through the Keep Calm strategy. Focus especially on Step 3, giving students the following specific instructions:

Take in a deep, slow breath through your nose while you count to 5.

Hold it while you count to 2.

Breathe out through your mouth to another count of 5.

Repeat until you are sure you are calmer.

Students may be uncomfortable trying Keep Calm for the first time, or they may not take it seriously. It is important to validate their reactions and to emphasize that if Keep Calm is done properly, others will not even know that they are using it.

5. Introduce YOUR Keep Calm.

Let students know that many people have personal ways of keeping calm, ways that work especially well for them. Ask them to tell you some of the different ways they stay calm and keep their self-control. Sample responses include the following:

- Imagining a peaceful scene

- Thinking about how much someone loves me
- Counting to ten
- Remembering advice given by a valued person
- Playing some favorite music in my head

Record students' responses as they give them. If you wish, volunteer your own ways of keeping calm.

6. Assign the task of watching for self-calming strategies.

Ask students to remember or write down times they use Keep Calm or YOUR Keep Calm, or times they recognize that if they or their classmates did use these strategies it would have been helpful. Their observations will be shared in the sharing circle at the start of the next topic.

7. Provide a summary.

Ask students to share the one or two things they will remember most from this topic. Encourage use of the skill and prepare students for the activities of the next topic.

IMPLEMENTATION TIPS

1. Keep Calm and YOUR Keep Calm will be learned to the extent that students are prompted and reminded to use these skills in everyday situations, such as while moving from class to class, when being teased at lunch, while anticipating a test, before an important meeting, when they are upset at home—or in performance situations like reading aloud, presenting a report in front of the class, being called on by the teacher, showing their work in music or art, or participating in sports activities. Be sure faculty and staff who work with students in your groups know about these strategies and how to prompt them.

2. Here are some ways you can prompt a student's use of Keep Calm or YOUR Keep Calm. When the student is upset or beginning to lose control, say:

   Use "YOUR Keep Calm."

   Stop and think about what's happening and how you can calm yourself down.

   Let's take a look at what's going on—tell me what you see.

(Or ask for "what you saw," "what happened," "how you are feeling," or whatever seems likeliest to evoke a clear answer.)

Take a deep breath, think about how you can calm yourself down, and relax—then we can talk about it.

3. Testimonials, in which students discuss their actual or potential use of Keep Calm or YOUR Keep Calm and give each other reinforcement and feedback for future use of these strategies should be solicited regularly. These discussions will promote transfer and generalization of the skill.

Keep Calm Procedure

1. Tell yourself to STOP.

2. Tell yourself to KEEP CALM.

3. Slow down your breathing with two long, deep breaths.

4. Praise yourself for a job well done.

From *Social Decision Making/Social Problem Solving for Middle School Students: Skills and Activities for Academic, Social, and Emotional Success.*
Copyright © 2005 by Maurice J. Elias and Linda Bruene Butler. Research Press (800-519-2707; www.researchpress.com)

4

Confident and Effective Communication and Social Literacy: How to Be Your BEST in Many Situations

Effective interpersonal behavior is essential for academic success as well as for satisfactory social interaction. Understanding how people communicate is a linking point between social-emotional and reading literacy. Middle school students benefit from some specific guidelines for how to interpret and react in a variety of social situations.

OBJECTIVES

- To teach confident and effective communication skills
- To teach students to distinguish passive, aggressive, and confident styles of the following four components of behavior:

  B—Body posture

  E—Eye contact

  S—Speech (Saying appropriate things)

  T—Tone of voice

MATERIALS

Chalkboard or easel pad

Whole-class display of "BEST Procedure" (Worksheet 3.4)

NOTES: After you have introduced BEST, keep a whole-class display of the components posted in the classroom. It is useful to prepare for this topic by assigning the task of collecting pictures of people communicating with each other.

LEADER'S GUIDE

1. Review past activities and skills related to SDM/SPS.

Ask students to give some examples of times they used the skills during the week.

2. Introduce the skill covered in this topic.

Tell the group:

> As we deal with different people in our lives, we can choose from among several styles of communication. These styles are passive, aggressive, and confident. Today, we will look at these different styles and learn how to use the confident style of communication, which is the best way to be successful in dealing with people.

3. Motivate the students and define the skill.

Tell students:

> Using the BEST way means acting in a way that respects others and also yourself. We usually refer to this as being "appropriately confident." We all have a right to express ourselves at the appropriate time and place and to do so in a way that is respectful of others' rights. There are three ways that people usually communicate, and we are going to start off by comparing and contrasting them.

If you gave the students a prior assignment to bring in pictures of people communicating in different ways, the next activity can involve students in sorting out the pictures according to how they match each of the three styles of behavior. Otherwise, you can simply describe and perhaps demonstrate the various styles for the class. Record students' examples of the styles on the chalkboard or easel pad.

The Passive Way

The passive way of communicating is used by people who, while they respect others' rights of expression, do not respect their own rights of expression. This style has also been called *wimpy* or *submissive*. Those who communicate in a passive way allow others to impose upon them, make decisions for them, or act hurtfully to them in some way.

Ask students for some examples of passive communication behaviors, such as not speaking up when you are unfairly accused of something, not approaching a friend who owes you money, letting someone bully you without saying anything to anyone, and so on. Then generate from the students some of the negative consequences of acting in a passive way: not getting what you need, having difficulty keeping friends or making new ones because you are overly quiet, having teachers think that you didn't do your work because you do not speak up and answer questions in class, and so forth.

The Aggressive Way

Explain:

The aggressive way of communicating is used by people who respect their own rights to say what they think and feel, but they do it in a way that does not respect the rights of others. This style has also been called cruel or bullying, and it occurs when a person communicates in a way that overpowers or is hurtful to others.

Elicit from the students examples of aggressive communication, such as screaming and yelling at a vice principal when you feel that you have been unfairly accused, threatening a friend in a verbal or physical way in order to get your money back, and so on. Then generate from the students examples of negative consequences of behaving aggressively: You may develop a bad reputation with the vice principal, which may make matters even worse in the long run; you may get into a fight with your friend over money and may even lose the friend and get hurt, too.

The Confident Way

The confident way of communicating involves expressing your thoughts and feelings in a way that respects both your rights and the rights of others. A confident way is the "BEST" way to say what you want to say in a way that people can understand. It is a style that can encourage others to work with you.

Direct students to the "BEST Procedure" display and explain its components:

B—Body posture

E—Eye contact

S—Speech (Saying appropriate things)

T—Tone of voice

4. Model the skill.

To compare and contrast aggressive, passive, and confident behavior, you should model the same situation using all three styles, one at a time (passive, aggressive, and then confident), and then discuss them with the group.

You may choose to model a student's asking a question of a teacher or get the class involved in role-playing students' asking one another to stop bothering them.

5. Provide opportunities for skill practice with feedback and reinforcement.

Have students pick situations to role-play and demonstrate the three alternative behavioral styles for each situation. Refer to and comment on BEST components of the role-plays. Have the group provide positive corrective feedback to help students express a confident style, if needed.

Here are some examples to try:

- Making a common request
- Initiating a conversation about a problem, first with an adult authority and then with a friend
- Asking for a favor

Have the students bring the contrasting styles to life, and then have them discuss as a group the impact of the three styles.

A follow-up to this exercise is to use examples from recent class events in which one student exhibited passive or aggressive behavior. This will give students a chance to try out confident responses in examples to which they can relate.

IMPLEMENTATION TIPS

1. Have students write, tell, or draw a story about a situation where they could have used Keep Calm or BEST. You can ask them to write a story comparing and contrasting passive versus aggressive reactions to a situation. Have one character be passive, one aggressive, and one confident.

2. Use the trigger situations from the Keep Calm role-play game. Have the students pick a situation from the bowl and role-play both keeping calm and being their BEST. Students enjoy a variation of this, in which they first behave passively or aggressively and then do it again in a confident manner. Assign other students to observe each of the BEST behaviors and provide feedback.

3. Find magazine pictures of people using appropriate or inappropriate BEST behaviors. Have children describe the behaviors that led to their decision as to whether the behavior was appropriate or inappropriate.

4. Role-play or write about the following situations and possible responses:

■ You spot your best friend coming out of a movie theater with another friend. Earlier in the day he told you he had to visit his aunt. You are feeling hurt. How should you handle this situation?

   I would not say anything to him because he might get angry at me.

   I would mention it to him in order to hear what he had to say.

   I would call him later and really let him have it for leaving me out.

   I may ignore him for a few days and also tell all my friends to ignore him, too.

■ A classmate borrowed two dollars from you and hasn't paid you back. It has been three weeks. How should you handle this situation?

   I would give him a piece of my mind and tell him that if he does not pay, he'll be sorry.

   I would not bother him and hope that he pays one of these days.

   I would remind him again and ask him when he will have the money.

For the following situations, indicate whether the person is acting passively, aggressively, or confidently. If the person is acting inappropriately, role-play appropriate behavior. If the person is behaving appropriately, see if the students can think of other ways of being their BEST for the situation.

■ Juan has been bothered by a boy in his class. For some reason, the boy keeps picking on him. Juan sees the other boy coming. He quickly starts walking in the other direction to avoid him. How is Juan acting? What else could he do?

■ Marie's mother has been very angry at her lately. Today Marie forgot to take out the garbage, and her mother grounded her for two days. Marie had really been looking forward to a sleepover that night. She went to her mother, apologized, and offered to help with some cleaning. She also promised to leave a note to herself on her desk to remind her about taking the garbage out next time. How is Marie acting? What else could she do?

It is important to explain that everyone acts passively or aggressively some of the time. Aggressive behavior does not mean that someone is bad. Passive behavior does not mean that someone is too good. The point is that these types of behaviors are less likely to enable people to get what they want. It helps to try to be confident, but no one gets it right all the time.

When role-playing, especially with aggressive behavior, some students will get carried away. Remind students of the rules in the constitution and that they apply even if students are pretending.

5. Encourage students to use BEST during the week both in and out of school. Give them positive feedback when they use confident BEST behaviors, even if they were not aware of doing so; in other words, "catch them being good" and put it in BEST terms. For example, if students who often argue or do not say anything ask questions in a polite manner, you can say how much you appreciated their using BEST, and you could tell because they used a nice tone of voice and they made excellent eye contact.

6. It should be noted that there are cultural and ethnic differences in what might be regarded as BEST behavior. For example, part of eye contact also involves understanding and respecting personal space and customs of different cultures. This can be a topic in itself. Make students aware of it and incorporate it into the role-plays and everyday practice. One such cultural difference involves some Latino children, who may be less likely to make eye contact with adult males, out of respect.

7. Some special education teachers have found it important to extend the BEST framework to include some standard procedures for what to say in certain situations. The most common example occurs during teasing situations on the bus, or at lunch, gym, recess, or in hallways. Prompting special education youngsters to use "Be Your BEST" seems quite effective in making them less fun to tease. It may be helpful to draw upon the resources of the group as a group to aid individual students as they try to respond to the teasing of others. This is one experience that most students in a special education class will probably have encountered and one that probably angered or upset them. If a group of students can relate to one another as recipients of teasing, it may be easier to get them to coach and support each other in their attempts to prevent it with confident behavior.

It is also useful to provide special education students with specific verbal strategies for responding to teasing. One teacher with whom we have worked taught children to use the following sequence when faced with persistent teasing:

> *First, ignore them; second, say, "Please stop"; third, say, "Please stop—what you're doing is bothering me"; fourth, say, "If you don't stop, I am going to tell the teacher [aide, bus driver] what you are doing"; fifth, tell the adult on duty and use your BEST as you tell what happened.*

This teacher encouraged her students to use BEST. Also important, however, is that the teacher empowered classmates to help each other when these situations occurred. On the bus, one boy told another during a teasing episode that his voice was not strong enough and that he was not standing tall. This kind of real-time coaching, teamwork, and camaraderie can be of significant help in giving special education youngsters the confidence and pride they need to function in school, as well as in peer, family, and ultimately job situations.

Note that the use of BEST can be reinforced easily throughout the school day by asking:

> *Did you use BEST? What parts? How well did you do it? How else could you do it next time?*

It will also be useful to refer to the BEST framework when teaching and practicing role-playing.

BEST Procedure

When you communicate in your "BEST" way, it means that you are paying attention to the following components of your behavior:

- **B**—Body posture: Standing up straight, being confident in yourself but not arrogant.

- **E**—Eye contact: Looking the person in the eye at a comfortable distance.

- **S**—Speech: Using appropriate language and saying what you really feel in an open manner.

- **T**—Tone of voice: Using a calm voice, not whispering or shouting.

After using BEST, tell yourself that you did a good job! Give yourself a pat on the back!

From *Social Decision Making/Social Problem Solving for Middle School Students: Skills and Activities for Academic, Social, and Emotional Success.* Copyright © 2005 by Maurice J. Elias and Linda Bruene Butler. Research Press (800-519-2707; www.researchpress.com)

Worksheet 3.4

5   Identifying Trigger Situations: How to Recognize Personal Sources of Stress

Another part of self-control, especially among middle school students, is to recognize situations students find so stressful and emotionally arousing that they can't use their problem-solving abilities as well as possible. These are called *trigger situations* because they trigger extreme reactions, usually fight or flight. Often, classroom disruption of academic learning is caused by students' reactions to experiencing their trigger situations.

OBJECTIVES

- To help students identify their trigger situations
- To begin to discuss strategies for addressing trigger situations

MATERIALS

Chalkboard or easel pad

A video or DVD that illustrates trigger situations for key characters and equipment for viewing it

Copies of "Trigger Situations for Others" (Worksheet 3.5) and "Trigger Situations for Me" (Worksheet 3.6)

A folder for each student

NOTES: This particular approach can be included as a part of a health or science activity. Knowing the history and biology of trigger situations tends to be motivational for many students, making the response something they can picture dealing with.

Some classic comedy series (such as *The Honeymooners, I Love Lucy,* and *Sanford and Son*) and movies (such as *Platoon, Cyrano, Ice Age, Shrek,* and *Toy Story*) provide excellent examples of characters' trigger situations.

LEADER'S GUIDE

1. Review the preceding topic and hand out folders.

Explain to students that the folders are for collecting completed SDM/SPS worksheets and other materials.

2. Introduce the concept of trigger situations.

Tell students that they will be learning about specific kinds of events that, if left unchecked, can get them to lose control and do something that they will regret later. These events are called trigger situations.

Write the phrase *trigger situations* on the board and tell the students that the group will be discussing the different stressful events—trigger situations—that can get people upset. You might say:

> *Trigger situations are the events or things people do that get us upset and angry. They make it hard for us to keep control. Different people may have different trigger situations, and we also might share some of the same ones.*

3. Discuss real-life trigger situations.

Ask students to brainstorm with you the types of situations, events, or things that can easily get someone upset or angry. You may want to begin with some self-disclosure to briefly model what you mean by trigger situations (for instance, getting stuck in traffic when you are on the way to school). This will help get the ball rolling and assure the class that this sort of reaction is something that everyone experiences. List the trigger situations described by the students on the board.

4. Generalize the concept.

Ask students:

> *Why do you think we react to trigger situations as we do? What would have happened to human beings as we were evolving, if we did not have a set response to trigger situations?*

Make the point that all of us, even the bravest and strongest people, have trigger situations and have to learn how to deal with situations that frighten or greatly upset us. Then explain the biology of trigger situations by explaining that the response to trigger situations used to be like the fever we get when we are sick or the pain we feel when we injure ourselves: something that makes us act to protect ourselves from harm.

Our bodies are equipped to respond to trigger situations with a fight-or-flight response. These two responses were really helpful to the earliest men and women, who had to protect themselves physically from violent creatures that were attacking them. What happens is that a surge of adrenaline energizes our bodies when we are confronted with such stressful situations. Scientist Hans Selye (1956) identified the "General Adaptation Syndrome," in which he said that as we move into gear for an immediate response to a stressful situation, our body is affected in these ways:

- Adrenaline is secreted.
- Respiration increases.
- Muscles tense.
- Heart rate and blood pressure increase.
- Sugar production and secretion into the blood increase.
- Skin capillaries and other blood vessels constrict.
- Digestion slows down.

This reaction has three stages: first, *alarm,* in which the body mobilizes for action; second, *resistance,* in which the body takes action; and third, *exhaustion,* in which the body has a hard time responding to another threat while it builds up its ability to respond again, if necessary. When the body takes action, it is often by striking out in self-defense or by running away to safety. In the days when human beings lived in constant danger from wild animals, this was not a bad thing. But now it may lead to some problems.

Ask:

What kind of problems might we run into now if our trigger situations set us off in school?

How can it help you to know what your trigger situations are—the situations that lead you to feel stress, lose your cool, and get angry or upset?

Make the point that people who can predict what it is that usually prompts their bodies to be inappropriately charged up find it easier to learn how to calm themselves down so as to think clearly and gain control of the situation. While learning how to stay calm, though, it's often best to avoid those situations, or at least handle them carefully, perhaps by seeking help from others.

5. Conduct a practice exercise.

Give a brief overview of the plot of the program that you are going to show, and tell the students which character to monitor for trigger situations. Distribute the "Trigger Situations for Others" worksheet and ask students to write down whatever bodily reactions their character displays in response to each trigger situation. They can do this either during or after the video.

6. Review.

Once the video has been viewed and the students have filled out their worksheets, discuss their responses. The idea is to have the students identify triggers and see how the characters handled (or mishandled) them. Chart the trigger situations observed and how they were handled, rating each as positive or negative. This effort also sets the stage for the next part of the discussion, in which the students use the list of triggers observed in the videos and identify which of these are also triggers for them.

7. Apply the insights from the exercise.

Read through the list of stressful situations offered by the group and ask for a show of hands for people in the group who can identify each of these as one of their own trigger situations. Collect these worksheets or ask the students to place them in their SDM/SPS folders.

If the group is not ready for self-disclosure of this type, you may want to switch to a "rate the trigger situation" activity on the chalkboard. Draw the following scale on the chalkboard or easel pad:

Not so upset   0   1   2   3   4   5   6   7   Really upset

Read one of the trigger situations identified from the video and ask the students to indicate how upset they would be in this situation.

Pass out copies of the "Trigger Situations for Me" worksheet and instruct students to write down three trigger situations that they find themselves in this next week. Have them keep their completed worksheets in their SDM/SPS folders. At the next opportunity, review them individually with students and help them learn how to predict and manage them. Tools such as YOUR Keep Calm, BEST, and the Trouble Trackers (discussed in Topic 6) will be helpful for students to use.

8. Provide a summary.

Ask for a volunteer to review the definition of trigger situations for the group. Emphasize with the group that when they hear the prompt "Watch out for your trigger situation," it will be a reminder to them to try to avoid the situation or, if they cannot, to be calm and careful when it occurs.

Student _____ **Date** _____

List at least three trigger situations for this character (Example: when his girlfriend talked to another boy at the party.) Also list bodily signs that this was a trigger situation for this character (Example: he got red in the face).

Trigger Situations   **Bodily Signs**

1. _____   1. _____

_____   _____

_____   _____

2. _____   2. _____

_____   _____

_____   _____

3. _____   3. _____

_____   _____

_____   _____

Others   Others

_____   _____

_____   _____

_____   _____

73

Student _____ **Date** _____

List at least three trigger situations for yourself (Example: when the vice principal corrects me during change of class). Also list bodily signs that this was a trigger (Example: I kicked my locker door).

Trigger Situations   **Bodily Signs**

1. _____   1. _____

     _____   _____

     _____   _____

2. _____   2. _____

     _____   _____

     _____   _____

3. _____   3. _____

     _____   _____

     _____   _____

Others   Others

     _____   _____

     _____   _____

     _____   _____

6

Tracking Troubles: Coping with Personal Sources of Stress

Once students know their trigger situations, they are ready to problem solve better ways to handle them. This also includes difficult or academic situations. In this activity, students learn about the Trouble Tracker and how to use it to learn more about trigger situations, how to recognize when such situations are likely to get the best of them, and how they can better handle such situations.

OBJECTIVES

- To introduce use of the Trouble Tracker
- To provide practice with self-monitoring trigger situations and coping with them

MATERIALS

Copies of "Trouble Tracker (Short-Answer)" or "Trouble Tracker (Open-Ended)" (Worksheets 3.7 and 3.8)

A whole-class display of the Trouble Tracker you choose

NOTE: Choose the short-answer or open-ended form, whichever is most appropriate for your group; the more open-ended format is suitable for most classes.

LEADER'S GUIDE

1. Review preceding topics.

Ask:

How can you tell when you are upset and may lose control?
How can you remind yourself to use BEST and YOUR Keep Calm?

2. Introduce the new tool.

Capture students' interest by saying:

> *Today we will learn another way to handle problems, using something called a Trouble Tracker. The Trouble Tracker can be used in situations where you are out of control (such as on the playground or with personal conflicts) or when you are dealing with your trigger situations. Writing down a problem begins the problem-solving process and makes it more likely that you can cope with what is bothering you.*

Pass out the Trouble Trackers and discuss their use.

Use a hypothetical example verbally or with the whole-class display and walk students through it (for example, a student who always forgets to bring homework back to class, or a student who always interrupts others when they are talking). Model how you would use YOUR Keep Calm and BEST in these situations.

3. Conduct a practice activity.

Have students choose one situation that upset them or was stressful for them during the prior week. Perhaps they experienced a trigger situation and want to use that as an example. Have students complete an individual Trouble Tracker.

Ask two or three students to volunteer to read their responses. Don't have others comment at first. Instead, ask if anyone else had similar situations. Focus on the warning signs of losing control and how students can use YOUR Keep Calm and BEST to help them.

Have children brainstorm ideas about how to better handle the situations shared, should they come up again. Role-play various responses to these situations to help students learn how to carry out their ideas. Have the rest of the group give feedback and help show how they would use YOUR Keep Calm and BEST in similar situations.

4. Provide a summary.

Review when the students may use Trouble Trackers and tell the group where the Trouble Trackers are kept.

Have students complete Trouble Trackers at other times when you feel it is important to self-monitor. Continue to use Trouble Trackers when students seem to have feelings they would like to get under control.

IMPLEMENTATION TIPS

1. Have students keep copies of the Trouble Trackers in their SDM/SPS folders. Monitor the folders and comment on them occasionally.

2. Share Trouble Trackers with small groups or individuals, when necessary. Sometimes it is best to create hypothetical versions of problem situations to keep them confidential. Have students role-play Trouble Tracker situations and proposed solutions for group discussion.

3. For children with reading or writing problems, the Trouble Tracker can be completed as an interview with the teacher or aide or recorded on tape. It is important to keep a student's reading or writing problems from interfering with the process of tracking problems and generating solutions.

4. Have Trouble Trackers available in your room, in classrooms, and elsewhere around the school. Any adult who encounters a student who is having a problem that cannot be dealt with at the moment should have the student complete a Trouble Tracker. This gives the student the message that the school takes problems seriously and will give students the thorough discussion that they deserve.

5. Before negotiating fights between students, have each participant complete a Trouble Tracker. This will immediately defuse the conflict, give them time to reflect, and start them on a problem-solving process.

6. Some students have petty but frequent complaints. Having the students complete a Trouble Tracker every time before you discuss it can give you an idea of whether the problem was truly serious or the student was just seeking attention; a student who is serious about the problem will complete the Trouble Tracker, while most others will find they have better uses for their time.

7. Have a specific time when Trouble Trackers are reviewed, such as during a sharing time.

8. Allow students to write "PRIVATE" on their Trouble Trackers. This means that only you will read what they write. However, warn them that if information is revealed that can be of harm to the student or another person (suicidal thoughts, child abuse, drug abuse by a parent), you must report the information to the appropriate authorities or agencies.

9. Keep reminding students about the Trouble Tracker. Teachers sometimes forget about this tool about two months after introducing it. However, it is useful throughout the year.

10. Adapt the Trouble Tracker to the individual circumstances and needs of your students. For example, if the music room is often a place where trouble starts, add this specifically to the form. It is also useful to tailor the feelings words to the vocabulary level of your students.

Student _____ **Date** _____

Time: A.M. P.M. *(Circle one.)*

1. Where were you? *(Circle where the trouble happened.)*

Classroom   School bus   Neighborhood

Hallway   Special class   Friend's house

Lunchroom   Home   Gym

On the way to or from school   Other _____

2. What happened? *(Circle what happened.)*

Somebody teased me.   Somebody called me a name.

Somebody took something of mine.   I did something wrong.

Somebody told me to do something.   Somebody started to fight.

Other _____

3. How did you feel? *(Circle how you felt.)*

Embarrassed   Angry   Hurt   Guilty

Ashamed   Jealous   Happy   Surprised

Sad   Upset   Scared   Other _____

4. How strong were your feelings? *(Circle how strongly you felt.)*

Not strong at all   A little strong   Medium strong   Very strong   Too strong

5. What did you do? *(Circle what you did.)*

Hit back   Told an adult   Broke something

Ran away   Walked away calmly   Ignored the person

Yelled   Talked it out   Used Keep Calm

Cried   Told my friend about it   Used BEST

Other _____

6. How did you handle yourself? *(Circle one.)*

Poor   OK   Good   Great

7. What would you do next time?

_____

_____

Student _____ **Date** _____

Time: A.M. P.M. *(Circle one.)*

1. **Briefly describe the trigger situation.** *(Answer who, what, where, and when.)*

   _____

   _____

2. **How did you feel?** _____

3. **What did you say and do?** _____

4. **What happened in the end?** _____

5. **Did you notice physical signs of stress in yourself?**   Yes   No *(Circle one.)*

   If so, where in your body were the signs? _____

6. **How calm and under control were you before you did or said something?** *(Circle one number.)*

1	2	3	4	5
under control	mostly calm	so-so	tense and upset	out of control

7. **How satisfied were you with the way you communicated?** *(Circle one number for each part of BEST.)*

Body posture	1	2	3	4	5
Eye contact	1	2	3	4	5
Spoken words	1	2	3	4	5
Tone of voice	1	2	3	4	5
	Not at all	Only a little	So-so	Pretty satisfied	Very, very satisfied

8. **What did you like about what you did?** _____

9. **What didn't you like about what you did?** _____

10. **What are some things you could have done and might try if it happens again?**

    _____

    _____

7

How to Be a Good Decision Maker and Problem Solver: FIG TESPN

In school, with friends, during after-school activities, and with parents and other adults, students need good social decision making and social problem solving skills. Without them, it's hard to pursue goals and have satisfying relationships with others. Further, problem solving underlies health decision making, scientific and historical inquiry, and the writing process. It is a basic intellectual skill. This series of activities introduces students to a powerful strategy for decision making and problem solving that they can use throughout their time in middle school, and beyond.

OBJECTIVES

- To introduce students to FIG TESPN
- To show students how to use the steps together and in sequence
- To provide students and teachers with a prompt for use of this strategy

MATERIALS

Whole-class display of the steps in FIG TESPN (Worksheet 3.9)

Copies of "FIG TESPN: My Social Problem Solver" (Worksheet 3.10)

Newsprint and markers

NOTE: After you have introduced FIG TESPN, keep a whole-class display of the steps posted in the classroom.

LEADER'S GUIDE

1. Review preceding topics.

Go over "YOUR Keep Calm," "BEST," and the Trouble Tracker, and discuss how students have used them.

2. Introduce the new tool.

Refer students to the whole-class display of FIG TESPN. Tell them:

> *Today we are going to learn to use a new tool called "FIG TESPN" (after the first letter of each of the steps). FIG TESPN helps you solve problems and figure out how to do things in the best way possible. It helps you use your own resources and abilities so you don't need me or anyone else to do it for you. FIG TESPN helps you think before acting and decide the best thing to do to get what you want. It is something you bring on the scene when your feelings become strong and you have difficulty deciding what to do.*

Generate examples of what such a tool might be like. If the students are having difficulty, talk about people who have the job of providing guidance and helping others succeed without acting directly for them. If students cannot generate examples, suggest local or national sports coaches or managers and relevant television or movie characters (Obi Wan Kenobi and Yoda from *Star Wars* or Jiminy Cricket from *Pinocchio*). Stress that FIG TESPN does not solve the problem for the student or tell the student what to do; instead, FIG TESPN helps the student solve the problem.

3. Distribute and personalize the FIG TESPN worksheet.

Explain that people can help themselves solve problems by using FIG TESPN to remind them to be good problem solvers and decision makers.

Give each student a copy of Worksheet 3.9. Encourage them to develop their own visual image of FIG TESPN. Have them discuss their ideas in small groups, and then each create a personal visual reminder of FIG TESPN that they can draw on their FIG TESPN handout. Then have them share their images with the full group.

4. Illustrate the use of FIG TESPN.

Model a problem-solving situation using FIG TESPN to show how it guides your decision making. Use something suitable from your own life: a time when you had to solve a problem, make a decision, or resolve a conflict with someone—for example, deciding which activities to present to the class to help them understand a concept, what to do on a Friday afternoon, whether or not to assign something for homework, or how to cope with two conflicting meetings or responsibilities.

5. Conduct a practice activity.

Present a situation for students to deal with by using FIG TESPN. Divide the class into groups. Give each group a piece of newsprint and a marker. Here is a sample situation you can use, or you can substitute any situation you like, as long as it is hypothetical:

> *Imagine you just moved into a new house, a house you have really wanted. It seems perfect in every way. The first night, after a day of unpacking, you lay your head on the pillow to go to sleep and you hear a dog barking. It barks and barks for almost an hour, but you are so tired, you fall asleep. Next day, you do more unpacking and the place is starting to look really good. At the end of the day, you again get ready to sleep, and again, the dog starts barking, for over an hour. The same thing happens every night for five nights.*

Then say to the students:

> *Take out your FIG TESPN worksheets. I want you to use FIG TESPN to try to solve this problem. Take one step at a time and write out your responses on the newsprint. One person should be the recorder for the group, and then we will share ideas.*

Use this as a time to reinforce students' using their SDM/SPS skills to work as a team and as a diagnostic to see their problem-solving strengths and weaknesses. Don't worry about correcting students at first; focus on helping them enjoy and value the problem-solving process. Then, in the future, when a problem arises, you can have them work it out in subgroups or as a full group, using the FIG TESPN format.

IMPLEMENTATION TIPS

1. Have students draw a comic strip involving FIG TESPN.
2. Show the film *Pinocchio* or videos of the old television show *The Wonder Years* and discuss comparisons between FIG TESPN and

Jiminy Cricket or between FIG TESPN and the voice that helps the main character think through his problems.

3. Give a writing assignment with a beginning (feeling and problem) and an end. Have the students fill in the middle of the story, using FIG TESPN.

4. Use FIG TESPN as a prompt for problem solving. For example, you might ask, "How could FIG TESPN help you with this?"

5. Do not expect that students will completely understand or be able to use FIG TESPN after this brief introduction. Remember that FIG TESPN will be learned through repetition. Also, in subsequent activities, always do a complete run-through of FIG TESPN at least once in the activity.

Steps in FIG TESPN

F —**Feelings** cue me to problem solve.

I —**Identify** the problem.

G—**Goals** give me a guide.

T —**Think** of many possible solutions.

E —**Envision** outcomes.

S —**Select** the best solution.

P —**Plan** the procedure, anticipate pitfalls, and practice.

N —**Notice** what happened and remember it for next time.

F —**Feelings** cue me to problem solve.

I —**Identify** the problem.

G—**Goals** give me a guide.

T —**Think** of many possible solutions.

E —**Envision** outcomes.

S —**Select** the best solution.

P —**Plan** the procedure, anticipate pitfalls, and practice.

N—**Notice** what happened and remember it for next time.

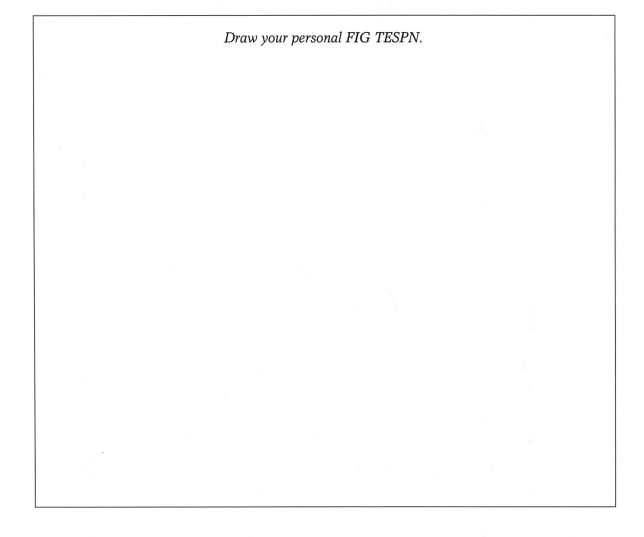

Draw your personal FIG TESPN.

8 Extra Practice in Recognizing Feelings

In middle school, hormones often play havoc with students' ability to be clear about the feelings shown by others, as well as how they are feeling. Some extra practice helps students over-learn a skill they will need in highly emotionally charged situations, including many that occur in the classroom and elsewhere in school.

OBJECTIVES

- To reinforce the skill of identifying signs of different feelings
- To help students further understand and deal effectively with feelings

MATERIALS

Chalkboard or easel pad

Any book of fiction that is familiar to all students

A video or DVD and equipment to play it *(optional)*

LEADER'S GUIDE

1. Review the SDM/SPS program.

Ask students to share with the group when they used "YOUR Keep Calm" or FIG TESPN and how they and others felt about the situations they were in.

2. Introduce the new topic.

Tell the group that the day's activity will help them practice identifying feelings a little more. Say:

The reason to keep practicing these skills is that the practice can help you in real life. The times you need these skills most— when you need to ask someone to do something and you're afraid they won't want to say yes, or when something happens and you're about to lose your temper—are exactly the times when it's hardest to remember what to do. The more you practice, the likelier you are to do things that get the results you want when you're under real pressure.

Remind students that awareness of a feeling is the first step in problem solving. Go over the steps of FIG TESPN. Have students take turns reading each step aloud, using a different kind of voice (for example, loud, soft, with different accents, emphasizing every other word).

3. Present a fictional situation.

Select a book that the students are reading or have read. Review the plot. For each of the characters, take the most recent (or final) situation they were in and make a chart with three columns. Title the columns as follows:

"Which Character?"

"Had What Feeling?"

"How Could You Tell?"

Generate a list of various situations each character experienced and the feelings associated with each situation.

4. Apply FIG TESPN.

Discuss one or more of the situations from Step 3 in detail by introducing FIG TESPN and asking:

How could FIG TESPN help the character out? What's the first thing it would remind the character to do? What should the character do next?

The first answer is that the character should figure out what he or she is feeling. Be sure to ask "what next" about each of the other seven questions.

Encourage students to be aware of different feelings in themselves and others and how FIG TESPN may be helpful to them. Discuss several situations such as these:

- You are talking to someone you want to impress, and they look bored.

- You want to ask your parents if you can go out, and they look angry.
- You want to be cool but sense yourself getting nervous.

5. Provide a summary.

Recap the skills, then ask students to remember situations in which awareness of feelings, either their own or those of others, was helpful to them. Have them record this in journals and give them opportunities to share with the group at the next opportunity.

IMPLEMENTATION TIPS

1. Stress the importance of identifying feelings both in others and in themselves. Students may find it easier to identify feelings in others than in themselves.

2. Consider using a videotape or DVD in addition to a book. A classic movie or situation comedy can be very effective for getting the concept across. Animated videos are often especially useful because the characters' feelings are exaggerated and easier to detect. Be sure to watch your chosen movie prior to showing it to the group, and give the class a brief synopsis. When you show it to the group, be sure to highlight and explore at least two feelings. You can repeat, as desired, focusing on additional feelings.

4

Transition to the New Learning Tasks of Middle School: Organizational and Study Skills Activities

In many middle school teachers' rooms, the following lament is heard every year: "Wait until you get next year's class. They can't take notes. They don't know how to study. They lose track of their assignments. They are too disorganized. I don't know what happens to their memories when they take tests."

Add this disorganization and lack of study skills to the many new pressures and experiences that students must contend with throughout the middle school years and you have a recipe for disaster. For the first time, the students have to deal with different teachers—with varying demands—for each particular subject area, and they have to move from classroom to classroom. The expectation that students will be more responsible for their own behaviors and academic performance means they need additional self-control and self-management techniques—just at the time when the onset of puberty and the increasing peer pressure they face undercut whatever self-control they built in elementary school. Many children entering middle school do not make a smooth adjustment, to put it mildly.

To a growing extent, educators are coming to believe that the acquisition of a systematic set of organizational and study skills can help students cope with these new demands and counteract the shortcomings with which they enter middle school (Anderson-Inman, 1986; Deshler & Schumaker, 1986; Elias, 1987).

Good study habits are learned, not something students inherit from their parents. Most students do not know how to change their study habits and many do not see the value of learning new study strategies. But how to study and how to organize work responsibilities are important skills that students will use for the rest of their lives. In

Thanks to Karen L. Welland for her contributions to this chapter.

school, study skills help to improve grades. Later on, these skills can help with learning on the job. Good study habits improve both use of time and recall of what has been read. And as study skills improve, similar gains can be seen in the ability to work well with others.

It is worth noting that the first Organizational Study Skills activities using SDM/SPS began in Von E. Mauger Middle School in Middlesex Borough, New Jersey, led by guidance counselor Karen Welland. She started this program to replace study hall, during which many students fooled around—often to the point of getting detention—because they were neither prepared for studying nor sure how best to do it.

Often, clinical interventions can be avoided or at least supplemented by the activities focused on study and work habits contained in this chapter. Throughout this chapter, teaching methods combine social decision making with hands-on practice. Modalities used include presentations, pictures, worksheets, small-group discussions and projects, guided practice. Students begin by learning how to organize their lockers and notebooks, track assignments, and establish study environments. A problem-solving approach is taken to help all students come up with practical solutions that they are likely to implement. This aspect of instruction provides for cultural sensitivity. The students then move on to more familiar domains related more directly to academics. After a skill-building emphasis, time is spent in review, consolidation, and practice of what has been learned, using vehicles such as the creation and sharing of study manuals.

The very nature of the activities allows for close articulation with all academic subject areas. Further, the social decision making instructional perspective and the overall structure of the activities allow for integration of other materials, as needed, to bolster a group's skills or to extend the program to a longer period of time. The vast array of materials on the market allow for variety and creativity in addressing the students' various learning styles, as needs indicate, and these also can be adapted to the SDM/SPS structure.

GENERAL IMPLEMENTATION TIPS

1. *Involve guidance counselors.* Since the activities in this chapter are designed to aid in the smooth transition to middle school, the guidance counselor could play a major role in carrying them out. This might mean leading or co-leading some of the activities in a subject-area classroom or advisory, or infusing the program with a guidance curriculum directed toward developing self-esteem and building skills for overcoming obstacles and solving everyday problems.

2. *Fit into school routines.* Every school is unique, and fitting in the activities for the general school population (as opposed to selected subgroups of students) depends on local logistics. In some cases, integrating study skills with the curriculum is done on a daily basis in the classroom. In others, activities are carried out in varying subject areas as one class period per week. For example, the language arts teacher could incorporate it into the curriculum on a given day each week for one marking period, the social studies teacher for another marking period, and so on.

3. *Use group or individual formats.* Sometimes, working on study skills with a single individual is necessary. Facets of the activities can easily be individualized based on need. However, the emphasis in the activities in this chapter is on small groups. Small groups allow instructors to engage students in tasks through active participation. The interactions within small groups of students working on a common project can facilitate the learning of skills through shared problem solving and mutual learning. There is also a greater likelihood of peer reinforcement and support outside the formal meetings that take place.

4. *Involving parents is optional.* Relatively little is presented regarding systematic involvement of parents. It is obvious that the more parental involvement, the better. However, the activities are designed to benefit students whose parents are not going to provide coordinated, supportive assistance and follow-through in the home. Still, the communication techniques presented in Chapter 9 lend themselves very well to communicating with parents about the kinds of organizational and study skills their children need for academic success, and what they can do to support school efforts to build students' skills in those areas.

TOPICS OF ACTIVITIES IN THIS CHAPTER

1. Locker Organization
2. Locker Cleanout and Student Feedback
3. Learning About and Improving Your Study Habits
4. Organizing Notebooks and Assignments
5. Literacy-Based Projects for Students' Internalizing Their Own Study Patterns and Habits

SUGGESTED RESOURCES

Burkie, C. R., & Marshak, D. (1986). *Home study skills program* (Student text, levels 1 and 2). Washington, DC: National

Association of Elementary School Principals/National Association of Secondary School Principals.

Campbell, L. (2003). *Mindful learning: 101 proven strategies for student and teacher success.* Thousand Oaks, CA: Corwin.

Chuska, K. R. (2003). *Fourteen connections, or how to study everything* (Fastback No. 502). Bloomington, IN: Phi Delta Kappa Education Foundation.

Creative Visuals. (n.d.). *Study skills series No. 40* (Transparencies). Big Spring, TX: Creative Visuals.

Frender, G. (1990). *Learning to learn: Strengthening study skills and brain power.* Nashville, TN: Incentive Publications.

Gleason, M. M. (1988). Teaching study strategies. *Teaching Exceptional Children, 20,* 52–53.

How to teach study skills (Video). (2000). Alexandria, VA: Association for Supervision and Curriculum Development.

Lobb, N. (1984). *Following directions—An activity pack* (Masters and cassette). Portland, ME: J. Weston Walch.

Marzano, R. J., Pickering, D., & Pollack, C. (2001). *Classroom instruction that works.* Alexandria, VA: Association for Supervision and Curriculum Development.

Mason, G. (1984). *Scoring higher on tests.* Portland, ME: J. Weston Walch.

Ohme, H. (1986). *Learn how to learn study skills.* Los Altos, CA: California Education Plan.

Perfection Form Company. (1982). *Making the grade: A time-effective knowledge system.* Logan, IA: Author.

Perfection Form Company. (1982). *Strategies for study: The learning-how-to-learn handbook.* Logan, IA: Author.

Sunburst Communications. (1988). *Students' skills for success.* Pleasantville, NY: Sunburst Communications.

The Right Combination Co. (1986). *Research proven test-taking tactics* (grades 6–8). Conyers, GA: The Right Combination Company.

1 Locker Organization

The first step in organization is students' lockers. For too many, lockers are a mess and make it more, rather than less, difficult for their owners to come to class adequately prepared.

OBJECTIVES

- To teach the necessary skills for keeping a neat, well-organized locker
- To introduce the idea of scheduled opportunities for locker cleanup
- To establish the potential benefits of a clean, organized locker
- To have students determine what it is they can do to improve the organization of their own lockers

MATERIALS

Copies of "Organizing and Cleaning Out Your Locker" (Worksheet 4.1)

Drawing paper

Markers, crayons, and rulers

NOTE: Be careful not to spend too much time on this activity. Set a time limit that will allow you to complete the remainder of what you wish to accomplish for that day.

LEADER'S GUIDE

1. Introduce the *sharing circle* format.

Assemble the group in a circle and have students each say their name and answer one or two impersonal questions, such as favorite bagels or sandwiches, last live performance seen or listened to, or favorite car. (See the "Implementation Tips" section for more detailed information.)

2. Distribute the locker management worksheet.

This worksheet begins by asking the students to consider the benefits of organization. Ask:

What are the benefits of having a neat, well-organized locker?

Have each student answer this question. Then discuss these answers as a group.

3. Distribute materials for the locker drawings specified in the "Classroom Activity" section of the worksheet.

Explain the purpose to the students. Walk around to each student, stressing the importance of neatness and organization in the drawing. Be sure that, as a group, you go over the ideas that the students have for improving their individual lockers. This will benefit those students who could not come up with their own good ideas.

Go over and clarify the section regarding periodic locker cleanouts. Do not tell the students when these cleanouts will occur. Simply tell them to hold on to their locker drawing (and all of their Organizational and Study Skills materials) so that you can compare the drawing to the actual locker. Post a chart to acknowledge those students who have a clean, organized locker at each check.

If you wish, you may revisit the students' locker drawings periodically. They sometimes come up with better layouts, or they must make modifications as the books and other materials they need change over time.

4. Explain the follow-up assignment.

Tell students:

On the back of your locker drawing you have made a list of five steps that you can take to improve the neatness and organization of your locker. Sometime between now and our next class meeting you are to complete those five steps. In other words, if we should happen to have a locker cleanout next week, your locker will look identical to the one that you have drawn in class today. We will be discussing this assignment during next week's sharing circle.

If you wish, tell students about any incentive plan you have for locker cleanout.

IMPLEMENTATION TIPS: THE SHARING CIRCLE

The sharing circle is an organized method by which students will be giving reviews and testimonials about what they have learned and put into practice. Through the use of the sharing circle and testimonials, the following will be accomplished:

- The teachers and students will have an opportunity to learn more about each other as people.
- The group will become more cohesive.
- Instructors will be able to correctly determine who has and who has not completed their home study assignment.
- Students will be exposed to the successes and problems of their fellow students. This represents an outstanding opportunity for the students to learn from one another.

The sharing circle is to be conducted in the following manner:

1. If the sharing circle is a part of the day's agenda, then it is always the first activity in that meeting.

2. The students do not have to be in a circle. However, it is important for your group to take a consistent form and to try to position students so they can see one another.

3. To help the students feel at ease with this group activity, your first question should always be something nonthreatening. For example:

   Going around the circle from right to left, I would like everyone to share with the rest of the group the name of their favorite movie or their favorite ice cream.

   If students do not all know one another's names, ask them to say their names before they answer.

4. When everyone in the group has had an opportunity to answer the initial question, it is time for the testimonials. Here is one way to begin this part of the activity:

   Going around the circle from left to right, I would like each of you to share with the rest of the group a situation in which you used the skills from the activity we did on [day of last lesson]] If you did not use the skills, then share a time when using these skills might have been helpful.

   The first time you do an organizational and study skills activity, you might want to start with the question,

   What is most helpful to you when you study? What is least helpful?

5. If a student is uncomfortable answering a particular question, then that student should be allowed to "pass." However, do not allow students to abuse this privilege. (Some leaders give each student one written pass to use per month.)

6. Once the class has completed this activity, you have the option of either rearranging the room or teaching the lesson from the students' sharing circle positions. This is a matter of personal preference.

Student _____ **Date** _____

Today you will be learning how to improve the organization and neatness of your locker. A neat, well-organized locker will give you many benefits. Can you think of any? Write your answers on the lines below:

1. _____

2. _____

3. _____

4. _____

5. _____

CLASSROOM ACTIVITY

You will receive one piece of drawing paper. With that piece of construction paper, you are to do the following:

1. Fold it in half so that it is the same shape as your school locker.

2. Using the markers, crayons, and ruler, draw the outside of your locker.

3. Using the same materials, draw the inside of your locker as you would like it to appear. Make it as neat and as well organized as you possibly can.

4. On the back of the construction paper, list five things that you can do to improve the neatness and the organization of your locker. We will then share and discuss these ideas as a group.

LOCKER CLEANOUTS

During the course of the school year, your teacher will announce locker cleanouts. Locker cleanouts give you the opportunity to make your locker look identical to the one you drew today. They also provide members of the school staff with the opportunity to evaluate all the lockers. In other words, if at the end of a locker cleanout your locker looks identical to the one that you have drawn, then you will receive any agreed-upon recognition.

2   Locker Cleanout and Student Feedback

The first part of this activity is a continuation of the locker organization process. The second part focuses on helping students self-monitor their progress and track their utilization of skills. This is a procedure that is valuable not only in the context of this activity but in virtually any academic endeavor.

OBJECTIVES

- To provide students with time for cleaning out their lockers
- To provide teachers with an opportunity to evaluate the students' lockers
- To provide the teachers with an opportunity for correcting poorly kept lockers
- To promote more active student involvement in organizational and study skills tasks
- To determine if the students are using the skills that they have been taught
- To both obtain and review the students' ideas for improving the activities

MATERIALS

Several trash cans

Copies of the "Organization and Study Skills Student Feedback Form" (Worksheet 4.2)

LEADER'S GUIDE

1. Conduct a sharing circle.

End the sharing circle by having the class discuss the follow-up assignment from the preceding activity.

2. Explain your rules for completing today's task.

The rules that you choose to enforce will be your decision. However, make sure each student works alone. Students who are allowed to work in groups get very little locker cleaning done. Also, before you let the students out into the hallway, remind them that they must bring their locker drawings with them. Inform students that when they finish their work, their lockers should look exactly like the drawings.

3. Perform and review locker cleanout.

Release the students for the cleanup work, and tell them to signal you when they're ready for review. Once you've looked over a locker, send the owner back into the classroom to begin working on the feedback form.

4. Have students fill out the feedback forms.

Give the students enough time to complete the form. Tell them to write down the activity for which you want feedback (in this case, locker cleanout). Do not rush them. Make sure the students know that they should not put their names on the form so that it can be confidential. It is not to be used against any student in any way!

Once these forms have been collected, keep them. When you are reading them, keep an eye out for good suggestions. It is pleasantly surprising to see the quality of some of the students' ideas. (In fact, several student suggestions have had an influence on the procedures presented here.)

Date _____

I am very interested in your suggestions about activities designed to help you with your organization and your study skills. Therefore, I would appreciate it if you would answer the following questions *honestly.* Do not write your name anywhere on this paper. When you are finished, place the paper face down. One of the students will then collect the papers and mix up the order and then return them to me. The activity that I would like to have your suggestions and feelings on at this time is this:

_____

1. How much have you liked this activity? *(Circle one.)*

   Very much   OK   Not at all

2. What have you liked the most about this activity?

   _____

   _____

3. What have you liked the least about this activity?

   _____

   _____

4. If you had been leading this activity, what would you have done differently?

   _____

   _____

5. Have you used anything that you have learned in this activity either in school or at home?

   Yes   No   If yes, what? _____

6. Have the skills that you have learned in this activity helped you in any way?

   Yes   No   If yes, how? _____

7. In the space below, write anything else you feel it would be helpful for me to know about this or related activities:

   _____

   _____

3 Learning About and Improving Your Study Habits

Success in school depends on sound study habits. As students enter middle school, the quality and quantity of work required changes. Often, study habits that worked for students in elementary school are no longer adequate. Most students do not know how to change their study habits, and many do not see the value of learning new study strategies. This topic is designed to provide both the how and the why of efficient study.

OBJECTIVES

- To provide students with an opportunity to determine their study strengths and areas in need of improvement
- To teach students an ongoing process to monitor and plan to improve their weakest study habits

MATERIALS

Chalkboard or easel pad

Copies of the "Study Habits Rating Scale" (Worksheet 4.3) and "Study Skills Planner" (Worksheet 4.4)

LEADER'S GUIDE

1. Begin with a sharing circle.

Use the time to review recent study skills activities.

Ask the group:

What does the word study *mean to you?*

Get at least four or five responses. Help the students get the idea that studying is about preparation and learning. Then ask:

When do you do your best studying? Let's go around the group and see what all of you think.

Give everyone a chance to answer, and record their responses on the chalkboard or easel pad. Check off those responses that are repeated. Next, ask:

OK, now I would like you to think about when you find you do your worst studying. When is it hard to study?

As before, go around the room and record responses.

2. Distribute the "Study Habits Rating Scale" worksheet.

Tell students:

How well you do in middle school depends a lot on your study habits. We've discussed a number of things that help you study well, and that make it hard for you to study well.

Take a moment to review what was discussed.

Besides those things, studying has some other aspects that are important for you to pay attention to. I am going to pass out a sheet that lists a lot of different study areas. Read them over and rate them according to the instructions.

Have the students fill out the ratings scale individually.

3. Review the ratings.

Tell students:

In the next activity, you will be paired up with a study skills partner. Together, you will review each other's study habits rating sheets and decide, for each of you, which three areas you want to improve. Then, take a copy of the Study Skills Planner and help each other make a plan to improve the study skills that you have chosen to improve. When you are finished, raise your hand and I will review your sheets. When we are all satisfied, we will all sign them.

Divide the class into pairs. Either assign pairs so a more and less compent student are together or match students of similar study ability.

Circulate among the pairs of students and help them set goals and make plans. Use the sharing circle time periodically, or at some other available time, to have students review their progress and make revised plans. Repeat this process regularly. The first two or three times, waiting a week between reviews of goals and plans is a good idea; gradually, you can extend this to two or three weeks, though some students may need weekly reviews. This activity can be used flexibly and repeatedly, as you wish.

As you close this activity, remind students that you expect study skills partners to work together. It is their job to help each other, check up on each other, and support each other.

If a study problem comes up that they can't solve, they should try to use FIG TESPN to solve the problem (see Chapter 3), ask another study partner team for help, or ask you. What they are *not* allowed to do is to let the problem hang around. You want to make it clear that your students are a problem-solving team, and that among all of them, there is enough study power and skill to help everyone.

4. Follow up.

Praise students for their continued work on study habits. Re-administer the Study Habits Rating Scale toward the end of the school year and have pairs of students compare it to their original ratings and evaluate their overall progress during the year. This can take the form of an essay written by the students about their partners and about themselves, stating where they improved most and least and making some recommendations for what to do over the rest of the school year and the following year.

Student _____ Date _____

Circle one of the numbers to the right of each study skill listed to indicate how often you do each one.

Rating scale: 1—Never; 2—Almost never; 3—Sometimes; 4—Almost always; 5—Always

CLASSROOM-RELATED SKILLS

Arrive at class on time	1	2	3	4	5
Come to class prepared with materials needed	1	2	3	4	5
Come to class with work due	1	2	3	4	5
Pay attention during class	1	2	3	4	5
Show self-control	1	2	3	4	5
Seek extra help when needed	1	2	3	4	5
Follow directions	1	2	3	4	5
Participate in class activities	1	2	3	4	5
Work well in small groups	1	2	3	4	5
Work well independently	1	2	3	4	5
Use time well	1	2	3	4	5
Take your time going through work	1	2	3	4	5
Prepare written work carefully	1	2	3	4	5
Complete classwork on time	1	2	3	4	5
Write down assignments	1	2	3	4	5
Complete homework on time	1	2	3	4	5
Make up absentee work	1	2	3	4	5

HOME-RELATED SKILLS

Work in a place as quiet as possible	1	2	3	4	5
Study in a comfortable place	1	2	3	4	5
Avoid distractions	1	2	3	4	5
Study at a regular time each day	1	2	3	4	5
Start work early enough	1	2	3	4	5
Plan the order of studying	1	2	3	4	5
Allow a certain amount of time per subject	1	2	3	4	5
Get all needed materials in a timely way	1	2	3	4	5
Get to work immediately	1	2	3	4	5
Stick even to the most difficult assignments	1	2	3	4	5
Use a dictionary for unfamiliar words	1	2	3	4	5
Make notes on important points	1	2	3	4	5
Summarize what is read	1	2	3	4	5
Work until the subject is mastered	1	2	3	4	5
Check over your own work	1	2	3	4	5
Prepare thoroughly for tests	1	2	3	4	5
Relax briefly between subjects	1	2	3	4	5
Do something enjoyable when finished	1	2	3	4	5

Student _____ Date _____

STUDY SKILL YOU PLAN TO IMPROVE

1. _____

2. _____

3. _____

WHAT WILL YOU DO TO TRY TO IMPROVE?

1. _____

2. _____

3. _____

How well did your plan go? *(Circle the best answer for each step.)*

1. Very well	OK but still more to go	Not well
2. Very well	OK but still more to go	Not well
3. Very well	OK but still more to go	Not well

Take a new planning sheet and list your next set of goals. You can choose all new goals, keep some and add some, or keep all your current goals and work to improve them.

Your signature _____

Your study partner's signature _____

Group leader's signature _____

4 Organizing Notebooks and Assignments

It is essential for academic success that students learn to organize information, and their notebooks and assignments are two key elements of information they need to organize. Compared to elementary school, middle school demands more emphasis on notebooks and also requires students to keep track of more numerous and more varied assignments. Note that as students do more work on computers, this activity can easily be modified to focus on how files are organized and how information within files is managed, in addition to how students can use electronic reminders for keeping track of assignments.

OBJECTIVES

- To help students improve the organization of their notebooks
- To teach the students how to create and properly use an assignment sheet
- To recommend that students begin using a checklist of things to do before leaving school each day

MATERIALS AND PREPARATION

Copies of "Notebook Organization" (Worksheet 4.5), the "Daily Assignment Sheet" (Worksheet 4.6), and "Tips for Using and Assignment Sheet" (Worksheet 4.7)

Chalkboard or easel pad

Paper and pencils

NOTE: Make five copies of the Daily Assignment Sheet to start (one for each day of the week). Let students know where they can pick up additional copies as they need them.

LEADER'S GUIDE

1. Begin with a sharing circle.

Ask the students to discuss how they use their notebooks.

2. Introduce the day's activities.

Tell the class:

During the first half of today's class, we will be discussing suggestions for improving the organization of a notebook. Why is it helpful to have a well-organized notebook?

Be sure to get a few good ideas and to make the point that a well-organized notebook will help maintain good study habits and achieve better grades. Then go over Worksheet 4.5 with students, giving them a slow and careful review of each of the tips.

3. Practice cleaning out notebooks.

Ask students to follow and complete the directions for the notebook cleanout activity. Inform your students that from now on, they must bring their primary notebooks with them to class.

Whenever you have free time at the end of a class period, use it to give the students the opportunity to clean out their notebooks. Those students who do not bring their primary notebooks to class should be considered unprepared.

4. Work with assignment sheets.

Tell students:

In the next activity, you will learn how to properly use an assignment sheet.

Then go over Worksheets 4.6 and 4.7, on assignment sheet use. Discuss each point on Worksheet 4.6 and answer any questions.

5. Build a checklist.

Explain that part of doing assignments is to be sure to have the materials you need to do the work you have to do. With the students, create a checklist titled "Before I Leave School Today." Discuss what they should be thinking about and checking for before they leave school. On the chalkboard or easel pad, record students' responses.

Later, use a word processor to create the checklist (or have a student do it) and then make copies for everyone. Leave one or two blank lines so students can list things that are specific to their own circumstances.

One option is to have the students hang a copy of the checklist in their lockers. This helps to avoid the "I forgot" syndrome. If you choose to do this, then make looking for the checklist a part of your locker inspections. Another is to have the checklist routinely distributed at the end of the school day. Your students may suggest other options that are feasible.

Student _____ Date _____

TIPS FOR ORGANIZING A NOTEBOOK

1. Every notebook must be cleaned out regularly. If you are certain that you no longer need to keep something, then throw it away. However, if you have any doubts, do not throw it out. Instead, save it and ask the appropriate teacher whether you will need it or not. It is better to be safe than sorry!

2 It helps to divide your notebook into different sections (for example, class notes, homework) by using colored dividers and tabs. This can make it quicker and easier for you to find things.

3. If there's room, include a pocket or pouch for extra pens and pencils.

4. Write your name, address, and home phone number on the inside cover of your notebook. If you should ever lose your notebook, this information will make it possible for someone to return it to you.

5. Keep a list of your classmates and their phone numbers in your notebook. Then, if you are at home and you have a question, you will be able to call a classmate to get the answer.

6. Create a place in your notebook for storing the handouts that your teachers give to you.

DIRECTIONS FOR NOTEBOOK CLEANOUTS

7. Reread the tips for organizing a notebook. As you are reading, circle those tips that you believe will help you to improve the organization of your notebook. You will then have approximately ten minutes to complete the steps that you have circled.

8. From now on, you must bring your notebook to class with you. When we have free time at the end of a class period, it will be spent cleaning out notebooks.

Student _____ Date _____

Put a check mark in the "complete" column when you finish an assignment.

Subject/Class	Assignment	Date due	Complete

Student _____ **Date** _____

1. Use one assignment sheet per day.

2. Take your assignment sheet with you to every class.

3. When your teacher gives out an assignment, fill in the columns on the assignment sheet. If there is no assignment, write "none" in the appropriate space for that class.

4. Before leaving class, make sure that you completely understand the assignment. If you have any questions, ask the teacher.

5. Post a note in your locker that will remind you to take your assignment sheet home.

6. When you finish an assignment, cross it out or check it off.

5 Literacy-Based Projects for Students' Internalizing Their Own Study Patterns and Habits

Students need help to internalize their organizational and study skills. This can be done while also building literacy skills in multiple modalities. The activities in this topic allow students to develop manuals or skits as ways to accomplish multiple educational goals.

OBJECTIVES

- To help students elaborate and internalize their organizational and study skills
- To enable students to learn about their classmates' study strategies
- To provide a project format for building students' literacy in multiple modalities

MATERIALS

Copies of "Creating Your Own Study Skills Skit" (Worksheet 4.8)

Arts and crafts supplies

Props for skits

Computer access for creating manuals *(optional)*

Videotaping equipment *(optional)*

LEADER'S GUIDE

1. Begin with a sharing circle.

Choose a topic related to students' use of study skills.

Tell students that they are going to spend some classes making manuals and creating skits to help them remember their study patterns and share them with others.

2. Launch the study skills manual activity.

Divide students into groups of four to six to work together on the study skills manuals.

Explain:

Using any format you wish, you are to develop a booklet that details at least four and no more than seven important study skills.

Help students by having a purpose for the manuals. For example, let them know that they will share them with parents, other students in their grade levels, or students who are entering middle school. Sometimes it can be helpful to create a competitive environment, to spur all groups on to do their best work.

3. Present guidelines for creating manuals.

Give students the following instructions:

Review study skills and organizing activities you have learned, share ideas within a group, and decide what is important in each of them. Consider also how you go about preparing for these study situations (for which you may or may not have learned strategies this year): creating a good study area; memorizing information when studying for a test; improving your test-taking skills for different kinds of tests; improving your skills at listening when adults and peers are speaking in class; reading for meaning; taking notes from textbooks and from the Internet; taking notes when teachers are lecturing; organizing time and prioritizing different assignments; and studying for tests, reports, projects.

Here are some helpful hints to offer the class:

- Design a cover page.
- Prepare a table of contents.
- Draw pictures.
- Look at some of the manuals other students have prepared.
- Be creative.
- Use a lot of color.

Provide a time frame within which you would like to see students complete this activity, and then help keep them on track. Encourage students to use FIG TESPN during all parts of the process of working together.

4. Create study skills skits.

Tell the class:

> *Using the study skills activities that you have learned, you will be creating your own short study skills skit. Who knows what a skit is?*

Help students come up with a definition. Then go over Worksheet 4.7 with the group.

Ask students for some of their ideas about skits. An example of a skit would be a group of friends deciding to study for a test together. Either the positive or the negative approaches could be presented. The narrator would help explain these. Following presentation of the skit, the class could actively participate by sharing what they noticed as good and bad study and organizational skills.

You could choose to share this with students as an example or hold this idea in reserve if they are unable to come up with any viable ideas or approaches. The topic will also depend on the intended audience for the skits.

Follow the general guidelines for the manual activity to have students work in groups to create skits. In these skits, between two and four skills are sufficient to represent.

Student(s) _____ **Date** _____

RULES FOR CREATING YOUR SKIT

1. You will have _____ class periods for completing this assignment. During the _____ period, you are to write and rehearse your skit. During the _____ class period, you will be rehearsing and performing it.

2. Your skit must show the audience how a skill that you have learned can be used either in school or at home.

3. The cast of each skit must consist of a minimum of two or maximum of five actors.

4. Each skit must be at least five minutes long.

5. Skits may be videotaped so we can share them with other classes.

SUGGESTIONS

1. Give your skit a title.

2. Designate someone in your group to be the narrator. The narrator will describe the setting of your skit to the audience.

3. Write a copy of the script for each cast member. This will help you avoid the embarrassment of forgetting your lines.

4. Consider showing your characters both before and after they have learned a study skill.

5. Be creative.

Part 3

Applications to Academic Content Areas and Group Counseling Formats

CHAPTER

5

Applying a Social Decision Making Approach to Social Studies, Current Events, and History to Promote Citizenship and Community Service

Participatory citizenship requires a free and critical intelligence.

—S. Natoli (1989, p. 336)

The types of critical thinking skills upon which good citizenship depends cannot be acquired incidentally (Engle, 1990; Gerzon, 1997). Rather, education for citizenship depends on the systematic instruction of critical thinking and decision-making skills. The same holds true for the kinds of careful thinking needed for effective everyday interaction with peers and adults. In all aspects of life, students benefit from instruction in the skills they need to be productive citizens, whether of the school, family, workplace, or community (Fredericks, 2003). However, teaching students isolated critical thinking skills is not sufficient to ensure thoughtful evaluation and action in response to social and historical issues. A framework for organized application of these skills must also be taught.

One promising framework involves teaching students how to view historical and current events as the outcome of decision-making activities on the part of significant persons. In traditional social studies instruction, a decision-making perspective can easily be lost, given the heavy instructional reliance on textbooks and lectures that tend to present historical events as facts on a par with natural events like the ebb and flow of the tides rather than as the outcome of a decision-making process. Equipping students with a decision-making framework allows them to begin to recognize how world events might have differed if alternative decisions had been reached. By extension,

Thanks to Karen Haboush for her contributions to this chapter.

121

understanding how history might have been changed can help students consider how current world conditions and events might be modified through responsible decision making and problem solving.

As an example of its application, a decision-making framework could be used to examine the alternative solutions to the same problem offered by different candidates in either a public election or a student council election. Students could evaluate the possible consequences of each candidate's proposed solution in deciding on the best candidate. Students could also apply a decision-making framework to determine whether their personal choices may have consequences for larger societal problems (for example, whether to buy clothes or sneakers made in the United States or in a foreign country).

The kind of learning essential for citizenship can be applied to students in both classroom and group, club, or counseling contexts. The instructional demands already facing social studies teachers make an approach that allows teachers to teach decision-making skills with existing social studies content most desirable because it avoids creating additional demands on teachers. The activities in this chapter allow teachers to provide a decision-making framework by having students apply it to whatever topic area is already under study. Similarly, the activities lend themselves well to group and counseling formats that are designed to build problem-solving and decision-making skills in a positive, nonclinical, and unstigmatizing context that emphasizes empowerment rather than remediation.

Dissatisfaction with the extent to which existing approaches to both education and counseling are helping students understand and enact the concept of responsible citizenship requires that we reexamine our assumptions about what kind of instruction is necessary to accomplish this task (Seif, 2004). Understanding the nature of the democratic process may ultimately serve as the best instructional guide (Gerzon, 1997). While consensus exists among educators about the need for students to possess a thorough knowledge base in the social studies, greater knowledge alone does not appear to guarantee better citizenship; what is also required is the ability to *use* this knowledge in probing, well-grounded, and thoughtful examinations of current and historical issues (Engle, 1990; see also Hergert, 2002, and Massialas, 1990).

Ultimately, democracy itself may present the best guide for modifying instructional practice (Gerzon, 1997). To better understand the types of thinking skills students must develop for good citizenship, we need to recognize that what really defines democracy is the *freedom to question available information*—that is, to freely examine, evaluate, and challenge what is presented for public consumption (Engle, 1990; Natoli, 1989). This process must occur if people are to participate fully in democratic government. Thus to be able to identify issues for social reform, students must learn how to systematically think about the knowledge they acquire (Engle, 1990; Natoli, 1989). This is also true for enabling troubled students to make personal changes in their own lives. They need to be able to look at the world around them—and at their interactions within it—in new, more open and questioning ways. When students directly participate in the SDM/SPS instructional activities in this chapter, social studies—whether in the classroom or other group contexts—can become an arena for students to learn by experience what *active participation* actually means and build the skills to do it effectively and constructively (Boyer, 1990; Haboush, 1989).

GENERAL IMPLEMENTATION TIPS

1. *Make sure the students learn the content.* That is, give the students a sense of the relevant subject matter that will be the focus of the SDM/SPS discussions. For example, it is useful to teach new vocabulary words and use maps and other instructional aids such as brief articles to ensure students' comprehension. Some teachers prefer to use the SDM/SPS activities as a vehicle for integrating knowledge after students have finished a unit of study. For example, upon completing a chapter of a social studies textbook, teachers might conduct a class discussion of the main topic using the framework. Alternatively, teachers have substituted a social decision making worksheet for the review questions at the end of a textbook chapter.

2. *Start with the sequence.* Once teachers understand the concept of teaching from a social decision making perspective, variations on the instructional sequence may be attempted. However, it is recommended that teachers follow the suggested sequence when first teaching the approach.

3. *Use varied sources of instructional materials.* As noted, the social decision making framework can be applied to whatever topic area is under study. The following represents a partial list of possible instructional sources:

   - A topic from a social studies textbook
   - A newspaper article or an article from a weekly current events news magazine
   - A historical document
   - A story on the evening news
   - A letter to the editor or a newspaper editorial
   - A docudrama

- A historical play or drama

- A political speech or pamphlet

- A debate by several political candidates

- A resolution passed by local government officials

- A Supreme Court decision

- A resolution by the United Nations on a particular issue

- A recently passed state or national law

An outstanding and continually improving source of reference materials and ideas is www.smithsonianeducation.org. At the teacher section of the Web site, you can find information retrievable by grade, keywords, or museums; lessons, interactive activities, and teaching tools aligned with national standards; professional development opportunities, and a guide to planning field trips to the Smithsonian and other museums. The student section contains interactive exhibits, streaming video, sound, photos, maps, techniques on how discoveries are made (for example, gathering artifacts, space travel). The site also has a family section that shows how parents can make the most of museum trips.

4. *Work with groups.* Teachers should attempt to maximize opportunities for students to work collaboratively in practicing application of the framework. This approach lends itself particularly well to small-group work in which students represent members of either heterogeneous or homogeneous groups. In this manner, students gain additional experience in understanding how democratic participation requires discussion among individuals with differing opinions. Working collaboratively can assist students in better understanding other viewpoints.

5. *Assess in various ways.* Naturally, comprehension of subject matter will be of concern. In addition to whatever methods you would normally use to determine students' level of comprehension, responses to the social decision making worksheets and framework questions should also be evaluated. An incorrect discussion of the issues or a set of incomplete responses to questions may reflect limited comprehension. The level of ability to systematically discuss a particular issue from the perspective of the decision-making framework should also be indicative of students' degree of comprehension.

In addition to comprehension of subject matter, you will also want to assess students' application of the decision-making framework. Students' ability to apply the framework systematically and thoroughly should be evaluated. Has the student completed all of the steps of the framework? Has the student completed all steps of the framework for each goal and solution suggested? Do the responses to each step of the framework reflect some degree of thoughtfulness—or does the student appear to be providing information taken verbatim from text? Is the student able to describe the personal thought process used in deciding upon a final solution? These are all questions that should be considered in assessing students' abilities to apply the framework. In addition, the completed sample assignments included in this chapter can serve as a further guide to evaluating students' use of the framework.

Finally, students should also be graded on participation because the activities are designed to increase students' level of participation. Student participation in small-group work and class discussion can be assessed. Students should be able to generate various goals and solutions as well as to critically examine the solutions offered by other students.

TOPICS IN THIS CHAPTER

1. Introducing the Concept of Decision Making in Social Studies, History, and Civics
2. Creating a Newspaper Article
3. Decision Making Around Current Events
4. Making History Relevant: Linking the Present and the Past

1

Introducing the Concept of Decision Making in Social Studies, History, and Civics

The purpose of this activity is to help students begin to view historical and current events as the outcome of decision-making activities. This activity involves teaching an expanded version of the social decision making framework. By elaborating on the questions from the original framework, students can more easily learn how to apply the steps to social studies and current events. This activity is particularly useful when students are first becoming familiar with the decision-making steps.

OBJECTIVES

- To introduce or review the process of SDM/SPS with students
- To help students view historical and current events as the outcome of decision making and problem solving by individuals and groups

MATERIALS

Copies of "Making Decisions About Important Events" (Worksheet 5.1)

LEADER'S GUIDE

1. Present the underlying subject matter.

Begin by discussing the social studies topic area under study or by introducing an area. Define any new vocabulary words.

2. Introduce the idea that historical and current events represent the outcomes of decision-making activities.

Stress that just as personal problems require solutions, world problems also require them. Provide students with examples of how different solutions to the same problem result in very different consequences. The examples can come from local (even school) issues affecting students' own lives in order to better make the point. Be sure students understand how to think about current and historical events as problems before proceeding.

3. Hand out copies of the worksheet.

Distribute the "Making Decisions About Important Events" worksheet. Ask the students to describe an aspect of the topic as a *problem*. Often, the main point of a selection can be restated as a problem.

4. Identify the participants.

Once the group has agreed on the problem, have students identify those individuals or groups who are involved in the problem. Students can refer to their textbooks, newspaper articles, Web sources, and so on to do this.

5. Assess feelings and goals.

After students have identified the different groups, ask them to imagine what the *feelings* of each group might be. Next, have them identify *goals* for each group.

6. Develop solutions.

Allowing students to work either independently or in small groups, have them generate different *solutions* to the problem. If working in groups, students can either represent a unified group and generate solutions for their group or pretend to be composed of members of different groups working as a team (like the United Nations) that is attempting to reach a mutually agreeable solution.

7. Assess consequences.

Have students, either independently or in small groups, envision and identify possible short- and long-term *consequences* for each solution.

Ask students to select the *solution* that will best reach their goals, based on their evaluation of the consequences.

8. Make a plan.

Request that students describe how their chosen solution should be carried out. Students should devise an operationally defined *plan* for doing this.

Allow different students or groups to discuss how they chose their solutions and how their solutions compare.

9. Introduce questions for reflection and discussion.

After students have completed the worksheet and shared their ideas, the following questions can be used to stimulate further discussion:

- How did you feel when others disagreed with your pick for best solution?

- How did you feel when someone with a different solution first began to speak? Were you fully listening to them or did you tune them out?

- Did you feel more favorably toward another solution after hearing it being discussed?

- Is it ever possible for people to completely agree on a solution? If not, how can we accept differences of opinion?

IMPLEMENTATION TIPS

1. Prior to conducting any lessons, it is useful to assess students' knowledge of FIG TESPN or related problem-solving strategies. FIG TESPN is built implicitly into the structure of Worksheet 5.1. Although this assessment is not essential, some instructors find the information helpful in deciding how much time to spend teaching about an SDM/SPS framework and concepts. (See Chapter 2 for ways to provide this background and Chapter 3 for a sample short course.)

2. Clarify any new vocabulary words and concepts before asking students to apply the decision-making framework.

3. This activity lends itself well to small-group work, allowing students to gain experience in collaborative teamwork. Be sure to review the ground rules, Classroom Constitution, or whatever the group is using to manage internal communications before beginning the group work. Groups can be identified as representing

either a homogeneous group (say, the Democratic or Republican Party) or a group composed of heterogeneous members (say, the U.S. Senate). Current events can also be studied using small groups.

4. When first using this activity, do not allow students to begin working in small groups until they have demonstrated that they understand how to apply the framework.

5. The worksheet can be used with a variety of instructional materials, including social studies textbooks, newspaper articles, current events magazines, historical documents, educational videos, documentaries, Web sources, and plays.

EXAMPLES OF COMPLETED ASSIGNMENTS

The first example is an assignment completed by a sixth grader. The student worked as part of a group, but then each group member was asked to complete an individual essay. The second example is a consensus essay that a group arrived at together. The topic is the decline of Egypt. The social decision making steps have been capitalized in order to draw attention to them. The responses are discussed in greater detail following each example.

Example 1

One PROBLEM that made Egypt decline was that the priests and pharaohs were almost always struggling. Another is that too much money and energy was spent for war. Also, Amenhotep IV changed the Egyptian religion. All because of this, Egypt was losing power.

The PEOPLE involved are Egyptian priests and pharaohs. Other people involved are Egyptian government officials, temple workers, administrators, Amen-Re, and the Assyrians. The GOALS of the Egyptian people were to stop the pharaohs from taking money and weapons from them. Another GOAL was to conquer Amenhotep IV. Other GOALS were to open the temples of Amen-Re, to get iron ore, and to get food.

Some possible SOLUTIONS to stop the decline of Egypt would be for priests and pharaohs not to struggle, not to spend money on wars, and spend money on schools and medicine.

If the priests and pharaohs stopped struggling, they could regain control (CONSEQUENCE) and if the Egyptians don't spend money on weapons for war, they could spend money on food and crops (CONSEQUENCES).

Discussion of Example 1

The main problem, Egypt's decline in power, was identified. Three more specific causes of this problem were also cited. However, more information could have been provided as to why Amenhotep IV's decision to change Egypt's religion contributed to its declining power.

Specific individuals as well as important groups were identified. The goals listed pertained to those of the common people, while the goals of other individuals and groups were not included.

Although a number of solutions were listed, not all of the identified goals have solutions. The possible consequences of these solutions were presented. However, a plan for implementing each solution was lacking.

Overall, this work sample illustrates how additional specificity would have enhanced the completeness of the essay. However, the sequential nature of the decision-making framework has been followed carefully. This student also demonstrated an understanding of how different groups can have different goals that require divergent solutions.

The following essay on the same topic reflects a more integrated application of the decision-making framework. The decision-making steps are identified in parentheses that precede the students' response to each step.

Example 2

The following statements are our opinions on how Egyptians could have prevented the (PROBLEM) decline of their empire. Egypt declined because of its (PROBLEM) grudge between the priests and pharaohs, pharaohs' attempts to keep the neighboring countries of Egypt under Egyptian control, and money being spent on things that are not necessary. The main people involved in this situation are basically the (PEOPLE) Egyptians and outsiders. We think the solution that could have prevented this from happening is to (SOLUTION) elect a pharaoh that will care for his country and not about ruling other ones. If the (CONSEQUENCE) pharaoh elected tries to gain control of other countries, simply select another one that has responsibility. One idea that could have possibly worked would have been to (PLAN) elect a female pharaoh to the throne because females are usually not interested in violence. Since the main problem is the (PROBLEM) grudge between the priests and pharaohs, somehow the (SOLUTION) priests and pharaohs must gain friendship again to keep the country strong. Another main problem is that of the (PROBLEM) pharaohs spending money on products that will not profit the country. I think (SOLUTION) the people should vote on what will profit the country and what will not. (SOLUTION) Instead of the pharaohs buying weapons to create wars, they should use them to defend themselves. (SOLUTION) They should buy things such as food, clothing, etc., that will do the country good.

Discussion of Example 2

This essay clearly reflects a more integrated use of the decision-making framework. The students also applied the framework to generate a solution of their own to the problem of Egypt's decline. As a result, this essay provides a nice illustration of how application of the social decision making framework can help to stimulate students' divergent thinking. When applied to current events, the framework allows students to feel as if they are able to make contributions to the problems being discussed.

Student _____ Date _____

1. What is the event you are thinking about? When and where did it happen? Put the event into words as a *problem*.

   _____

   _____

2. What people or groups were involved in the problem? What were their *different feelings* and points of view about the problem? Try to put their *goals* into words.

   _____

   _____

3. For each group, name some *different* decisions or *solutions* to the problem that they thought might help them to reach their goals.

   _____

   _____

4. For each solution, think of all the *things that might have happened next*. Think about short-term and long-term consequences.

   _____

   _____

5. What were the *final decisions?* How were they made? By whom? Why? Do you agree or disagree? Why?

   _____

   _____

6. How was the solution carried out? What was the *plan?* What obstacles were met? How well was the problem solved? Why?

   _____

   _____

7. Rethink it. What would *you* have chosen to do? Why?

   _____

   _____

   _____

2 Creating a Newspaper Article

Because newspaper articles contain only the most critical points about an issue, attempting to write one provides practice in learning how to summarize information concisely. This lesson will help students learn how the social decision making framework can be used to summarize the main points of an issue. Additionally, by working together to create an article, students may better understand how current events represent problems that require solutions. The task of creating a newspaper article is often highly engaging for students, as many of them will enjoy creatively designing front pages and other aspects of the task.

OBJECTIVES

- To help students understand the process used in creating a newspaper article
- To provide an opportunity for students to build teamwork skills
- To build students' decision-making and problem-solving skills
- To create a vehicle for students to have positive visibility in their school

MATERIALS

Copies of "Creating a Newspaper Article" (Worksheet 5.2)

Samples of articles from different newspapers.

NOTE: Collecting articles can be an assignment given to students before the activity.

LEADER'S GUIDE

1. Present the underlying subject matter.

Begin the class by discussing the topic area under study. Define any new vocabulary words. Discuss the "who, what, where, when, and why" of the topic.

2. Hand out copies of the worksheet.

Distribute the "Creating a Newspaper Article" worksheet. Use the following questions to help orient students:

How was information about current events communicated before the invention of newspapers?

Talk about this as a problem.

How is information about current events communicated now? How do you get most of your current events information?

Talk about this as a problem as well, and look into the potential strengths and weaknesses of the various sources, and especially of relying on only one source.

Proceed with Steps 2 through 9 of the instructional sequence described in Topic 1, using Worksheet 5.2.

3. Provide a reflective opportunity.

At the end, ask this question:

What problems do you think most reporters face in trying to write an article? What problems did you experience in writing this article? How did you solve them?

IMPLEMENTATION TIPS

1. Although the worksheet asks the student to write a newspaper article, the topic does not have to be a current event. Topics can be drawn from a variety of instructional sources (history textbooks, videos of historical dramatizations, news broadcasts).

2. Have students bring a current events article to class and present it to their classmates using the social decision making framework.

3. Letters to the editor and editorials often reflect attempts by citizens to generate solutions to problems. Ask students to read an editorial or a letter to the editor and have them critique it by applying the decision-making framework to examine how systematically the writer thought through the presentation of and response to a problem.

EXAMPLES OF COMPLETED ASSIGNMENTS

The following assignments on the history of the alphabet were completed by two sixth graders, based on the "Creating a Newspaper

Article" worksheet. The steps of the social decision making framework are capitalized and precede each student's responses to those steps.

Example 1

The (PROBLEM) Phoenicians' alphabet was too complicated for keeping trade records. It took too long to write down all that they needed to remember because they used a system of picture writing. (PEOPLE) Traders, sailors, merchants, shopkeepers, carpenters, craftsmen, and a lot more people had these problems. As you can guess, these people wanted another writing system. Their GOAL was to find and have a new alphabet, one that was easier. Some possible SOLUTIONS were to assign people to invent a new alphabet or to borrow from another country. They decided to borrow from another country. Their alphabet was similar to the Egyptians' hieroglyphics. By the time it reached Phoenicia, it had become an alphabet with twenty-two symbols. This is the history of our alphabet.

Example 2

The Phoenicians and the Hebrews were very interested in trade, but there was a problem that needed to be resolved to make trading easier.

The traders had (PROBLEM) trouble keeping records. Since people used a system of picture writing in those days, it was (PROBLEM) much too difficult to keep track of trade records.

There were many PEOPLE involved in trade. Sailors, craftsmen who worked on the ships, carpenters, traders, and merchants. They were from all over the world. They were Romans, Greeks, Aegeans, and Hebrews.

So the Phoenicians' GOAL was to find an easier writing system to keep trade records. For that (SOLUTIONS) they could go to other cities and countries to borrow an alphabet or make up their own alphabet.

If they would find an easier system, it would really be to their benefit. They (CONSEQUENCES) would be able to write faster and be accurate and keep track of all their records. They could also spend more time trading, and they would have more free time.

The final DECISION should be to carry the new easy system to other countries. It would make trade better, and easier. And it would make people understand each other better, and they could learn from each other better.

A PLAN to do this would be to send all trade ships to other countries with special teachers to teach the new alphabet. I would make sure that these teachers would be high officials to carry out such an important task.

Discussion

Although Example 2 is slightly longer, it restricts itself to the elements of the social decision making framework. Therefore, its greater length is not due to inclusion of nonessential information but rather reflects the thoroughness of the student's response.

Student _____ Date _____

Imagine that you are a newspaper reporter for *USA Today* or *The New York Times*. You have been asked to write a newspaper article on the social studies topic you have just finished studying in class.

Think about some part of the topic as an event or *problem*. Then use the following problem-solving outline to help you write your article. Be sure your article starts with a headline and then answers the following questions:

1. What is the *problem* you are thinking about?

2. What *people* or *groups* of people are involved?

3. What *feelings* and *goals* does each person or group have?

4. What are some possible *solutions* to achieve each goal?

5. What are some of the *consequences,* both long-term and short-term, for each possible solution?

6. What solution was chosen? Do you think a different choice should have been made? If so, why?

7. What could have been done to *improve* the chosen plan?

8. *Summarize* the information in the article and draw some conclusions.

HEADLINE: _____

From *Social Decision Making/Social Problem Solving for Middle School Students: Skills and Activities for Academic, Social, and Emotional Success.* Copyright © 2005 by Maurice J. Elias and Linda Bruene Butler. Research Press (800-519-2707; www.researchpress.com)

3

Decision Making Around Current Events

The purpose of this lesson is to reinforce students' knowledge of the decision-making steps with prompts based on each step of the framework. The chart format of this topic's worksheet uses key words rather than the lengthier questions that make up the framework. Students can more easily remember these cues, making it increasingly likely that they will be able to internalize the framework and generalize its use to other situations.

OBJECTIVES

- To provide a framework students can use to understand current events articles and related contemporary news sources
- To use the FIG TESPN strategy to show students how to plan action in response to situations presented in current events articles

MATERIALS AND PREPARATION

Copies of the "Social Decision Making Chart" (Worksheet 5.3)

Article or other basis for current events discussion.

NOTE: You can use Worksheet 5.4 ("Current Events Outline") if a greater degree of structure is needed or if students have less familiarity with FIG TESPN or the social decision making approach in general.

LEADER'S GUIDE

1. Present the underlying subject matter.

Begin the class by discussing the current events story under study. Define any new vocabulary words.

Discuss the "who, what, where, when, and why" of the topic. Ask:

Does this problem affect your life in some way? Do people behave differently when something affects them directly?

2. Hand out the worksheet and conduct an exercise with it.

Distribute the "Social Decision Making Chart." Proceed with Steps 2 through 9 of the instructional sequence described in Topic 1.

IMPLEMENTATION TIPS

1. As a variation on the instructional sequence, the decision-making chart may be copied from the worksheet onto a whole-class display. The class can then work together to generate answers rather than work independently or in small groups.

2. Because Worksheet 5.3 uses key words to prompt students' use of the social decision making steps, it should be used when students have had previous exposure to the framework. However, when students are first learning the approach, teachers might opt to use the "Current Events Outline" (Worksheet 5.4) instead, as it clearly spells out each step of the social decision making framework to be applied.

3. This activity is adaptable to situations unfolding in the news, such as those related to war, violence, or terrorism. In addition, this activity works well with problems occurring in one's state, local community, or school. Examples of the latter include school violence, bullying and peer harassment, drug use, separation or exclusion of groups in the school, school government, and local homeland security and school safety issues. It can be reused on a weekly basis with changing content.

EXAMPLES OF COMPLETED ASSIGNMENTS

The following examples were completed by seventh graders writing about current events topics.

Example 1

PROBLEM: Should the United States pay more to house the homeless?

PEOPLE/GROUPS: U.S. government, U.S. people.

FEELINGS: Government feels they can't afford to pay for all the homeless people. U.S. citizens have mixed feelings—some feel the government can pay for all the needs of the homeless, others feel the government can't.

SOLUTIONS: Congress voted to spend $35 million on the homeless for emergency aid. The government could build houses that the homeless could afford.

SHORT-TERM CONSEQUENCES: The homeless could temporarily be helped or get homes.

LONG-TERM CONSEQUENCES: Programs might not last when a new president is elected.

PLAN: Have $5 from all taxes be given toward the homeless until there are no more homeless. Have a marathon to raise money for them. Have a telethon like Jerry Lewis does but for the homeless people.

Example 2

PROBLEM: Should the United States pay more to house the homeless?

PEOPLE/GROUPS and FEELINGS: Thomas Demery thinks being homeless is a local problem. Local governments want to help as much as possible. The federal government is interested in trying to save money for the homeless. The homeless want homes.

SOLUTIONS: The local government could provide permanent homes. Food drives could be organized. Clothing can be donated. Try to raise more money.

SHORT-TERM CONSEQUENCES: The homeless may get homes, food, and clothing for a little while,

LONG-TERM CONSEQUENCES: Supplies for the homeless will run out after a while.

PLAN: I will try to help by giving some money to charity.

Example 3

PROBLEM: Should the United States allow the death penalty?

PEOPLE/GROUPS: Amnesty International, the government, the Supreme Court, local citizens, convicted criminals.

GOALS: To reach a decision about whether or not to allow the death penalty. To decrease the murder rate.

SOLUTIONS: Allow the people to vote.

SHORT-TERM CONSEQUENCES: People could become outraged if murderers go on killing and killing. People will stop killing out of fear of losing their own lives.

LONG-TERM CONSEQUENCES: The murder rate could go down because people would be afraid to die themselves. People could continue to protest the death penalty.

EVALUATION: If the death penalty isn't used, then that person could still kill others. But the death penalty shouldn't be brutal.

FINAL DECISION: I think the death penalty should remain because if killers are let out of jail, they could go on hurting people.

PLAN: Compare the percentages of murder rates when the death penalty is and isn't used in order to make a final decision.

Discussion

These examples display a range of thoroughness in regard to completion of each step of the framework. Although the decision-making chart differs from the previous worksheets in that key words are used rather than sentences that state each step of the framework, it is still necessary for students to respond to all components of the decision-making framework. Example 2 contains a plan the student has developed for personal implementation. Example 3 makes evaluation of effectiveness part of the plan. These reflect the kind of ownership of problems and responsibility for change that is critical for building active citizenship.

Student _____ Date _____

1. Event and problem

   _____

2. People involved

   _____

3. Goals

   _____

4. Possible solutions

   _____

5. Consequences

   _____

6. Evaluation of solutions

   _____

7. What do you think the final decision should be? Explain your choice.

   _____

8. Design a plan to help carry out your solution. How will you know if it works?

   _____

Student _____ Date _____

1. What is the event you are thinking about? When and where is it happening? What people or groups of people are involved? What are their different points of view? Try to put into words what you think the *problem* is:

   _____

   _____

2. What *goals* do the different people or groups have?

   The goal of _____ is to _____.

   The goal of _____ is to _____.

3. For each group, what are some *different ways* they can reach their goal? Write some *different things* they might say or do.

   Three ways _____ could reach their goal are:

   1. _____

   2. _____

   3. _____

4. For each of the *solutions* (each of the ways to reach their goals), think of all the positive (+) and negative (–) things that might happen next.

   Solution 1:   **Consequences**

       Short-term   (+) _____

                      (–) _____

       Long-term   (+) _____

                      (–) _____

   Solution 2:   **Consequences**

       Short-term   (+) _____

                      (–) _____

       Long-term   (+) _____

                      (–) _____

Solution 3:   **Consequences**

Short-term   (+) _____

(−) _____

Long-term   (+) _____

(−) _____

5. What do you think the *final decision* about the best way to reach the goal should be? How should the decision be made? Who should make it? Why?

I think the final decision should be _____.

It should be made by _____ because _____.

6. Think of a *plan* to carry out the final solution. What could you do to make your solution work?

My goal is to _____.

My plan is to _____.

(Think of who, what, where, when, and how it can happen.)

7. *Make a final check.* What might happen that might keep your plan from working? Who might disagree with your plan? Why?

Some things that might be *obstacles* to the plan and keep it from working are

1. _____

2. _____

3. _____

8. *Make a new plan.* Go back to Step 3 and think of other solutions, consequences, and a new plan.

Make another check.

If _____ happens, I would change my plan in this way:

_____

_____

_____

_____

4 Making History Relevant: Linking the Present and the Past

The purpose of this lesson is to make the study of a historical event more meaningful to students by allowing them to gain perspective on the way a teenager living during a different era might have felt about a problem. While earlier lessons required that students assume the perspective of different historical groups, this lesson asks students to imagine *themselves* living in another time period. Through this lesson, students may also come to recognize how many of the problems faced by today's teenagers are similar to those confronted by teens living in past eras. When students understand the similarities between present and past problems, the study of history can become more meaningful.

OBJECTIVES

- To improve students' perspective-taking ability
- To deepen students' appreciation of the role of human decision making in historical events
- To improve critical thinking skills as applied to historical analysis

MATERIALS

Copies of "Linking Present and Past Problems" (Worksheet 5.5)

LEADER'S GUIDE

1. Present the underlying subject matter.

Begin the class by discussing the historical events under study. Define any new vocabulary words.

2. Introduce the concept of moving your own viewpoint back in time.

Ask students to discuss what life was like for teenagers during this era. What were the conditions under which they lived? What was their role in society? Be sure to spend sufficient time on this topic so that students can really gain some understanding of what their lives might have been like if they had lived in the era being studied.

3. Hand out copies of the worksheet.

Proceed with Steps 2 through 9 of the instructional sequence described in Topic 1. Use the "Linking Present and Past Problems" worksheet. The identified problem can be either one specifically faced by teenagers or one with an impact on teenagers as well as other groups. In either case, students will be asked to describe the problem from a teenager's perspective.

4. Provide a reflective opportunity.

Upon completion of the activity, ask the following questions to broaden and deepen the integration of students' knowledge:

- What problems did teenagers face during the time period that you are studying that aren't faced by teenagers today? What solutions were available to them?

- What problems do today's teens face that are specific to our times? Try to suggest some solutions.

- How would someone other than a teenager living during that time period have felt about the problem under study?

- What factors besides age influence the way people feel about problems? Would a teenager from a different social class or religion have felt differently, despite living at the same time?

IMPLEMENTATION TIPS

1. To enhance the relevance of studying historical events, it is recommended that this lesson initially be conducted using a problem that resembles one facing today's teenagers (such as individual rights or family roles). However, this lesson can also be used with a topic area that illustrates how different, rather than how similar, are the problems faced by teenagers of different eras. Understanding differences is also important for developing a solid knowledge base in the social studies.

2. This lesson can be varied in order to study a problem currently facing teens in another country (for example, in the Middle East, Eastern Europe, Africa, or Central America). In this way, students may come to better understand the feelings of other individuals and identify commonalities as a way of building empathy.

3. As with any of the other activities, students can complete the worksheet as a homework assignment.

Student _____ Date _____

Directions: Imagine yourself as a teenager in the historical period you have just studied. What type of clothing would you wear? Where would you live? At your age, would you be in school, or would you be working? On the back of this paper, draw a picture of what you think you would look like if you were a teenager during this period.

Next consider how you might feel about the problem that your group has been discussing. Based on your viewpoint as a teenager during this period, how would you feel about this problem?

1. What is the *problem?*

2. What *people* or *groups* of people are involved?

3. What *feelings* does each person or group have? From a teenager's viewpoint, what are *your* feelings about the problem?

4. What *goals* does each person or group have? What are your goals?

5. What *solutions* were considered to achieve each goal? What other possible solutions can you think of?

6. What were some of the *consequences,* both long- and short-term, for each possible solution?

7. What *solution* was chosen? Do you think a different choice should have been made based on its consequences? If so, describe that solution.

8. How well was the problem solved? Why?

9. In what ways is this problem similar to a problem faced by today's teenagers? In what ways are things different now?

CHAPTER

6

Building Social Problem Solving and Social Decision Making Skills Through Literature Analysis

The natural environment for the exercise of literature analysis using an SDM paradigm is in the English classroom. The middle school English classroom often encourages students to think about books in new, thought-provoking ways. Adding an SDM component helps make literature analysis more systematic and makes it easier for students to personalize important themes and messages. Further, teaching students to think carefully, critically, and responsibly is a broad mandate that affects all school areas. In the SDM approach to literature analysis in the middle school, as such literature is discussed with a good SDM paradigm in mind, students see themselves in similar situations outside of class. Subsequently, they apply the thought processes they used during school discussions to their personal circumstances. Thus time devoted to SDM skills becomes time devoted to enhancing all aspects of social and academic success.

OBJECTIVES

- To give students a framework for reading that helps them see literature as involving problems to be solved and decisions to be made
- To increase students' sensitivity to the emotional reactions and interpersonal situations of characters in books they read
- To create added enjoyment and depth of appreciation to reading

MATERIALS

Age-appropriate literature

Thanks to Margaret I. Naftel for her contributions to this chapter.

Copies of "FIG TESPN: A Strategy for Everyday Decision Making and Problem Solving" (Worksheet 6.1) and "Literature Analysis: SDM/SPS Questions" (Worksheet 6.2)

Student journals

Recommended Readings

Blume, J. *Starring Sally J. Friedman as Herself.*

Set in 1947, this story is about a young girl whose family is touched by the war, discrimination, and health problems.

Blume, J. *Then Again, Maybe I Won't.*

This book is about a boy whose father becomes wealthy and how the boy and his family cope with the difficulties involved in moving and dealing with new peer groups.

Dahl, R. *Matilda.*

This is about a girl who has some problems with her school principal, and how she outsmarts everyone by the end.

Frank, A. *Anne Frank: Diary of a Young Girl.*

The diary of a young Dutch Jewish girl hiding from the Nazis during the Holocaust.

Geller, M. *My Life in the Seventh Grade.*

The everyday adventures of boys and girls in a middle school.

Johnson, T. *A Rock and a Hard Place.*

The autobiography of fourteen-year-old Tony Johnson, who overcame an abusive childhood only to find out that he was diagnosed with AIDS.

Hinton, S. E. *The Outsiders.*

How groups of teens deal with growing up, competition, and each other.

Hunter-Gault, C. *In My Place.*

How and why Charlayne Hunter-Gault found the courage and commitment to become the first African American to register for class in the 175-year history of the University of Georgia.

Parks, R. *Rosa Parks: My Story.*

The inspiring autobiography of the woman who is often called "the mother of the civil rights movement," focusing on the many choices she had to make in her life. (Accompanying video materials, which often help bring historical books to life for middle schoolers, can be ordered through www.tolerance.org.)

Peck, R. *Close Enough to Touch.*

The girlfriend of a teenage boy dies suddenly, and this book tells about how he struggles to cope with her death.

Peck, R. *Princess Ashley.*

A high school girl moves into a new town and has trouble trying to figure out who her real friends are.

Raskin, E. *The Westing Game.*

A spunky, rebellious thirteen-year-old girl solves the plot-twisting mystery of a dead man's will.

Taylor, M. D. *Roll of Thunder, Hear My Cry.*

The story of an African-American family trying to keep their land and dignity in Mississippi in the 1930s.

Wiesel, E. *Night.*

Elie Wiesel's moving and profound personal account of his experiences in Nazi Germany.

White, R. *Ryan White: My Own Story.*

Ryan White tells the story of his valiant fight against AIDS.

Zindel, P. *The Pigman.*

Two high school sophomores meet Mr. Pignati, a lonely old man, and they learn about his secret.

Anthologies of Stories Reflecting America's Diversity

In the Spirit of Peace (New York: Defense for Children-International-USA)

Goodbye, Vietnam (New York: Knopf)

Growing Up Asian American (New York: Morrow)

Visions of America: Personal Narratives from the Promised Land (New York: Persea Books)

LEADER'S GUIDE

1. Assign a book for the class to read.

Students can be given time to do this reading in class or given several chapters as homework. The "Materials" section suggests a range of readings to which the SDM/SPS framework has been applied.

2. Provide an overview of FIG TESPN.

Ask if any students have heard of FIG TESPN. If so, allow them to explain and then work from their explanation. If none have, say that in many books, characters have problems and have to solve them. Ask if they can think of any examples. After taking a few examples and adding more, as you feel is necessary, tell students:

> *We are going to read some books with the goal of under-standing how the different characters look at the problems they face and try to solve them. To do this, we will use a framework called "FIG TESPN."*

Distribute the FIG TESPN worksheet and then review each of the steps with the class.

F —Feelings cue me to problem solve.

I —Identify the problem.

G —Goals give me a guide.

T —Think of many possible solutions.

E —Envision outcomes.

S —Select the best solution.

P —Plan the procedure, anticipate pitfalls, and practice.

N —Notice what happened and remember it for next time.

Try applying the worksheets to a book that the class most recently read and discussed as a way of illustrating their application.

3. Conduct a practice exercise.

For the next book to be read, assign questions about the plot and characters to the point at which students are to read the book, based on the "Literature Analysis: SDM/SPS Questions" worksheet. Have students answer these questions in journals.

After students have done the assignment, call them together to form small discussion groups. The groups discuss each student's individual response to the question at hand.

The group discussion begins with each student reading the written response to a question. Everyone listens to each response. When all responses have been read, encourage students with differing points of view to discuss the reasoning behind their responses. Sometimes a good way to do this is to work with one discussion group while the others listen, to learn the kinds of questions they can be asking to one another. It's also useful to generate and distribute a list of sample follow-up questions. Encourage students to incorporate the FIG TESPN steps; for example, ask them to identify the way they perceive the characters to be feeling, and then reflect in their explanation whether they have felt the same way in similar situations. They can discuss what they believe a character should do at a particular point in the story, thus leading to further practice of FIG TESPN, such as envisioning results for options, selecting best solutions, and planning for roadblocks.

Also of value is encouraging students to explain why they think characters chose as they did, or to think about whether one option will be better for one character than for another. Literature often provides a chance to look at the decision-making process used by characters and allows students a chance to compare how they might think things through and act if they were in a similar situation. This is the type of practice of SDM skills that encourages transfer from the classroom into the world beyond it.

Throughout the discussion, ensure that students listen respectfully to one another and remind them that all points of view are important. There are no right or wrong responses to these questions during discussion. (In appropriate sections of books, for a change of pace, and especially at the end, bring students together for full-class discussion.)

IMPLEMENTATION TIPS

This section addresses the most common issues that have emerged from the teaching of literature analysis using SDM.

1. Who can lead these discussions of literature?

An English teacher is well suited to this effort, but counselors, librarians, parents, after-school program leaders, or anyone with the time and inclination to read and discuss literature with adolescents can pursue this exercise. A literature analysis group makes an excellent alternative to traditional counseling or clinical groups and can also serve as an adjunct to health and family life education classes, especially if books are chosen that reflect themes of overcoming difficulties and dealing with specific problem areas such as bullying, shyness, depression, eating disorders, cancer, HIV/AIDS, and the like. Well-chosen biographies can also be useful. Social skills are built not only by monitoring and guiding behavior in discussion groups but by having students role-play different parts of the story, different ways characters would proceed at various points, even different ways of enacting parts of the text that everyone has read.

2. How long is the typical discussion?

A discussion lasting about twenty-five or thirty minutes gives a group of five to seven members time to state each response and then to discuss the responses, as well as other topics that may arise. The discussion will vary with group size, amount of reading material assigned, and the degree of heterogeneity in groups. Especially at first, discussions should not be undertaken too quickly because this does not allow time for the careful critical thinking that social decision making steps are designed to encourage.

3. How does this approach mesh with existing and ongoing programming?

In the English classroom, this approach meshes very well with existing programming. This is because the teacher often assigns books to be read by the entire class during the semester. A few questions using FIG TESPN as a guideline can easily be constructed and assigned to the class, and soon group discussions of responses may be held. This exercise occurs during time otherwise consumed by the students' reading and responding in writing and the teacher's then checking the numerous questions usually asked. Also, the class can be engaged in using FIG TESPN to discuss the forms of the literature, such as the style of the author. In counseling and other contexts, the approach can fit naturally into existing time frames and constraints.

4. What is the linkage with academics?

Because this program meshes so well with the existing program of English classrooms, the linkage with academics is firm. This program conforms to curriculum objectives on many points. Written and verbal use of grammar may be checked by observing the written responses contained in journals and spoken during discussions. Vocabulary and spelling are reinforced in the same manner as grammar. When the author uses unusual words to describe people, events, or environments, the general meaning and specific use of these words can be discussed to build vocabulary. Creative writing skills are also practiced in journal responses, because, again, students are encouraged to be thoughtful in responding to these questions.

Study skills such as listening, summarizing, and following directions are encouraged because the questions asked and the responses students give usually do not rely on information-based answers that can be looked up in the book. Students must thoughtfully consider what they have read and craft their responses to the questions asked, and they must defend their answers when their points of view differ from those of their peers. Listening skills are focused on when students are asked to repeat others' responses during discussion. Voice projection and body language are also factors in group discussion—for example, when a soft-spoken student is encouraged to repeat an inaudible answer in a voice that others will hear and understand. Often, students will ask one another to repeat remarks, encouraging the give-and-take of discussion. (Communication skills like "BEST" can be taught to students if a framework for behavior during discussion times is needed. See Topic 4, in Chapter 3.)

Finally, the study of different forms of literature is practiced. Classifications of writing, literary terms, and specific writing techniques and interpretation can be part of group discussion when appropriate.

5. What are the relevant instructional considerations with regard to cultural sensitivity and racial and ethnic diversity?

The books chosen for this exercise open the door for emphasis on cultural and racial diversity. An excellent source of books on diverse cultures is the Web site www.tolerance.org. For example, a book about a family that lives in Argentina will probably contain many cultural aspects that differ from family life in the United States. Discussion of such a book with an SDM paradigm can elicit students' thoughts concerning these differences and encourage them to examine their reasoning behind what they think about these differences. Racial and ethnic diversity can be discussed in the same manner, depending on the subject matter of the book selected.

For example, *Not Separate, Not Equal,* by Brenda Scott Wilkinson (1987), tells the story of a young African-American girl growing up in the South during the early years of segregation. The story is told from the girl's point of view. It was written for the middle school to high school age group. Discussion of this book within an SDM/SPS paradigm can encourage students to think about what they might have done during segregation and also about the way they interact with people of a different race today.

6. How can learner outcomes be assessed?

The purpose of this exercise is to encourage students to transfer the skills they learn and practice in the classroom into their world outside the classroom. The intent is that they will ultimately use the skills in real-life situations to make decisions and solve problems they encounter. However, short-term benefits are also available from this exercise.

- Short-term benefits may be observed by checking samples of the student's writing throughout the year. Perusal of journals where discussion questions are first answered can frequently indicate the degree of growth in the way students are approaching written material with critical thinking. As the student becomes familiar with discussion groups, the time taken with a thoughtful journal answer often increases, and the answer, as well as the writing style, improves.

- Journal answers or other writing samples from a class practicing SDM/SPS skills may be compared to samples from a similar class that is not practicing the skills in order to observe a difference in writing skills and thoughtfulness of response. The writing skills may be similar, but there should be distinct differences seen in the class that practices the skills.

- Another way that students can be evaluated for short-term benefits is through observation. For example, teachers can assess students' participation in discussions. A student who does not participate much in the larger class can be encouraged first to take an active role in a small-group discussion. Student self-expression should improve as the discussions continue. A related way to measure benefits from literature analysis within an SDM/SPS paradigm is through anecdotal records. Anecdotal record keeping can provide teachers and discussion leaders with a way to assess students during the process of discussion.

- Observations of students in the process of everyday reading and writing allow teachers to see for themselves the reading and writing and problem-solving strategies students use and their responses to reading and writing. By using anecdotal records and discussing them periodically with students, both teacher and student may observe progress in the use of social decision making.

- Yet another way of observing short-term benefits involves parental reports. Since the focus of this exercise is to give students a place to practice skills that they will hopefully translate to life outside the classroom, parents can be helpful. Parental support may be elicited by the teacher; then an interested parent may receive an explanation of the skills being taught and shown how to look for signs of skills being practiced as the child interacts at home. The parent can then meet with the teacher or send in written reports and be involved in a plan to bolster students' skills as needed.

- The long-term benefits of transferring SDM/SPS skills to real-life situations may be best verified in longitudinal study. Where skills are introduced in elementary grades and practiced every year, there is perhaps the best opportunity of such a study. Also, parents may be enlisted to help researchers keep in touch with children as they become adults and go out into the working world. Yearly reports may shed some light on the long-term benefits of SDM/SPS skills training.

FIG TESPN: A Strategy for Everyday Decision Making and Problem Solving

Student _____ **Date** _____

FIG TESPN is an acronym for a strategy that characters in literature as well as people in real life use to solve problems and make decisions:

F—Feelings cue me to problem solve.

I—Identify the problem.

G—Goals give me a guide.

T—Think of many possible solutions.

E—Envision outcomes.

S—Select the best solution.

P—Plan the procedure, anticipate pitfalls, and practice.

N—Notice what happened and remember it for next time.

1. Think of an event in the section of the book assigned. When and where is it happening? Put the event into words as a problem to be solved or a choice or decision to be made.

2. What people or groups were involved in the problem? What are their different feelings? What are their points of view about the problem?

3. What do each of these people or groups want to have happen? Try to put their goals into words.

4. For each person or group, name some different options or solutions to the problem that they think might help them reach their goals. Add any ideas that you think might help them that they might not have thought of.

5. For each option or solution you listed, picture all the things that might happen next. Envision long-term and short-term consequences.

6. What do you think the final decision should be? How should it be made? By whom? Why?

7. Imagine a plan to help you carry out your solution. What could you do or think of to make your solution work? What obstacles or roadblocks might keep your solution from working? Who might disagree with your ideas? Why? What else could you do?

8. Rethink it. As you read, see what the author wrote and compare it to what you anticipated or how else it could have been presented. Is there another way of looking at the situation that might be better? Are there other groups, goals, or plans that come to mind?

9. What questions do you have, based on what you read? What questions would you like to be able to ask one or more of the characters? The author? Why are these questions important to you? If you had to write a sequel to this book, what would the plot be? How might you approach it?

From *Social Decision Making/Social Problem Solving for Middle School Students: Skills and Activities for Academic, Social, and Emotional Success.* Copyright © 2005 by Maurice J. Elias and Linda Bruene Butler. Research Press (800-519-2707; www.researchpress.com)

7 Prepare Your Students to Understand and Use the Tools of Media Literacy and Social Decision Making

Middle school students truly are children of the video age. They participate daily in a revolution in media, communication, and information technologies through their use of television sets, VCRs CDs, DVDs, MP3s, video and computer games, Instant Messenger, chat rooms, blogs, and e-mail discussion lists. Those working with students need to engage these new technologies to provide an enjoyable, rich, and rigorous experiential approach to building students' critical thinking and social decision making skills.

Kubey and Csikszentmihalyi (1990) did a classic study of television watching in America, and their conclusions are fascinating. Middle school students spend more time watching television than studying. They have absorbed the grammar of television in a way that actually inhibits their critical thinking skills. To attempt to close them off from television and other recordable digital formats, like DVDs, is impractical and unrealistic. To change the way they view and interact with these powerful media, however, is quite possible. In fact, the medium of television has been shown to serve as an exciting springboard for the development of critical thinking skills, including higher order cognitive skills (Salomon, 1979) and social decision making skills, even in emotionally and behaviorally disturbed and learning-impaired students (Elias, 1983).

The SDM/SPS curricula have made use of video technology through the concept of "Television, Discussion, and Role Play/Rehearsal and Practice," better known as TVDRP (Elias & Maher, 1983; Elias & Tobias, 1996). Once a new skill or idea is presented to students, they view a video related to the topic (TV). They then discuss the concepts as represented in the video (D) and finally role-play or in other ways

---

Thanks to Howard (Haim) M. Rubinstein for his contributions to this chapter.

practice the new skill with each other to incorporate what they have learned into their behaviors (RP).

The overall goal of the activities in this chapter is to capitalize on the attraction of television and video technology by engaging students in video-related projects that require them to use their critical thinking and decision-making skills. As students work on their projects and learn new social skills, they receive immediate audio and visual feedback on their progress from videotapes of themselves.

This chapter presents two separate units. "Media Literacy, Advertising, and Commercials" works within the social decision making framework to teach students about the advertising appeals used to sell products. It encourages students to view most video or television productions from the perspectives of video maker and critic. "Social Decision Making and Video and Documentary Making" expands on this theme to further enhance students' decision-making and problem-solving skills as they explore the art of video making and produce their own video documentaries. This process also teaches students to actively analyze television commercials and programs from a critical perspective: trying to differentiate fact and fiction, critiquing the elements of a commercial or full-length show, and challenging programming that is poorly presented.

Turning children into active viewers of visual media may help them become more selective in deciding what they believe from these media. It may also result in their being more selective in the programs they view.

The activities in this chapter also involve students in making their own video commercials and documentaries, using their social decision making and critical thinking skills to help them carry the projects to completion. These activities take advantage of the special attraction television and videos hold for adolescents, using it to teach and reinforce social decision making and critical thinking skills. Many students imagine being part of a television program, movie, or music video, and this unit's activities turn dreams into reality by offering a class or group of students the chance to develop, produce, and act in their own television commercials or public-service messages.

Videotaping students' behaviors and playing them back to the class or group can enhance the acquisition of new social skills. Feedback is critically important to learning any new skill, and often the more immediate the feedback, the greater the impact. Video technology gives educators the advantage of almost instantaneous audio and visual feedback. With the help of videotaping, it is possible to say to children, "You should see how well you just did that!"—and to then *show* them how well they did. Students can also watch themselves more than once and focus on different aspects of their behavior each time.

Using video technology in this manner offers young adolescents the extra incentive of observing themselves from a unique and important vantage point—that of the other person. Adolescence is, for many, the age of self-consciousness, in which peer acceptance is vitally important. "How do I come across to the kids in my class?" is a question on the minds of most, if not all, middle school students. Many topics in this chapter allow students to learn about themselves in a supportive group setting. Guided practice with feedback is an integral part of social decision making lessons as a means for helping students transfer their newly learned social skills to everyday interpersonal situations. If they see things they do not like, the social decision making program offers skills for making changes and opportunities to practice them in social situations.

TOPICS IN THIS CHAPTER

Unit 1: Media Literacy, Advertising, and Commercials

1. Critical Viewing of the Media: Learning the Importance of Active Versus Passive Viewing

2. Critical Viewing of the Media: Looking at Commercials and the Feelings They Try to Create in Us

3. Creating Scripts and Storyboards for Commercials

4. Videotaping Students' Commercials

Unit 2: Social Decision Making and Video and Documentary Making

1. Using Social Decision Making as a Critical Thinking Guide for the Media

2. Looking for Signs of Different Feelings: A Workshop on Acting

3. Put the Problem into Words: An Introduction to Documentaries

4. The Video Critique Club: An Approach to Creating Public Service Spots and Prevention Messages, and to Running Counseling and Clinical Groups

Supplemental Activity

Videotaping Feedback on BEST for Skill-Building Practice

SUGGESTED RESOURCES

Baldwin, H. (1989). *How to create effective TV commercials.* Lincolnwood, IL: NTC Business Books.

Hampe, B. (1997). *Making documentary films and reality videos: A practical guide to planning, filming, and editing documentaries of real events.* New York: Henry Holt.

Johnson, D., Broida, R., Stauffer, T., & Fahs, C. (2004). *How to do everything with your digital video camcorder.* Emeryville, CA: McGraw-Hill.

Rosenthal, A. (2002). *Writing, directing, and producing documentary films and videos* (3rd ed.). Carbondale: Southern Illinois University Press.

Rubin, M. (2001). *The little digital video book.* Berkeley: Peachpit Press.

Underdahl, K. (2002). *Digital video for dummies* (3rd ed.). New York: Wiley.

UNIT 1

Media Literacy, Advertising, and Commercials

1

Critical Viewing of the Media: Learning the Importance of Active Versus Passive Viewing

Every set of standards addresses the issue of literacy, and the more sophisticated sets of standards address literacy across multiple modalities. For middle school students, exposure to sophisticated media while their powers of reasoning and moral direction are still developing creates the potential for considerable harm and negative influence. This topic begins the process of sharpening students' skills in the area of televised and film media, but it also exposes them to skills that can be useful for analyzing print media.

OBJECTIVES

- To teach students to become active viewers of audiovisual media
- To raise awareness of the appeals used to sell products and help students evaluate commercials critically

MATERIALS AND PREPARATION

Chalkboard or easel pad

Copies of "Advertising Appeals" (Worksheet 7.1)

A variety of old magazines—you may need to supply these, though it is also possible to have students bring in the magazines from home (see Step 8 in the "Leader's Guide" section)

LEADER'S GUIDE

1. Introduce the topic.

Tell the students they will be participating in a special mini-course on video media. Describe briefly that they will learn about television advertising and then make their own commercials.

2. Talk about commercials.

To promote group building, have students think of their favorite television commercial. Ask them to think about why the commercial attracts them and how it makes them feel. Go around the room and have the students share their responses to these questions.

3. State the goal of the activity.

We are all often in situations where someone is trying to persuade us to buy a particular product or to agree with a certain point of view. Today we will learn how this happens.

Ask the students for examples and put them on the chalkboard or easel pad. As needed, give the following examples, or offer your own. Be sure that the list winds up including something about television commercials, magazine ads, and students' friends.

- Our friends may try to get us to do what they are doing or support their point of view.
- Art designers for music CDs, DVDs, and videos are hired to create covers that make us interested in purchasing the product.
- Automobile dealers try to convince customers to buy their cars.
- Producers of cigarettes and alcoholic beverages often give away hats, mugs, and T-shirts to get us to drink or smoke.
- Politicians participate in local events and parades to get us to support their campaigns and to vote for them.
- Makers of television commercials and magazine advertisements try to get us to buy their products by appealing to our feelings.

At some point, summarize these examples as indicators of *persuasion,* and introduce the term as a vocabulary word. Then encourage the students to share additional situations in which they were the targets of persuasion.

4. Elicit the difference between being active and being passive.

Discuss the difference between being an active or a passive participant in the situations listed in Step 3. Here are some useful prompts:

Should we believe everything we see, hear, or read?

What might happen if we don't think about what we are doing in these situations?

5. Explain the problem.

Television shows and magazines are full of commercials and advertisements that try to persuade us to buy products or to think in certain ways, and many people are not even aware that the media are trying to do this. So, in effect, people are often passive viewers of these media. Say:

> *This mini-unit will help us become more active viewers of mass media.*

Here introduce the term *mass media* and elicit definitions and examples. Summarize and continue by saying:

> *Television and magazines are part of the mass media, which also include newspapers, radio, videos, and movies.*

The following questions can be discussed in a full-class group or in subgroups, with reporters sharing each group's ideas with everyone else, orally or on the board.

> *What is a passive viewer?*

(Someone who does not do much thinking but tends to accept what is being shown without question. You may want to introduce the term *couch potato* at this point.)

> *What is an active viewer?*

(Someone who evaluates, judges, and appropriately challenges what is being shown.)

> *What are the most important differences between active and passive viewers?*

(The answer to this question may be self-evident after discussing the two preceding questions.)

> *What are the advantages of being an active viewer?*

(Active viewers have the advantage over passive viewers since their impressions are the result of their own thinking about what is shown to them, rather than the result of the thinking of people who may not have the viewers' best interests at heart.)

6. Discuss tricks and techniques.

Ask students, as a class or in subgroups, to generate a list of the techniques and approaches advertisers use to persuade consumers to do what they would like. After the class has produced an initial list, hand out Worksheet 7.1, which lists advertising appeals commonly used by producers of commercials and advertisements.* Be sure to link these appeals with those offered by the students and add extra appeals mentioned by the students. This list may be used for the assignment, although it is best to have the class generate its own unique list and create a handout from that.

7. Apply the list of techniques to real life.

After generating a list of appeals with the students, ask if students can think of commercials or advertisements that fit into any of these categories.

This is an appropriate time to discuss how advertisements and commercials sometimes portray characters in stereotyped roles and exploit certain groups of people (such as women and nonwhites). Discuss with the students how these portrayals are inaccurate and how advertisements, commercials, and programs teach and reinforce them. An important point to get across to your students is that this type of programming can shape their views in a way that creates barriers in their relationships with others. You may want to show an example of an exploitative advertisement to illustrate your point.

8. Assign the task of finding magazine advertisements that represent the listed kinds of ads.

The appropriate number of ads is left for you to decide, as is the format for making this an individual, dyad, or small-group assignment. Some teachers have asked each student or group of students to find one ad for each appeal; others have asked that students find ads for five or six of the appeals.

To complete this assignment, students will need copies of the "Advertising Appeals" worksheet, either the version provided here or a version you create. This activity can serve either as an in-class assignment or as homework, depending on time constraints and your preference. If you use it as an in-class assignment, you will need to supply old magazines and scissors or have the students bring in old magazines from home before this lesson begins.

---

*This list is adapted from *Basic Skills at Work,* a media course taught by Sal Calcaterra, a faculty member in the Woodbridge School District, Woodbridge, New Jersey. (See Calcaterra & Rippas, 1981.)

Student _____ Date _____

Find magazine advertisements that illustrate the advertising appeals listed below.

1. **Bandwagon:** Everyone is doing it.

2. **Beauty and good looks:** This product will make you better looking.

3. **Romance:** This product will bring you true love.

4. **Happiness:** This product will bring you happiness.

5. **Masculine:** This product will make you more of a man.

6. **Feminine:** This product will make you more womanly.

7. **Sex appeal:** Sexy models attract consumers' attention.

8. **Snob appeal:** It costs more, but aren't you worth it?

9. **Testimonial:** Famous person claims to use the product.

10. **Youth appeal:** Rock music, current slang make it seem to belong to young people.

11. **Excitement:** This product will make your life exciting.

12. **Scientific:** Scientist or doctor uses charts and big words to sell a product.

13. **Humor:** You laugh in a way that makes you remember the product.

14. **Healthy and natural:** Outdoor scenes are featured—making it look like the product has nothing artificial about it.

15. **Paranoia:** You will feel weird about yourself if you don't use the product.

16. **Best price:** This product is the cheapest; may offer coupons.

17. Other: _____

18. Other: _____

2 Critical Viewing of the Media: Looking at Commercials and the Feelings They Try to Create in Us

Commercials exercise a great deal of influence over middle school children. They are especially susceptible to ads that suggest that they are the only ones not doing, owning, or seeing something, or that they will be uncool unless they purchase some desired object. Helping them take a step back and understand how television commercials create feelings and impulses in them is the first step in making them less impulsive and more thoughtful consumers of media, and more thoughtful consumers in general. The critical thinking skills they will be learning are applicable to virtually any academic subject area.

OBJECTIVES

- To provide practice in identifying the elements of a television commercial
- To encourage students to become active viewers of television commercials

MATERIALS

Videotape of a variety of commercials

Copies of "Viewing Commercials" (Worksheet 7.2)

Copies of "Planning Commercials" (Worksheet 7.3)

LEADER'S GUIDE

1. Reinforce the importance of being an active, critical viewer of mass media.

Review students' work from Topic 1. You may want to allow each student to present several advertisements and explain how they illustrate the advertising appeals. Compliment the students on working hard to become active readers of these advertisements.

2. Apply the concepts to television commercials.

Ask the students to what extent they think these appeals are also used in television commercials. Summarize, and say that this lesson will focus on students' becoming active viewers of television commercials. Explain that you are about to show several commercials and that you would like the students to watch for the advertising appeals used in them. Ask students to also look for how the commercials are designed to shape the viewer's thinking. They should be aware of the feelings the commercials stir up in them.

3. Show video clips of one or two commercials.

Use the "Viewing Commercials" worksheet as a guide. You may want to use it as an outline for discussing the commercials, or it may serve as a worksheet for students to fill out as they watch the commercials. In the latter case, you will probably need to show each clip more than once for students to get all of the information.

Begin with a full-group discussion. Identify and discuss the advertising appeals used in the commercials, the feelings that they created, and what it was like to be an active viewer. Ask if anyone saw something new in the commercials as an active viewer that they had not seen before. Continue by showing additional clips and allow students to carry out small-group discussions based on the worksheet and then report back to the large group.

4. Form groups to start planning commercials.

Students should break into small groups to start the process of producing their own video commercials. The products they are trying to sell can be real or imaginary. Groups are to decide on answers to the following questions:

- What type of product will be advertised, and what will it be named?
- To whom will the commercial appeal?
- What advertising appeals will be used?
- What feelings do the students want to elicit in the consumer?

Introduce the "Planning Commercials" worksheet to help groups organize and record their plans. It is especially important for each group to brainstorm the alternative ways of presenting the product and consider the consequences of each one as they attempt to reach this goal. Remind students that the goal of their commercial is to sell the product. They want to convince consumers to buy it.

Optional Homework Assignment: Assign two copies of the "Viewing Commercials" worksheet to be completed as homework. Ask students to use it to analyze two commercials they see on TV. Emphasize that special thought should be given to Question 7. This may be a graded assignment.

ALTERNATE FORMATS

Note that this topic's activities can also be conducted using public service announcements instead of commercials. This allows a bridge to be made to issues such as alcohol and drug use, smoking, drinking and driving, child abuse, and the environment. Videotapes of public service announcements can often be obtained from local television or cable television stations and from such groups as the Advertising Council and the National Clearinghouse on Alcohol and Drug Information. Ultimately, students will make their own public service announcements about key health problems, prevention, mental health, and environmental and community issues. They can show these to other students and even offer them to local television and cable television stations for airing.

A further adaptation of this topic can be made to radio advertising.

Student _____ Date _____

1. Type of product: _____

_____

2. Name of product: _____

3. To whom does the product appeal? _____

_____

4. What advertising appeals did you notice in the commercial? _____

_____

5. What feelings did you experience while viewing the commercial?

_____

6. Would you consider buying this product?

_____

7. If you were remaking the commercial, what would you do differently? Here are some questions that may be useful to answer:

   a. Is the name of the product a catchy one? Do you remember it easily?

   _____

   _____

   b. Would you choose to appeal to a different group of buyers? Why or why not?

   _____

   _____

   c. Would you choose alternative advertising appeals? What would be the consequences of those changes?

   _____

   _____

Student _____ Date _____

1. Type of product: _____

   _____

2. Name of product: _____

   _____

   Things to think about:

   a. Is the name of the product a catchy one?

   b. Do you remember it easily?

3. Who are the consumers of your product? _____

   _____

4. What advertising appeals could you use to sell the product?

   a. _____

   b. _____

   c. _____

   d. _____

5. List two consequences of using each alternative here.

   a. _____   _____

   b. _____   _____

   c. _____   _____

   d. _____   _____

6. Choose your best appeal.

   _____

   _____

From *Social Decision Making/Social Problem Solving for Middle School Students: Skills and Activities for Academic, Social, and Emotional Success.* Copyright © 2005 by Maurice J. Elias and Linda Bruene Butler. Research Press (800-519-2707; www.researchpress.com)

3 Creating Scripts and Storyboards for Commercials

Understanding the mechanics of creating scripts brings students in touch with the processes involved in creating a range of media. Part of removing the hypnotic effect of media, and especially commercials, is helping students get backstage and realize the way in which audience influence motivates the creation of commercials. At the same time, students also learn the importance of taking the perspective of their audience, which includes the teacher as a consumer of many student products.

OBJECTIVES

- To define the terms *audio, video, script,* and *storyboard*
- To assist students in creating scripts and storyboards for their commercials

MATERIALS

Whole-class displays of the "Completed Script Sheet" (Worksheet 7.4) and "Completed Storyboard" (Worksheet 7.5)

Copies of the "Script Sheet" (Worksheet 7.6) and "Storyboard" (Worksheet 7.7)

Videocamera and monitor *(optional)*

LEADER'S GUIDE

1. Review Topic 2.

To promote group building, ask the students to share their experiences planning a commercial. Have them share any problems they encountered while trying to reach their goal. As a group, have them brainstorm solutions to some of the problems expressed.

2. Launch the activity.

Tell the students that today they will begin to complete preparation for their commercials. Now that students have decided on the best advertising appeals for their products, they need to plan their commercials and check them before the final videotaping.

Introduce the concepts of script sheets and storyboards by asking for definitions or hypotheses of what these might be. Define script sheets and storyboards as tools to help advertisers carefully plan their commercials. Explain that these sheets are used by professional video makers and movie makers. They are designed to organize all the important information for shooting a video so that everyone will understand what they have to do.

3. Describe the audio side of the script sheet.

Show students the example of a completed script sheet (Worksheet 7.4) and explain how it is divided into two sections: audio and video. Explain that the audio section, on the right-hand side, contains the actual spoken words for the commercial and indicates who is to say them. The writing is in both lowercase and uppercase letters. Each audio entry applies to one particular video shot. It starts with identification of who will say the words. This identification is in capital letters, and it is underlined to cue the script reader not to read it aloud. Different audio entries and video shots are separated by a horizontal line across the page.

4. Describe the video side of the script sheet.

Continuing with the same example, explain that the video portion of the script sheet includes instructions especially important for the person running the camera. Point out that these directions are written in uppercase letters. The video directions should include who or what is to be included in the shot and how they are to appear on the screen. Some of the most basic video directions are FADE IN; CLOSE-UP OF [WHATEVER]; DISTANT SHOT OF [WHATEVER]; ZOOM IN TO CLOSE-UP OF [WHATEVER]; ZOOM OUT TO DISTANT SHOT OF [WHATEVER]; FADE OUT. The blank lines are to be filled in with the subject to be included in the shot. Here are some examples of video directions: CLOSE-UP OF ANNOUNCER; ZOOM IN TO CLOSE-UP OF PRODUCT; DISTANT SHOT OF JOHN RIDING AWAY ON HIS BICYCLE; FADE IN TO SHOT OF SUSAN AND JANET WORKING NEXT TO EACH OTHER.

You can use a video camera and an accompanying monitor to illustrate the meanings of these terms. Turn the monitor so it is visible to the entire group. Zoom the camera in and out as it is pointed at different objects and people. You may ask students to call out different video directions for you to follow as they watch the monitor. Once it appears that students understand the directions, have some of them come up to operate the camera while others offer the video commands.

5. Introduce the storyboard.

Remind the students that in a video script, it is important for the visual effect to match the words being spoken. Show an example of a completed storyboard (Worksheet 7.5). Ask the students to identify and explain the difference between the script sheet and the storyboard. The storyboard matches a rough sketch of the visual image to be videotaped with the audio and video portions of the script sheet. The video instructions and audio portion of the script sheet are written below the scenes. The purpose of each square is to give an idea of what each scene will look like; lumps and stick figures will do for that, so it's not necessary to be an artist to complete a storyboard.

6. Work on the activity.

Pass out blank copies of the script sheet and storyboard worksheets (Worksheets 7.6 and 7.7). Instruct the students to break into their commercial-making groups from the preceding lesson. Today's task is creating a script for their commercial and entering the words onto the script sheet along with directions for each video shot. Before students begin this work, it is important to set a time limit for the length of their commercials—probably between thirty and sixty seconds. Once the script sheet is completed, members of the group may begin the accompanying storyboard.

Once students have planned out their commercials, they should make a list of the props they will need and decide who will be responsible for obtaining them. It will also be important to decide the roles of each group member in the videotaping. Each part is to be assigned, a camera operator should be chosen, and additional assistants should be given jobs to help with props or directing the action. Assist as needed.

Group members: Lisa, Bob, and Maria

Name of video: Getaway Bug Spray

Video	Audio
Distant shot of person sitting in chair, slapping neck	<u>Announcer:</u> Has this ever happened to you?
Close-up of announcer holding can of "Getaway Bug Spray"	<u>Announcer:</u> New "Getaway Bug Spray" will end your problems with mosquitoes, gnats, and pesky flies by keeping them away from you.
Distant shot of person spraying arms and legs	<u>Announcer:</u> Just spray "Getaway Bug Spray" on the exposed skin of your arms and legs before going outside, and then prepare to relax without being bothered by bugs.
Distant shot of person relaxing in chair	<u>Announcer:</u> See, isn't that better?
Close-up of spray can	<u>Announcer:</u> Get "Getaway Bug Spray" today and tell the bugs to "get away!"

Worksheet 7.5   **Completed Storyboard**

Group members: Lisa, Bob, and Maria   **Name of video:** Getaway Bug Spray

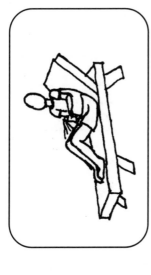

Video: Close-up of announcer holding spray can

Audio: New "Getaway Bug Spray" will end your problems with mosquitos, gnats, and pesky flies by keeping them away from you.

Video: Distant shot of person spraying arms and legs

Audio: Just spray "Getaway Bug Spray" on the exposed skin of your arms and legs before going outside and then prepare to relax without being bothered by bugs.

Video: Distant shot of person sitting in chair, slapping neck

Audio: Has this ever happened to you?

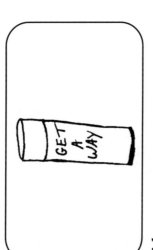

Video: Close-up of can

Audio: Get "Getaway Bug Spray" today and tell the bugs to "get away!"

Video:

Audio:

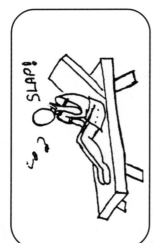

Video: Distant shot of person relaxing in chair

Audio: See, isn't that better?

From *Social Decision Making/Social Problem Solving for Middle School Students: Skills and Activities for Academic, Social, and Emotional Success.* Copyright © 2005 by Maurice J. Elias and Linda Bruene Butler. Research Press (800-519-2707; www.researchpress.com)

Group members: _____

Name of video: _____

Video	Audio

Group members: _____

Name of video: _____

Video:

Audio:

Video:

Audio:

Video:

Audio:

Video:

Audio:

Video:

Audio:

Video:

Audio:

4 Videotaping Students' Commercials

Building skills from feedback is a powerful form of learning. By creating their own commercials, students learn how to craft a final product carefully and then critique it with a view to improvement. These are skills fundamental to character education and both academic and social-emotional learning.

OBJECTIVES

- To assist students in the videotaping of their commercials
- To complete the process of demystifying commercials by giving the students a feel for their construction

MATERIALS

Video camera and monitor, and blank videotape

Students' props

Worksheets completed in Topic 3

Blank copies of "Viewing Commercials" (Worksheet 7.2, from Topic 2)

LEADER'S GUIDE

1. Briefly review Topic 3.

Be sure to include script sheets, storyboards, and audio and video directions. Take several minutes to discuss the process of planning for the commercials that went on in the last lesson. Ask for ideas of what might go wrong if the groups do not use their script sheets and storyboards to plan well.

2. Introduce the review process.

Explain that, now that the commercials are planned, the next step is to make a final check. This is done by practicing and rehearsing the commercials according to the script sheet and storyboard. Actors should practice their lines, camera operators should review their directions, and assistants should make sure they know when and where to do their jobs. Someone must also keep track of the time and pacing of the action. Once everyone feels ready, the commercial should be rehearsed several times to make sure everyone has it right.

As the groups rehearse their commercials, take the video camera around to one group at a time to give the camera operators a chance to practice their video directions with the camera. Those in groups waiting for the camera should pretend that they are operating the video cameras according to the video directions.

3. Videotape the commercials.

Once every group has had a chance for a full rehearsal, start the actual videotaping of the commercials with the group that appears to be the best prepared. Depending on what seems most useful, have the remaining groups either continue rehearsing or watch the group that is videotaping. Be prepared for this step to take more time than you expect. It is likely to require more than one lesson period. The short span of commercials can be deceiving—they usually take much longer to film than their running time.

4. View the commercials.

Run the tape either at the end of this session or at the beginning of the next.

After students have watched their commercials once or twice for fun, have the students fill out "Viewing Commercials" worksheets for one another's commercials. Discuss the sheets. This is a good time to have groups rethink how they planned their commercials. It is also important at some point to talk about how students used social decision making and social problem solving skills throughout this unit, whether it be formally or informally.

IMPLEMENTATION TIPS

1. *Linkage with academic subject areas.* These materials may be linked with several academic subjects, such as civics and current events. Creating scripts for commercials and short video skits involves proper grammar, writing skills, and imagination. Word usage and the power of adjectives is particularly important for writing commercial scripts. Some middle school civics curricula include units on mass media and consumerism. This SDM/SPS unit can

bring the civics material to life for students. Current events can be tied in with a variation on the unit with an additional video project in which students plan brief news reports about current topics. Another variation is for the students to make public service announcements. In this context, the video projects can be linked with health, family life, education, substance abuse, and other related issues.

2. *Appropriateness for different students.* After deciding that you are ready to try these materials, the question may arise as to their appropriateness for your students. This unit has been used successfully by special education teachers, who have found that their classes enjoyed the active nature of the format. As expected, additional adult guidance and structure greatly facilitated group projects in these classes. The unit can be taught as a time-limited curriculum during regular class periods, as a "pullout group," or as a before-school or after-school club.

3. *Avoiding cultural and gender stereotyping.* When choosing commercials and programs for these lessons, it is important to remain sensitive to students' ethnic and cultural backgrounds. The idea of promoting cultural diversity should help to guide programming decisions, and whenever possible, a variety of races and cultures should be represented in video examples. Programs, movies, and commercials that portray characters in stereotyped roles, and those that exploit certain groups of people (such as women and nonwhites) are not appropriate for use as exemplary video material, although such materials can and should be used to teach students how harmful stereotypes and exploitative attitudes are taught and reinforced through commercials, movies, and television programs.

UNIT 2

Social Decision Making and Video and Documentary Making

1

Using Social Decision Making as a Critical Thinking Guide for the Media

Building sound problem-solving and decision-making skills is important throughout the curriculum. Since students spend a great deal of their time watching video-based media, having them associate the SDM/SPS curriculum with real life by applying it to those media fosters generalization of skills.

OBJECTIVES

- To provide students with practice in applying the FIG TESPN strategy
- To exemplify carryover of the social decision making approach to making and viewing videos, films, and television programs
- To illustrate that most successful interpersonal contacts are the result of thoughtful decision making and problem solving

MATERIALS AND PREPARATION

Whole-class display or copies of "FIG TESPN: Steps in Social Decision Making" (Worksheet 7.8)

A videotaped segment of a popular television show or video—preferably one that has been recognized for its quality and content

Chalkboard or easel pad

Copies of "Critical Thinking Guide for the Media" (Worksheet 7.9)

LEADER'S GUIDE

1. Review or introduce the FIG TESPN strategy for SDM/SPS.

If necessary, introduce FIG TESPN. Here is one introduction that has proved useful to many teachers:

FIG TESPN is a strategy to help us make important decisions and solve problems more easily. It can be used in our day-to-day lives as well as in our video making.

Ask for volunteers to explain how good decision making might help them in their lives and in their video making. When it fits into the discussion, say:

Many decisions have to be made in making a video, and our FIG TESPN decision-making skills will be important tools as we pursue this project.

Hand out or display a poster of the FIG TESPN steps worksheet (or both) and read it as a group. Tell the students that they will learn more about how to use this approach to guide their work on this project.

2. Stress the need for careful planning.

It is at this point that you want to relate that a video or film is usually the result of careful planning.

The makers of a video start out with a goal of trying to create a certain impression in their audience. A maker of a beer advertisement wants you to feel, at the end of the ad, that having a beer will make you cool, or make you accepted or popular. The maker of a video or film to be shown in high school guidance or health class may want to impress you with the importance of talking to someone when you have a problem.

Ask the students for additional examples of goals for making a video or film.

3. Show and review the video.

Explain to the students that they will be viewing a video show for the purpose of understanding how the decision-making steps were used while producing the show. Show the students the segment and then discuss according to the FIG TESPN guidelines.

F—Feelings cue me to problem solve.

Remind students that video programs and movies often try to reach your mind and heart in order to change your opinion or persuade you. Show the video, then ask:

How did you feel after watching?

What made you feel that way?

Which of the characters did you agree with the most?

Did you feel anger, joy, disappointment, or other emotions with any of the characters?

Elicit positive answers to the last question in a discussion and identify these feelings as a first step in social decision making.

I—Identify the problem.

Usually, a central social problem emerges in interesting, successful video programs. Often it involves two or more people in some sort of a conflict: two best friends disagreeing, a teacher and a student not getting along, a boyfriend and girlfriend quarreling, an employee having a problem at work, and so on. Ask the students:

What is the central problem that the makers of this video have chosen to concentrate on?

What theme do they want us to focus on the most?

G—Goals give me a guide.

What is the main goal that the makers of this video had in mind? Why did they make this video?

Students often propose "making money" as a goal here, and although this answer is correct, try to expand the discussion beyond this point. Write the video makers' goal or goals at the top of the chalkboard, and separate the rest of the board into two columns, labeling one column "Video Makers" and the other "Student Reviewers."

T—Think of many possible solutions.

There are countless ways to present any theme or problem in a video program. Help the students identify elements of the video used by video makers to present their theme. This may include the show's setting, characters, costuming, story line, special effects, dialogue, and so on.

How did the video makers create in us the impression that they wanted?

Summarize students' responses in the "Video Makers" column. One can always find different angles within a program that could be embellished, deleted, or changed. This is the time to allow the students to become video critics. What would they have done differently to make the same point? Elicit from the students alternative means for creating the same or a similar effect on viewers of the program, and summarize them in the "Student Reviewers" column.

E—Envision outcomes.

Discuss the consequences of the video makers' choices to achieve their goal and those of the alternatives offered by the students.

How do you feel the audience reacted to the solutions the video makers chose?

How might the audience react to your suggestions about making the video different?

If the group needs guidance or encouragement, the following questions may help them:

How would the video be different:

> *If the story took place in a different setting?*
>
> *If you knew more about certain characters?*
>
> *If particular scenes had been played out differently?*

S—Select the best solution.

Of the alternative ways to make this video, what main changes would the students make to convey the theme of the show or to create the impression they wanted? Have them explain their answers.

P—Plan the procedure, anticipate pitfalls, and practice.

> *How well planned was the video?*

This may be difficult for students to answer, since they were not present to witness the organization of the video in the making. Nonetheless, there may be clues as to how well it was planned in the video itself. The following may help spark students' thinking:

> *What are the factors that need to be considered in planning a video?*

- Finding a site—restaurant, school, outdoor setting
- Keeping within a budget
- Selecting the right actors for the roles
- Choosing the wardrobe
- Making sure that the video is not too short or too long
- Selecting the music
- Deciding how much information to include about characters and themes

You can also ask questions like these:

> *What other obstacles might emerge during the process of putting together a video, and how would you deal with them (for example, actors' strike, director's getting sick, disagreement between director and producer)?*

N—Notice what happened and remember it for next time.

Ask the students to recall their thoughts on the goal of the production (Step 3 of these guidelines). Then have the group rate the video makers' success at getting their theme across, using this scale:

| 0 | 1 | 2 | 3 | 4 | 5 | 6 | 7 | 8 | 9 | 10 |

Did not come close   **Very successful**

Then have the group rate particular actors on their performances. Remind the students that the rating should be based not on how well they liked the actors' characters but on how well the individual actors portrayed their characters (as an irritated high school senior, a happy teacher, a frustrated employee, or whatever). Use this scale when judging how well the character was portrayed:

| 0 | 1 | 2 | 3 | 4 | 5 | 6 | 7 | 8 | 9 | 10 |

Unsuccessful   **Very successful**

Now ask students to rethink the entire video production and give it an overall rating, using this scale:

| 0 | 1 | 2 | 3 | 4 | 5 | 6 | 7 | 8 | 9 | 10 |

Poor   **Excellent**

As always, reinforce the appropriate contributions of the students with verbal compliments given throughout the activity. Close with a summary of the major themes of critical thinking that emerged. Encourage the students to use the FIG TESPN strategy for social decision making in all areas of their lives.

4. Assign homework, if you wish.

As an optional homework assignment, provide each student with a copy of the FIG TESPN steps worksheet and a copy of the "Critical Thinking Guide for the Media" worksheet. Ask students to apply Steps 1 through 8 to a television program by writing a paragraph about each step. This may be considered a literacy-related assignment.

It is a good idea to have students discuss the programs they plan to watch so you can approve them. Examples of appropriate television programs for this activity would be after-school specials, public television programs aimed at young adolescents, History or Discovery Channel programs on cable, and some network television programming. Find a way to share the products of the students' work by displaying their summaries or creating a movie and television review newsletter summarizing all the students' reviews.

F —Feelings cue me to problem solve.

I —Identify the problem.

G —Goals give me a guide.

T —Think of many possible solutions.

E —Envision outcomes.

S —Select the best solution.

P —Plan the procedure, anticipate pitfalls, and practice.

N —Notice what happened and remember it for next time.

1. **Feelings cue me to problem solve. (F)**

   Remember, video programs and movies often try to reach your mind and heart in order to change your opinion or persuade you to do something. So let's take a closer look at the kinds of feelings that this program generated in you.

   - How did you feel? What made you feel that way?

   - Which of the characters did you agree with the most?

   - Did you feel anger, joy, disappointment, or other emotions with any of the characters?

2. **Identify the problem. (I)**

   There is usually a problem or conflict that emerges in interesting, successful programs, and it needs to be put into words.

   - What is the central problem that the video makers have chosen to concentrate on?

   - What is it that they want us to focus on the most?

3. **Goals give me a guide. (G)**

   - What is the main goal that the makers of this show had in mind?

4. **Think of many possible solutions. (T)**

   There are countless ways to present any theme or problem in a video program. The elements used by video makers to present their theme may include the show's setting, characters, costuming, story line, special effects, dialogue, and so on.

   - How did the video makers create in us the impression that they wanted?

   - What would you have done differently to make the same point? Brainstorm and list alternative means for creating the same or a similar effect on viewers of the program.

5. **Envision outcomes. (E)**

   Discuss the consequences of the video makers' choices regarding setting, characters, story line, special effects, dialogue, and so on. Picture what might happen, in the short term and the long term, to main characters and others.

   - How do you feel the audience reacted to the video makers' choices in these areas?

   - How might the audience react to your suggestions about making the video differently?

6. **Select the best solution. (S)**

   - What are the main changes you would make in this program to create the impression you want? Explain.

7. **Plan the procedure, anticipate pitfalls, and practice. (P)**
   - How well planned was the program?
   - Would you have planned it differently?
   - Do you think each of the actors planned all of their words? If not, what scenes and individuals are you referring to?
   - Would you have planned for a different setting?
   - What do you think were important factors that need special consideration in planning this video? (Some examples could be organizing special effects and stunts or securing the health and safety of the video crew for a video made in the desert or in the mountains.)
   - What kinds of logistics would be involved in carrying out your improvements? How feasible would they be?

8. **Notice what happened and remember it for next time. (N)**

   Remind yourself of what you thought the goal of the production was (see Step 3). Rate the video makers on how successful they were in achieving their intended goal, using this scale:

0	1	2	3	4	5	6	7	8	9	10

   Did not come close   Very successful

   Rate the actors on how successful they were in playing their roles, using this scale:

0	1	2	3	4	5	6	7	8	9	10

   Unsuccessful at portraying the character   Very successful at portraying the character

   Now rethink the entire video production and give an overall rating of it on the scale below.

0	1	2	3	4	5	6	7	8	9	10

   A poor video production   An excellent video production

2 Looking for Signs of Different Feelings: A Workshop on Acting

Underlying academic success and interpersonal effectiveness with peers and adults is the ability to be sensitive to feelings in others and in oneself. This basic human attribute is required for correct interpretation of literature, history, and current events, as well as art and music. As cultural trends toward faster, more digitized imagery and general speed in decision making and task performance increase, more and more children lose opportunities to build and refine their skills in recognizing feelings. This activity provides some tools to help reverse that trend.

OBJECTIVES

- To practice applying the first step of FIG TESPN, looking for signs of different feelings, both internally and in others
- To demonstrate how the expression of different feelings is important for students' video performances

MATERIALS

Whole-class display of FIG TESPN steps (Worksheet 7.8)

Video camera and monitor

LEADER'S GUIDE

1. Review Topic 1.

Ask for a volunteer to review the ways good decision making will help the group make better videos. If no one is able to do this, give one of these examples: A conflict might arise between the director of a video and the star because each one wants to shoot a scene a different way, or an action scene might wind up looking silly if it wasn't planned and checked carefully to make it as realistic and exciting as possible.

2. Present the first social decision making step in FIG TESPN.

Explain that "Feelings cue me to problem solve" means that it is a good idea to look for signs of feelings in ourselves and in others. Ask the students why recognizing feelings in these ways is important. Here are some suggested reasons that you can present if the group does not generate them:

Recognizing our own feelings gives us the incentive to act. For example, if I didn't get irritated about being treated unfairly by a friend, I would never be motivated to straighten out the situation.

Being able to read others' feelings helps guide us in knowing what to do. For example, it's very helpful to know the signs your friends show when they are upset. For example, they might get very quiet.

Ask students for their own examples. Summarize by saying that if you recognized these signs in your friends, you would be better able to make a choice about what to do next. Say:

This is an important first step because being aware of our feelings and the feelings of others can help us find out what the problem is and what we want to have happen in this situation.

Ask if anyone can think of signs of different feelings.

What are these signs? What cues can we look for?

Discuss internal and external signs, or cues.

3. Introduce the Feelings Charades game.

Tell the students that being able to recognize and show signs of different feelings can make everyone in the group a better actor. Say:

When we think of great actors and actresses, we usually think of people who can play almost any role and convince us that they are the person they are playing. To be convincing actors, we should use signs of feelings when we are the talent in a video. Let's practice acting out different feelings as a game of Feelings Charades.

Suggest different feelings or different situations in which a range of feelings is likely to be displayed. Have several students take turns silently acting out scenes in which they portray different emotions. Some examples:

- Someone drops a fragile object and is then sad that it broke.
- Someone receives a present and is surprised to see what's inside the box.

It may be easiest for students to start by pretending they are actors from television shows or movies. Start simple and then add more challenge. Some simple feelings words are *sad, mad, glad, upset, calm, surprised, ashamed*. Some interesting feelings words to act out are *mischievous, proud, anxious, jealous, bored, outraged, elated, silly, worried, lonely, excited, dejected.* Once the scene is over, the rest of the students should try to read the signs and guess what happened and the feelings being played. (This can also be done in teams or subgroups.)

Have students explain what cues they used to help them get the right answer (facial cues such as raised eyebrows, pouting mouth, wrinkled forehead, wide eyes; changes in posture; gestures).

After it is clear that the group understands the game, videotape individual students acting out a charade in another room where no one else can see. Then play the entire tape of all the students for the group to watch and guess which charade each actor chose. This will help students become accustomed to being videotaped and watching themselves on the monitor.

4. Explore speaking parts.

Next, move on to a more advanced activity, the scripted practice of different feelings with dialogue. Pair students and have each pair think up a skit in which each person emphasizes a different, specific feeling. Challenge students to try demonstrating two feelings that sometimes come together, such as excitement and nervousness about something new. The actors should not mention the feelings they are portraying. It is the job of the audience to identify them. Videotape each pair as they act out their skit. Allow the group to watch the tape and determine what feelings they are seeing.

3 Put the Problem into Words: An Introduction to Documentaries

Another essential skill is to be able to put a problem into words clearly and accurately. This is basic to math and science, as well as to a variety of situations related to projects, homework, and interpersonal relationships with peers and others. Impulsive judgment in children often leads them to pay too little attention to identifying problems and carefully and accurately putting them into words. This activity will provide much-needed practice opportunities for students to improve this skill.

OBJECTIVES

- To practice applying the second step in FIG TESPN decision making, "Identify the problem"
- To define the term *documentary* as a form of media literacy and identify problems addressed by documentaries

MATERIALS

Chalkboard or easel pad

Videotapes or DVDs of one or two programs exemplifying documentaries or the documentary style (Commercial and public television programs such as *60 Minutes, 20/20, Frontline, CNN Presents,* or *Nova,* and videos from the History Channel, A&E, and Discovery Channel can be appropriate sources of documentaries.)

LEADER'S GUIDE

1. Review Topic 2.

Go over the first part of FIG TESPN, "Feelings cue me to problem solve." Ask why this step is important. At this time, you may briefly discuss with students how being able to recognize our own feelings of pressure, tension, happiness, and so on gives us clues about how to deal with situations. Likewise, learning how to read those signs in the faces, posture, and voice tones of others will alert us as to how to proceed or not to proceed. Consider reviewing videotapes made in Topic 2, if available, to further illustrate your points.

2. Introduce the next part of FIG TESPN.

Reiterate that the next thing to do is to identify the problem. Say:

> *A problem is a reason for upset or unpleasant feelings. Why is it helpful for us to be able to identify the problems we are facing?*

One of the major points that you would like to get across here is that using this step offers a clear advantage: When people run into a difficult or upsetting situation, the feelings that accompany it may be overwhelming. Putting the problem into words is a skill that helps convert what's happening into a more manageable experience. So, "I feel frustrated now" becomes "I feel frustrated because I received a poor grade on an exam," or "I feel disappointed" becomes "I feel disappointed because I missed a phone call from my best friend."

> *This step can help you pause and organize yourself. Also, putting your experience into a "problem statement" will give you the feeling that it may be solvable, just like a problem in math or science!*

Elicit from the students a number of examples of everyday problems that people their age face. Write down the examples on the chalkboard or easel pad. Ask the class to link the feelings that come with each example in sentences following this format:

"People our age feel _____because (or when)
                                    (feelings)

_____."
(problem)

3. Make the link to video production.

Say to the students:

> *Being able to identify problems is a useful tool to video makers in two different ways.*
>
> *First, it can help them define difficulties that arise while they make videos. Once they have done this, the problems are easier to solve.*

Ask the group for examples of several problems they had when working on recent video-related or other school projects. Continue:

Second, identifying problems is important to video makers who are choosing a topic for their videos. Most videos include social conflicts and problems in their plots, and some videos actually explore a particular problem.

4. Introduce the term "documentary" and ask for volunteers to define it.

A definition should include the following concepts:

A documentary explores a real-life problem and presents factual information and clearly labeled and justified opinions related to that issue. The problem studied in a documentary may be a scientific issue, a political issue, a social issue, or an environmental issue. The documentary style can be used in making films, television shows, or videos.

Ask students to list some of the documentaries they have seen and the types of problems they addressed. Commercial and public television programs such as *60 Minutes, 20/20,* or *Nova,* and videos by *National Geographic* are all good examples of the documentary style. Students may mention some they have seen on MTV, VH1, E!, ESPN, or other entertainment, sports, and music-related outlets. These may or may not be good examples of documentaries that follow the definition presented here. When an unfamiliar or uncertain source is mentioned, ask the students:

How can you tell if something you have seen is really a documentary or not? What might clue you in that something is not really a documentary, though it may look like one?

Ask the students:

What problems do you think are important enough to be the subject of a documentary?

If the students have trouble coming up with responses, you may want to give them some hints (school issues, pollution, teenage substance abuse, the homeless). Keep a list of their examples.

5. Discuss feelings and problems in the context of documentaries.

Say:

The first two FIG TESPN decision-making steps are important for making a documentary. The problem explored in a documentary must be stated clearly for the audience to understand what it is about. Documentaries often bring out strong feelings in their viewers. Actors or people being interviewed in them show us their feelings about the issue. Factual information is also presented about the problem being addressed. Both of these components of documentaries can bring out certain feelings in relation to the problem.

Show a segment from the documentary video you have selected. Ask students to identify the problem being addressed. Go around the room and ask each student what feelings they experienced while watching the video clip. Ask what it was about the video clip that made them feel that way.

6. Begin the documentary exercise.

Break the students up into groups. Assign them the task of choosing an issue or problem about which they would like to make a documentary. Have each group identify the problem and discuss the feelings they have about it. From there, the group should decide on the feelings they would like to bring out in the audience of their own documentary.

Have each group choose someone to report on film about the decisions made by that group. The members should coach the speaker to be aware of the "BEST" behaviors—body posture, eye contact, speech, and tone of voice—while reporting on camera. (Review Worksheet 3.4 if the class needs more practice on this point.)

Try to hold the videotaping away from the remainder of the students. Sometimes it works well to have a room set up for videotaping so students can come in for a few minutes during their lunch or recess time to do the taping.

Once all speakers have been filmed, the tapes should be viewed by the entire group. Discuss how well each group put their problems into words, and how their representatives presented themselves and their information.

IMPLEMENTATION TIPS

1. If you would like students to pursue creating a documentary, use Topics 3 and 4 of Unit 1 ("Media Analysis, Advertising, and Commercials") as a format for organizing documentaries. Worksheets can be adapted and multiple storyboards used for each segment of the documentary. Encourage students to incorporate video or DVD and computer-based resources into their presentation to serve as a substitute for going on location. This is an excellent way for students to

delve into greater depth in various academic subject areas, all of which can be the basis for documentaries. Topic 4 of this unit, "The Video Critique Club," can also be used, especially if you want students to work on modifying existing documentaries.

2. If students seem to have trouble recognizing signs of feelings, the Supplemental Activity at the end of this chapter, on using video to teach BEST skills, will provide useful practice for students in the component skills of being able to recognize feelings in themselves and others.

4

The Video Critique Club: An Approach to Creating Public Service Spots and Prevention Messages, and to Running Counseling and Clinical Groups

The "Video Critique Club" capitalizes on some students' tendencies to be oppositional or uninterested in just about anything introduced by an adult or an authority figure. It is also useful when one is working with a heterogeneous group and can guarantee that a significant minority of the class will not be able to, or wish to, identify with the age, ethnicity, gender, or coolness of a video's protagonists. As you may surmise, middle school students greatly enjoy the Video Critique Club format.

The club format is useful in health and family life classes, especially for creating prevention messages of the kind one might see, hear, or read in public service announcements. Topical areas include using drugs, smoking, consuming alcohol, bullying, teasing, carrying weapons, and cheating. The club format can also be used for character education to include such positive values as trust, responsibility, respect, honesty, fairness and justice, and citizenship.

The club format is additionally useful in that one can use it to form a counseling and clinical group but avoid the stigma and negative labeling involved. From the students' point of view, the rationale for a club—clinical or otherwise—is a chance to get together and do something interesting related to television and videos. It gives students an opportunity to be like their favorite movie critics, whether *Ebert and Roeper, Entertainment Weekly,* or reviewers on MTV. They are told that they will meet for a given number of weeks (at least four, and as long as one, two, three, or four grading periods) and review videos. This activity tends to produce some level of positive motivation in even oppositional and disaffected students.

The skill development aspect of the critique approach comes in several ways. First of all, students share their views about the videos, which helps build their accuracy in processing cues in the environment. When students disagree about whether something was or was not said or shown, the group leader need only replay the relevant passage and allow students to resolve the issue largely on their own. Second, the main skill learning comes in the group interaction. Here, the leader plays an important role in helping students to use "Keep Calm" and "BEST" skills with one another. Further, brainstorming, envisioning consequences, planning, and anticipating obstacles are prominent aspects of the group tasks, thus giving the group leader many opportunities to use FIG TESPN to promote students' critical thinking, perspective taking, and interpersonal skill development. Yet all this is done in the service of helping the groups complete tasks they are interested in completing, not simply as part of a clinical or special education or related official academic agenda.

OBJECTIVES

- To provide students with a structured approach to giving constructive criticism of video and related media
- To build students' group problem solving and planning skills

MATERIALS

A video or DVD of a public service announcement

Copies of the "Outline for the Video Critique Club" (Worksheet 7.10)

Video camera and monitor

LEADER'S GUIDE

1. Introduce the activity.

Go over the "Outline for the Video Critique Club" worksheet. Depending on the focus, tell students that the group is going to work on evaluating and improving public service announcements, prevention videos, or whatever other type of content will be your focus.

2. Present a video.

Select the video for the group to work on based on the focus you've chosen for the group. There is no need to be defensive about your choice, however. It is fine if the students adopt a critical attitude toward the video they watch. Use the first three items on the worksheet to orient students to the video.

3. Show the video.

Ask for general ratings, using Question 4 and the Popcorn Box Rating System (Question 5).

4. Establish working groups.

At this point, or shortly thereafter, it is advisable to have students work in subgroups of four or five. The exact grouping pattern depends on your larger purposes—you can split up the group by gender or mix genders; you can mix students of different racial, ethnic, or socioeconomic groups; you can also mix academic levels and use the groupings to foster mainstreaming or inclusion.

5. Continue with the framework.

Ask students to respond to Questions 6 and 7, first as individuals and then to come to a group consensus. Note that students are being moved to be critical thinkers and reporters about what they have observed. They also must arrive at consensus at some points, which exercises many SDM/SPS skills, especially listening to others, taking others' perspective, keeping calm, and giving and receiving praise, help, and criticism.

Moreover, they are challenged first to be constructive about what they have seen and then—and only then—to point out areas they disliked. The essence of the procedure is to move the children to identify what they dislike and then become engaged in doing something about it.

Move students to respond to Questions 8, 9, 10, and 11 over the time period available. This is the stage of greatest learning: The students work in small groups to create their alternative versions. The group work provides a venue to observe and give feedback on the students' interpersonal styles, especially the attributes described in BEST. Here, rather than offering didactic instruction, you can promote skill development in the context of real-life examples, in situations in which students are motivated to get along because they are interested in completing the project.

IMPLEMENTATION TIPS

1. Sometimes students who are oppositional and lack motivation tend not to be interested in the preparatory activities. If this is a

concern, just show the video, and then go back and elaborate on the issues, along with a more careful viewing of the video. Beginning with the video serves as a gateway to the activities, taking advantage of the attention-getting aspects of the approach.

2. You may want to acquaint students with the techniques for creating commercials presented in the first three topics of this unit, to broaden their options in planning how to improve the service spots.

3. To provide extra motivation for the project, the revised public service spots can be audiotaped or videotaped, after which other groups can give feedback, and then the creators can edit them into a final format. Then you can arrange to have the finished products shown at an assembly; presented to other schools; shown to (and perhaps created for) children in younger grades; presented to the board of education, town council, or other local government body; used as part of a local business roundtable or a prevention fund-raiser; and shared with the community over cable access television.

1. Name of critic: _____

2. Name of video: _____

3. What is the goal of this video? Why is it supposed to be worth watching?

4. How much did you like the video? *(Circle one.)*

   a. A lot   b. It was OK   c. A little   d. Not at all

5. Popcorn Box Rating System:

   On a scale of 1 to 5 boxes of popcorn, with 1 box being the worst and 5 boxes being the best, how many boxes of popcorn would you give it?

               1   2   3   4   5

6. What parts did you like the best?

7. What parts did you like the least?

8. Look at the parts you liked the best. With your group, discuss why you felt that way. Then look at the parts you liked the least. Again, discuss with your group why you felt that way. Then agree as a group on the three parts that your group would most like to change. Write them here:

9. Next, together with your group, pick one of these parts to work on. Write it down, and then discuss and write down three different ways to improve on the part you liked the least. (It is fine to combine two or three parts you liked the least and work on them together, if it makes sense to do so.)

10. With your group, discuss your ideas and plan a script change. Remember how much time you have to work with, both in terms of the video segment you are working on and the time you have to work on this critique. Be sure to picture in your mind the goal of the video, who will see it, and everything that will go into changing the video.

11. Rehearse your changes and improve your script. If possible, audiotape or videotape your changes. If you have time, go back and work on changing other parts that you liked least. Share your changes with other groups and get and give feedback.

Videotaping Feedback on BEST for Skill-Building Practice

OBJECTIVES

- To practice BEST (or alternate social decision making skills) and evaluate students' performances with the aid of videotape equipment
- To allow students to build skills necessary for identifying feelings in themselves and others

MATERIALS

Video camera and monitor

NOTE: Throughout this activity, BEST appears in parentheses to signify that this lesson can be used with other social decision making skills by replacing BEST and its components with those of the alternate skill.

LEADER'S GUIDE

1. Review the social decision making skill of (BEST).

Be sure to cover the four components of the skill:

B —Body posture

E —Eye contact

S —Speech (Saying appropriate things)

T —Tone of voice

2. Explain to the students that today they will be practicing (BEST) with a little twist.

This time, they will get the chance to see themselves doing it on video.

3. Record each student's efforts.

Ask students, as individual performers, to pretend they are going up to a group of unfamiliar students and asking to sit at their lunch table. Ask them to show you how they would handle the situation, using their (BEST) skills. You can videotape students demonstrating (BEST) in front of the group or in their seats.

4. Show the video.

Once everyone has been recorded, arrange the students to watch the videotape of themselves. Students are usually excited about seeing themselves on television, and it is best to show the videotape once without interruption for all to enjoy.

5. Replay the video and review it.

Before the second showing, divide the students into groups and assign each group the role of observing one of the components of (BEST) during playback of the videotape. Stop the tape after each student's segment and ask the performer to comment on the performance:

How well did you remember to do all parts of (BEST)?

Then consult with each group for its feedback to that student on the performance.

6. Conduct a practice activity.

After the students complete the review, pair them up for guided practice. Explain that they are to plan and act out a situation in which it is important to use (BEST). It is also possible to have students act out two versions of the same situation, one in which a student does not use (BEST) when it is appropriate (to illustrate the consequences of failing to do so), and the other demonstrating the appropriate use of (BEST) in the same situation (to show the positive outcomes of using this skill).

Encourage the students to plan their situations carefully, since they will be videotaped and replayed. Assist students in their preparation, as needed, and videotape each pair's situations while the remainder of the students practice. When possible, videotape in a separate room. This will heighten the excitement and novelty of viewing the videotape later.

Once every pair has been taped, replay the videotape for the entire group. Show the entire tape without interruption, and on the second showing, stop it after each situation to review students' performances. Repeat the group observation and feedback carried out in Step 5 of this exercise.

8

A School-Community Environmental Service Project to Promote Social Decision Making Skills

This chapter presents a series of lessons designed to help students develop individual and group plans for solving environmental problems by using SDM/SPS as a framework for doing research, writing it up, and presenting it. The approach can also be adapted to a variety of other interdisciplinary topics. For example, the ability to organize one's thinking and develop a process for working through problems has been identified as a critical aspect of effective education in the sciences (Abell, 1990; Brandwein & Glass 1991; Klopfer, 1991; Otto, 1991). Otto also identified instructors' questioning techniques as a key element in learning the scientific process. Otto and Schuck (1983) found that students taught science lessons by teachers trained in a questioning technique learned more science and retained it longer. Wise and Okey (1983) analyzed research in teachers' strategies over a thirty-year period and found that students of teachers who employed questioning strategies to promote independent thinking scored significantly higher than those students whose teachers did not do so; further, they showed greater general achievement, problem-solving skills, creativity, critical and logical thinking skills, and affective development.

In the area of environmental education, exemplary programs use cooperative learning and problem-solving strategies to teach children to think critically about their environment and improve their scientific thinking abilities (Abell, 1990; Barton & Washburn, 1991; Brandwein & Glass, 1991; Fay, 1991; Klopfer, 1991). More recently, Moulds (2004) identified the benefits of a problem-based approach to studying such topics as water quality. The program Moulds reported on asked the question "What is the water quality of a nearby river?"

Thanks to Rebecca L. Johnsen for her contributions to this chapter.

Students addressed this topic by reading about the geography and history of the river; its industrial, agricultural, and recreational uses; and its current state. They gathered data from water samples, presented the information in various modalities, and forwarded recommendations about the river to relevant government agencies, historical societies, and local university departments. Seif (2004) reported similar benefits when students begin with questions like "What problems do countries face as they expand?" and "In what ways is the United States geographically and culturally diverse, and what is the relationship between the two?" The resulting learning, which is deep, integrative, and engaging, can be guided by the procedures outlined in this chapter.

SUGGESTED RESOURCES

Geddis, A. (1991). Improving the quality of science classroom discourse on controversial issues. *Science Education, 75*(2), 169–183.

Hopper, J. H., & Nielsen, J. McCarl. (1991). Recycling as altruistic behavior: Normative and behavioral strategies to expand participation in a community recycling program. *Environment and Behavior, 23*(2), 195–220.

Jacobson, S. K. (1991). Evaluation model for developing, implementing, and assessing conservation education programs: Examples from Belize and Costa Rica. *Environmental Management, 15*(2), 143–150.

Oskamp, S., Harrington, M. J., Edwards, T. C., Sherwood, D. L., Okuda, S. M., & Swansorr, D. C. (1991). Factors influencing household recycling behavior. *Environment and Behavior, 23*(4), 494–519.

Thompson, S. C., & Stoutemyer, K. (1991). Water use as a common dilemma: The effects of education that focuses on long-term consequences and individual action. *Environment and Behavior, 23*(3), 314–333.

School-Community Environmental Service Project

OBJECTIVES

- To develop an ongoing commitment among students to continue to learn about the most pressing areas of environmental concern
- To build students' sense of personal responsibility to become stewards of the earth
- To provide opportunities for creating presentations of learning for a range of audiences in the community

MATERIALS

Copies of the following:

"Group Leader's Game Plan" (Worksheet 8.1)

"Social Decision Making Discussion on Environmental Problems" (Worksheet 8.2)

"Committee Meeting Summary Form" (Worksheet 8.3)

"Planning Interdisciplinary Projects (PIP)" (Worksheet 8.4)

"Presentation Planning and Selection" (Worksheet 8.5)

NOTE: Examples of students' possible responses are provided as "Sample Environmental Goals and Action Strategies" (Exhibit 8.1); "Sample Committee Meeting Summary" (Exhibit 8.2); and "Meeting of the Town of Gar-Baj" (Exhibit 8.3).

LEADER'S GUIDE—PART 1: DEFINING THE PROBLEM, BRAINSTORMING SOLUTIONS, MAKING PLANS

1. Spend some time reviewing FIG TESPN.

Use peer tutoring to update any students who are new to the SDM/SPS approach. (If all students are new, begin by introducing FIG TESPN using the activities in Chapter 3.)

2. Review the Group Leader's Game Plan.

Go over Worksheet 8.1 and provide any necessary introduction to students about environmental issues. Note that the game plan is a set of guidelines, not a rigid framework. It is designed to help students see themselves as able to take action on environmental issues.

Provide the students with a base of knowledge about the problems of the environment. It is often useful to motivate the students with a few shocking facts about environmental problems in general and in a focal area that the group will work with. Abell (1990) describes this technique as presenting a class group with "a mess": a statement of conflict in need of resolution.

3. Brainstorm a list of students' own environmental concerns.

Tell students that your plan is to use the social decision making framework as a guide to help them plan essays, write letters, and develop personal decisions and plans about how they could better take care of their own environment and health. Here is one sample of a sixth-grade class's concerns about the environment:

Animals dying	Landfills
Effects of environment on the health of humans	Destruction of land
	Ocean shores polluted
Changing the beauty of nature	People do not care
Holes in the ozone layer	Recreation areas dirty/destroyed
Destruction of the rain forest	
Running out of clean water	Tourism and fishing industries dying
Losing forests	
Acid rain	

4. Organize students into sharing circles and have them brainstorm specific goals they would like to address.

Overall, use the discussion guide in Worksheet 8.2. Begin by clarifying students' feelings about various issues, putting the problem into words, and then deciding on a goal. After writing down a record of several rounds of sharing and brainstorming, refine a specific set of goals. (See the example in Exhibit 8.1, at the end of this chapter.)

5. Once goals have been developed, brainstorm specific solutions or action strategies that students can use to reach these goals.

This phase can take several class periods to develop, as students work through a wide variety of alternative solutions, anticipate both positive and negative consequences or outcomes, and discuss what actions will be most likely to help accomplish their goals. The example in Exhibit 8.1 took several class sessions; it reflects a series of modifications as the project, and the actions it outlines were developed through the thinking of the group. Be prepared to spend time encouraging the use of the social decision making framework whenever students plan any aspect of their solution. As desired, assign a formal thinking assignment by distributing a worksheet, but also continually refer back to a whole-class display of the steps in FIG TESPN as a focus and guide for discussion and planning.

6. Continue to encourage students to work in committees or subgroups as they go through the rest of the problem-solving process.

Responses can be recorded on the "Committee Meeting Summary Form" (Worksheet 8.3). Exhibit 8.2, at the end of this chapter, provides a sample of a completed form.

I will:

1. Inform the students through reading and audiovisual materials.

2. Motivate the students with a few "shockers."

3. Encourage the students to identify some specific environmental problems (provide examples, if needed).

4. Use social decision making steps as a framework to arrive at simple everyday solutions and plans.

5. Integrate the curriculum by weaving study skills, health, science, reading, and other topics together.

An example of my expectations:

1. To inform—there is a limited supply of fresh water.

2. To motivate—about 1 percent of water is fresh, and much of that is locked in the polar ice caps.

3. To identify the problem—we could run out of usable fresh water.

4. To help the class use social decision making skills to identify goals and possible solutions. For example, to reach the goal of saving water, some possible student solutions include don't brush teeth at all; brush less often; wet toothbrush, turn water off, brush teeth, turn on water to rinse.

5. To integrate—write up a lab sheet for science on an activity whereby students measure the amount of water saved by the third choice noted in the preceding paragraph.

Worksheet 8.2
Social Decision Making Discussion on Environmental Problems

Student(s) _____ Date _____

1. Feelings

(Example: Anger, shock, fear, frustration.)

2. Identify the problem

(Example: If things continue the way they are, the environment will be in terrible shape by the time we grow up.)

3. Goals

(Example: To take individual responsibility and actions to help save and protect the environment.)

4. Think of solutions

(Example: Anything from "Storm Washington, D.C." to "Teach our families to do environmentally safe things.")

5. Envision outcomes

(Example: Whatever might happen, from "It would cost too much" to "People would get angry.")

6. Select the best solution

(Example: Teach our families to do environmentally safe things.)

7. Plan

(Example: Share information and facts at home; practice what we will say; develop plans at home to recycle, reuse, reduce.)

From *Social Decision Making/Social Problem Solving for Middle School Students: Skills and Activities for Academic, Social, and Emotional Success.* Copyright © 2005 by Maurice J. Elias and Linda Bruene Butler. Research Press (800-519-2707; www.researchpress.com)

Student(s) _____ Date _____

1. Feelings

_____

_____

2. Identify the Problem

_____

_____

3. Goals

_____

_____

4. Think of solutions

_____

_____

5. Envision consequences

_____

_____

6. Select the best solution

_____

_____

7. Plan

_____

_____

8. Follow up

_____

_____

LEADER'S GUIDE—PART 2:
DEVELOPING A WRITTEN PRODUCT AND A VISUAL PRESENTATION

1. Assign the report.

Distribute "Planning Interdisciplinary Projects (PIP)" (Worksheet 8.4) to the students. Inform them that the next step in the process is for each of the students to submit a written report that pulls together what they have learned. The worksheet encourages them to do so in different ways that you can further structure, depending on your curriculum and instructional priorities. Sometimes it is important for students to produce a standard research report format; other times, students can be engaged with other approaches, such as creating a documentary script, the dialogue for a panel discussion, an interview, a PowerPoint presentation, or a short book on their topic for children their age.

Using the worksheet, students are guided to think about their topic, their format of presentation, and ways to get additional information to supplement what they found in their group work. (*Note:* It is also possible to use this format to develop a written product without doing the group project, or prior to it.)

2. Assign the presentation.

Distribute "Presentation Planning and Selection" (Worksheet 8.5). Tell students they can use this worksheet as a way to help them present what they have learned to others.

A format that works well is a "presentation fair." This involves each student (or groups of students who have worked on similar topics and who would benefit from working together to build teamwork skills) in designing a visual presentation of key information they learned in their group discussion or written report. The audiences for such a fair can be students in the school, students in elementary school, parents, or members of the community at large who are affected by the problem chosen.

The fair gives students a chance to show others what they have learned and to help them think about and act on the problem. The worksheet helps students structure a plan for their presentation (which can involve work outside school) and encourages them to learn to keep the perspective of their audience in mind, both cognitively and emotionally.

Student(s) _____ Date _____

First: Define your problem and goal.

1. What is your topic?

2. What are some questions you would like to answer or learn about the topic? (Use the back of this page, if necessary.)

Second: Think of alternative places to look for information.

1. Write at least five possible places you can look for information:

   a. _____

   b. _____

   c. _____

   d. _____

   e. _____

2. Plan which one you will try first. (Use the back of this page, if necessary.)

3. Who else can you ask for ideas if these do not work?

Third: Think of alternative ways to present the topic.

1. Write at least three ways to present the topic in a written format:

   a. _____

   b. _____

   c. _____

2. Consider the consequences and organization for each way. Choose your best solution and plan how you will do it.

Fourth: Make a final check and fix what needs fixing.

1. Does your presentation answer the topic questions you asked? Is it clear and neat? Is the spelling correct? Is it proofread carefully? Will others enjoy it?

2. Does your presentation clarify the viewer/reader's understanding of the topic?

Student(s) _____ **Date** _____

Directions: It is time to give very serious consideration to the presentation that is to accompany your written report. Your presentation will be due _____. It should be visual so that someone walking around and looking at your presentation can understand it without too many questions. It should show some of your findings, learnings, or solutions to the problem you investigated. It may involve graphs, charts, tables, maps, photo collections, murals, models, experiments, diagrams, or other displays you find useful.

Use the following format to help plan and select your type of presentation. This plan is to be completed, signed, and turned in by _____.

1. What are some of the facts that you have learned?

2. What were some changes that have occurred over the years?

3. What are some solutions to problems you have studied?

4. Which of these categories of information (1, 2, or 3) would you like to highlight or focus upon for your presentation? Circle it.

5. What ideas do you have now about what would be the best way to present this information?

6. List dates below as a guide for completion.

   Make a plan (rough draft) _____

   Gather materials _____

   Start final version _____

   Midpoint of project completion _____

7. Review what you have written here for clarity, completeness, and neatness. When you are proud of it, sign it and turn it in. If you have questions, seek out help from classmates, teachers, librarians, or your parents or guardians.

AN EXAMPLE OF THE PROCESS IN ACTION

Berkeley Heights, New Jersey
Columbia Middle School
Rebecca Johnsen (Teacher)

During the beginning phase, we frequently worked together as a class, and I acted as a facilitator, guiding and helping to organize and structure the group's thoughts by using the social decision making steps as our guide. The students were able to clarify their feelings very early in the project. They did not like what was happening to the environment, and they wanted to take action to change and improve the situation.

In our initial large-group brainstorming sessions, students often came up with unrealistic or unworkable solutions. It was notable how often they were able to deduce for themselves the workability of an idea, if prompted to anticipate probable or possible consequences or outcomes of such actions. As a result, they discarded these ideas on their own. (One example of such a discussion is illustrated in Exhibit 8.1.) This example is a simplified version of what happened, as the students actually had too many suggestions to list them all here. The students developed strategies to become increasingly efficient in focusing on viable solutions, refining their thinking around realistic actions and considering both the positive and negative consequences that could result from alternative actions.

As a result of their work on this project, students became a driving force behind our community's decision to institute mandatory plastic recycling. They were invited to the town council meeting when the resolution was put to a vote. To prepare them, in one popular exercise, I had the students pretend to be a town council in Gar-Baj, a very environmentally careless town that had just been informed that in less than one month they will be totally responsible for their own solid waste disposal. (The highlights of this activity are recorded in Exhibit 8.3.) Part of this activity was filmed by CBS for a special titled *The Ecokids.*

The students planned and organized a meeting with our town mayor and thought of this as a great preparation for making a presentation at a town hall meeting. At the town hall meeting, they reported on a survey they had conducted in their neighborhoods that demonstrated public support for plastic recycling. They also shared the information they had learned at school with members of their families. In addition, several students had editorials published in the local community newspaper.

The students knew exactly what goals they wanted to accomplish, and because their social decision making skills empowered them to make the decisions they needed to plan out actions necessary to achieve these goals, they took true ownership of the project. It became a meaningful quest, not just a class assignment or rote exercise. That meant that a student, not a teacher, had to plan the call to the mayor, with feedback and input from peers, and then make the call to arrange for a meeting.

Throughout our unit of environmental studies, students were able to continually practice the entire range of social decision making skills that they had learned in their elementary curriculum. For example, students were able to use their readiness skills repeatedly when preparing and practicing their speeches for the town council and a later presentation to the New Jersey State Assembly. In particular, students used self-monitoring and group feedback to improve their Keep Calm skills. To make presentations increasingly effective, they practiced as key aspects of their communication the Be Your BEST skills of body posture, eye contact, careful planning of what to say, and tone of voice.

The class and I really needed our skills when we received national recognition. The group was honored at the White House by President Bush and awarded the President's Environmental Youth Award. Ten groups from across the nation are recognized each year for their environmental accomplishments. Since that time, we have been involved in local, regional, and national television productions. We enjoyed participating in the United Nations Environmental Youth Forum, and we had a write-up in *Environmental Magazine.* The participants remain active in the school, community, and state. And each year a new class of sixth graders determines its own goals and the strategies for achieving those goals.

The students used diverse social decision making skills in all aspects of the project. They were able to target specific behaviors and were therefore able to improve and perform admirably. It was noteworthy that New Jersey Assemblywoman Maureen Ogden specifically complimented the presenters on their poise and presentation at the State Assembly. Keep Calm was extremely important in all these situations. Even I found myself consciously using Keep Calm as we met President Bush.

Not every project will have this kind of impact, but each step taken gives the students a strong sense of empowerment and preparation for their roles as citizens—including dealing with disappointment when ideas are not accepted, as well as learning how to persist constructively in areas in which students feel strongly committed.

Social decision making has proven to be a powerful and viable vehicle to use in teaching if one's goal is to empower students to make their own decisions and take ownership of their own skills at making decisions and learning. Many students enter middle school with the enthusiasm and energy they need to be responsible decision makers—and emerge depressed and apathetic. Others have never realized that they can make a difference and never do so on their own. We need to conserve the students' natural enthusiasm and build the skills and confidence of all middle schoolers. These can be encouraged through practice and success. The environmental service application of social decision making provides a powerful, enjoyable, and viable framework for middle school teachers and students.

IMPLEMENTATION TIPS: HOW TO ADAPT THIS ACTIVITY TO OTHER FORMATS AND SUBJECT AREAS

Other academic topics

In addition to environmental issues, other academic topic areas that have lent themselves well to this project format are natural phenomena such as earthquakes, volcanoes, avalanches, hurricanes, floods, monsoons, typhoons, and cyclones; scientific discoveries; and explorers (both in the past and more contemporary, such as those who explore space, polar regions, and the ocean depths).

Project- and problem-based counseling groups

Counselors can use this format in place of typical remediation-oriented group approaches with students. For example, a group of children with social phobias or aggressive behavior or mixed social-emotional difficulties can be created with the rationale of helping them be better citizens of their school and community. The potential of creating a project that will inform the community—or younger students, parents, or some combination of these—is much more motivating to students than is the usual promise of personal remediation offered by counseling and clinical groups.

In such groups, the structure of the meetings provides the opportunity to teach students the skills they need to successfully complete their project. (Ideas for creating a positive group rule structure and supportive climate can be found in Chapter 3.) This can be the object of explicit discussion with students:

To do the research that is necessary and develop and do a presentation for parents (or whomever), what do you need to be able to do well? What skills do you need?

Brainstorm this list and keep it visible during group meetings. Make sure to cover FIG TESPN skills, skills for self-control, appropriate communication, cooperation, planning, organizational skills, writing skills, and the rest of the SDM/SPS toolbox. When there are breakdowns in group behavior, use them as teachable moments to point out the failure to use their skills and provide some practice opportunities to help them understand better ways to deal with the situations that derailed them. In all cases, use the other students as a problem-solving team to the extent possible. For example:

> *Tony and Keisha had a disagreement that led to name-calling and shouting. What are some other ways they could handle it when they disagree?*

> *Latia, Quesia, and Charles all started grabbing for the same interviewer's notebook and started to push and fight with each other about it. What are some better ways they could solve their problem?*

Keep in mind that a strong incentive for using these kinds of groups outside the academic context is the opportunity students have to showcase what they are learning. It is the eventual display of their work that provides the strongest reason for them to learn and use SDM/SPS skills in the service of group and individual work. Be sure these end products are clearly defined and are kept strongly and visibly in mind for students from the beginning of the group's work.

Exhibit 8.1
Sample Environmental Goals and Action Strategies

GOAL 1

To learn as much as possible about the environment and its problems by:

- Inviting guest speakers to the classroom
- Reading background and current information
- Viewing video, film, and television programs
- Interviewing people who have an impact on our environment, such as mayors, state representatives, fast-food restaurant owners, recycling location employees
- Researching an environmental topic

GOAL 2

To share our knowledge and concern regarding the environment with others by:

- Writing editorials to newspapers
- Participating in television shows (local programming)
- Developing "Help Our World (HOW)" information booklets
- Holding an environmental awareness night
- Publishing a newsletter, "HOW Highlighter"

GOAL 3

To act in a responsible fashion that demonstrates environmental concern by:

- Writing letters to companies (both "Shame on you" and "Good job!")
- Using the environmental 3 R's at home (reuse, reduce, recycle)
- Addressing the town council to encourage a plastics recycling program
- Adopting a whale
- Visiting and addressing the New Jersey State Assembly to express our concerns for our future in terms of the environment

Exhibit 8.2   *Sample Committee Meeting Summary*

Problem: No plastics recycling in Berkeley Heights.

Goal: Get plastics recycling in Berkeley Heights.

Solutions: Go door-to-door
Letter to mayor
Survey
Share information at home
Newspaper editorial
Booth at food store
Protests
Letters to president

Envision outcomes: Discuss problems in reaching our goal based on pros and cons of each solution, giving consideration to time, feasibility, and resources.

Select solution: A combination of ideas: Go door-to-door, visit town hall, set up a booth at the food store, and send letters to the president.

Plan: Practice and plan a call to the mayor.
Prepare for a meeting with the mayor.
Send out surveys to gain support—plan speeches.
Share information at home.

Follow up: Write letters to the newspaper.

Exhibit 8.3   **Meeting of the Town of Gar-Baj**

1. **Feelings**

   Panic, fear

2. **Identify the problem**

   Too much garbage (about 4 pounds per person daily) and not enough space to dispose of it

3. **Goals**

   To reduce garbage

   To have a workable plan for waste disposal

4. **Think of solutions**

   - Recycle all paper, bi-metal, aluminum, glass, cardboard. Compost all biodegradables (coffee grounds, vegetable peelings, grass clippings, etc.).
   - Reduce amount of garbage by buying items in least packaging, reuse materials whenever possible (aluminum foil, grocery bags).
   - Consider waste-to-energy facility for town.

5. **Envision outcomes**

   - Many of our ideas would be inconvenient, or lead to extra work, higher grocery bills.
   - Less garbage, cheaper fuel bills, etc.

6. **Select the best solution**

   A combination of ideas

7. **Plan**

   (beginning draft)

   - Would make recycling the law.
   - No curb pickup for lawn clippings and leaves, but composting directions sent to every household.
   - Careful checking of garbage as it arrives at local landfill; fines levied for throwing out recyclable materials.
   - Fines levied if homeowner has more than three pounds of garbage weekly.
   - Investigate sending waste to energy plant.

Part 4

Supporting Your Efforts in Building Students' SDM/SPS Skills

9 Parent Involvement and Engagement in Middle School: Communicating, Collaborating, Connecting

It is not easy to involve and engage parents in the education of their middle school students. Those who say otherwise have either been very lucky and have had circumstances that are hard to replicate elsewhere, or they are speaking hypothetically and not based on continuous experience.

AVAILABLE OPTIONS

That being said, a number of schools using the social decision making and social problem solving approach have found some modest success in reaching parents. Their activities take three forms: communicating, collaborating, and connecting.

Communicating

The essence of successful communication between home and school (as well as among parents) is to think in terms of conversations. Conversations can occur during formal school encounters like Back-to-School Night or conferences, or through informal contacts, arranged interviews, or personal telephone contact. Their purpose is to build an exchange of information. The adults who care about children need to get to know each other and share energies and ideas. Newsletter pieces, as will be described in this chapter, can be written to share information about what teachers and other educators in the school are trying to accomplish, but these pieces are not ends in themselves. They are a means to open ongoing channels of communication. The main

Thanks to Charlotte A. Hett, Louise McGarahan, Keli Bryan, Roger Weissberg, and Eva Patrikakou for their contributions to this chapter.

principle to remember in reaching out to parents with conversations and follow-up newsletters is to keep the exchange manageable and responsive. It will be a challenge to make sure that communications sent home from school are readable by busy parents—that is, clear and simple and free of jargon.

By setting a positive, encouraging tone, educators confirm their belief in the caring energies of adults and their commitment to a continuing process of sharing information and inquiry.

Collaborating

Parents of middle school children are dealing with a number of social-emotional development issues, and these often have a higher priority than academics. When home-school collaboration is too closely tied to academic issues, educators risk losing parents. And this seems to be what tends to happen, as parental involvement drops off sharply between elementary school and middle school. But when collaboration occurs around areas of mutual concern—areas that also have an impact on academics—there is a much greater chance of getting wider and more genuine collaborative participation. This is especially the case with urban, low-income, rural, and other contexts in which parents are traditionally less likely to be involved in their middle schoolers' education (often because of their own perceived educational shortcomings, discomfort with school, or preoccupation with household tensions and pressures).

Connecting

While it is valuable for parents to connect with the school, sometimes the school can do the greatest good for parents by helping them to connect with one another. That is the premise behind the groups known as "Emotionally Intelligent Parenting Circles," first developed in collaboration with the New Jersey Parent-Teacher Association. These groups help parents come together to share concerns and solutions, and to see themselves as resources for one another outside formal meetings. Educators play a significant role in convening and organizing such meetings as a form of conversation starter, but what comes from the effort can happen with or without school involvement, depending on the resources, motivation, and wherewithal of parents.

COMMUNICATING THROUGH SCHOOL AND HOME NEWSLETTERS

You probably receive a few newsletters, some on paper and some electronic. How often have you thought about their value, what goes into producing them, and their full potential? For example, consider the following purposes for which a newsletter is particularly useful:

- Communication about the status of a program and occurrences within it
- Sharing of ideas, accomplishments, and questions
- Improvement of students' social decision making skills

In this chapter, we share examples of a newsletter process that can foster communication and the development of social decision making skills. Specifically, we will give examples of a newsletter collaboration with parents. We will focus on the procedures used to make these newsletters into effective vehicles of communication so you can try to initiate versions at your sites.

Background

According to the Center for Early Adolescence, young adolescents need opportunities to express their developing feelings, interests, abilities, and thoughts. In a similar way, adults who are working with young adolescents can benefit from expressing and sharing discoveries they make as they move through stages of personal and professional growth. Newsletters are an ideal vehicle for building the partnership of adults who work with children and seek to promote the development of students' social decision making skills. Often overlooked, though, is how newsletters can promote communication beyond the printed word when they build a person-to-person exchange of resources and create opportunities for people to work in collaboration toward common goals.

Our view of newsletter collaboration is in part an outgrowth of citizen participation that occurred during the early years of court-ordered desegregation of the Boston Public Schools. Collaborating around newsletters was a natural extension of the activities promoted by Boston University through its partnership with the school district during the mid-1970s. According to Dr. Miriam Clasby, director of the Boston University District I Collaborative, newsletter activities gave parents a voice. For example, when the results of reading test scores were reported in the newspaper, the communication process stopped with the printed word. But parents had questions about what it meant to read on grade level. A collaborative newsletter process followed up the newspaper reports and engaged parents through interviews and group meetings to articulate and address their own questions. The next article that appeared in the newsletter on the topic then documented the information that parents discussed. The newsletter to parents thus went beyond the report of the test scores; it addressed the questions parents raised. Newsletter collaborators worked toward the goal of communicating with parents. To do that, they engaged parents in actual conversations.

The process of newsletter collaboration that resulted from activities led by the Boston University group was formalized through partnerships on behalf of children in several of the New Jersey schools where social decision making programs were implemented. The newsletter process was a vehicle for communication that promoted parental involvement and professional and programmatic growth.

How to Begin

An assessment of current school practices for sending messages to parents is a necessary part of building newsletter processes because of the many different assumptions and practices in place. For example, what is the climate for communicating with school staff? Are there already vehicles for communication that offer information to parents and encourage them to ask questions to learn more? How readable are these vehicles? How are they distributed? Is there a monthly calendar? Do current publications take into account the varied reading levels of parents and the languages they speak? Are they inviting to look at? Or do they appear dense and hard to read, like a telephone book? How are parents notified about new curricula or programs? If parents have questions, how do the staff find time and a comfortable place to answer those questions?

Once the current climate for communication and the current practices for notifying parents of new programs are uncovered, starting points for making a strong outreach to include parents as partners in a social decision making program initiative will become apparent.

The key to success is to find a starting point, get a few adults focused on common goals, and build from there. Those involved start the conversation but then invite a wider and wider circle of others to join, as listeners or readers and as participants. What follows next is an outline of how the process of creating a collaborative newsletter can proceed. It is focused on the medium of a written newsletter because most schools still have many parents who either do not have computers or, more likely, just do not use them regularly enough to serve as a reliable vehicle for broad communication. Further, many parents need something printed, usually posted on their refrigerator, to serve as a reminder of any task or technique requiring follow-through.

The Newsletter Collaboration Process

While this process can be initiated by parents, the assumption here is that school personnel—a guidance counselor, assistant principal, nurse, student assistance coordinator, or the like—will get things started.

1. Identify key contact people—principal, parent leaders, and additional parents or community volunteers.

2. Meet to get acquainted and establish a plan and agreement for the information-sharing process expressed through the newsletter (for example, monthly meetings for discussion of topics that will be informally researched in the particular school and the results written up and attached to a monthly calendar). The idea is that the newsletter is capturing and sharing things that are happening, thus giving life to the process and allowing the newsletter to be an extension of an ongoing interaction, or conversation.

3. Brainstorm a list of possible topics (questions that parents have about the school, children's development, testing and test scores, risk factors like drugs and alcohol, discipline issues, limit setting, how to help children succeed at school, how to help children solve problems and make decisions).

4. Select the topic of greatest interest to the newsletter group. Talk about the topic: What questions do people have about this issue? Who could be interviewed to learn more about the issue?

5. Plan information gathering: Who will talk to whom? What would parents like to know from teachers? What questions will the information gatherers try to answer?

6. Develop a draft piece from the information gathered. Introduce the question and tell parents what was learned about the question. Keep the piece small and interesting.

7. Circulate the draft among key people for final revision. (The principal usually is the final stop for review.) Determine a mechanism to encourage parental response to the article. Make it clear to parents that their response can also include questions. Will there be a box in the school for parents to drop off written comments? Will there be a dedicated phone line set up so parents can call in and leave messages with their comments? Will there be an e-mail address set up for sending responses? (If you use e-mail, you can set up an interactive format such as a bulletin board on which people can respond to one another or just post an e-mail address where messages will be read but not responded to individually.)

8. Rewrite as needed, including any additions or alterations, and hand the newsletter in to the principal for attachment to the monthly school calendar and distribution to parents. This can also include electronic distribution.

9. Set a time for the next meeting so that the process can begin again for the following month with brainstorming of possible topics. It is essential that each edition of the newsletter include a summary of comments and communications received about the prior month's article. Thus, after the first newsletter, all subsequent newsletters will include comments on the preceding topic as well as a new topic. At times, response to a topic will be so great that the new topic will be an extension of the preceding one. Still, there should always be clear sections in the newsletter that indicate comments on the past and current topic.

10. As an extension of Step 9, decide who will focus on comments and who will focus on the new topic. Who will collect and summarize responses, however they are coming in? In the beginning, it is often helpful to solicit comments by asking people if they have read the newsletter feature and inviting them to respond in whatever format the group has chosen. Note that those who respond can do so with their names or have their responses be confidential—this is always a choice that parents and guardians must be offered, and the newsletter coordinator needs to make sure that they clearly understand it.

A Sample Monthly Routine

Newsletter collaborators have found that two meetings per month make a reasonable routine for working together as a cooperative group. Note that the various roles can be handled on a rotating basis, as well as being assigned to those who may have the most skill and interest in doing them for a longer period of time.

First Meeting

- Pick a topic.
- Plan how to gather information.
- Put the plan to work: Who does what, and when?
- Bring and review the responses that have been made to the preceding topic.
- Decide who will summarize these responses and report next time.
- Decide on the date and time of the next meeting.

Second Meeting

- Information gatherers report on possible new topics and the summary of responses to the preceding topic.

- A meeting recorder writes a summary of main points on chart paper that all can see.

- Group puts ideas for the new topic in order—first, second, third, and so on.

- Group decides how much space to allocate for responses to preceding topic and what categories, plus examples of specific response, to present. The group also decides whether some continuation of the prior topic needs to be part of the next new topic or of a subsequent topic to be taken up later in the year.

- Coordinator watches time and keeps discussion moving, reminding group of tasks at hand if people get off track.

- Group decides date and time of next meeting.

- Key people are designated to handle finishing touches.

Examples of the Process in Action

In any school carrying out a collaborative newsletter, the process will be as creative and cooperative as the participants allow. The tasks can involve motivated teachers, support staff, administrators, parents, and community or business partner volunteers. The process can be limited to one person working with the principal and parent leaders, or it could be expanded to include a group if they are willing to work together as a team. These and other possibilities are suggested in the following brief case stories. Note that in each instance, the schools involved were carrying out SDM/SPS in one or more grade levels.

Hazelwood Happenings

As the key leader of a social decision making program at his school, the principal was the starting point for the collaboration process. Hazelwood School already sent home a monthly calendar of school events. Occasionally, the leader of the parent-teacher organization also attached pertinent information to the calendars for parents and guardians. Since this monthly calendar was established as a vehicle for communication, the newsletter team (principal, parent-teacher organization leaders, and university based volunteers) decided to build on this existing vehicle and plan outside contributions that would be written by the volunteers. The collaborators scheduled monthly meetings to discuss topics that could be addressed and to consider plans to cover selected topics in an article (not more than a page and a half) that would be developed, reviewed by the principal and parent leaders, revised, and then attached to the monthly calendar.

Parker Press

In this example, the newsletter process was described to the principal of Parker School, and he enlisted parent volunteers who were eager to take an active part in working on a newsletter team. The principal was enthused about this process and decided to meet with the team and encourage them to follow through and meet monthly on their own to discuss topics, articulate related questions, and plan interviews or other ways to address the questions that were concerning parents. The principal would take the final draft of a newsletter attachment and get it typed and attached to the monthly calendar already sent home to parents. One regular feature of the *Parker Press* was teachers' sharing information about new programs or activities they were doing with students. One month, the parents visited the local library to find out what books were in a parent collection that the children's librarian had established there. One of the newsletter discussions on peer pressure led to so much parent interest that a follow-up evening meeting was opened to all the parents in the school for a discussion of the topic.

An Example from Special Education

Another form of newsletter collaboration process occurred in a setting in which social decision making was implemented initially in special education classes. Student support staff worked closely with a teacher to implement the lessons in a middle school class for students classified educationally as emotionally disturbed, and capitalized on an excitement-sharing approach. The teacher was highly enthused about the work she was doing with the class, but also felt uneasy. With the help of her collaborators, she was able to use FIG TESPN to move forward in the communication process. Specifically, she was able to look for signs of different feelings in herself (eager, a little apprehensive, motivated), identify the issue (she was implementing social decision making with her class of students and wanted to explain it to parents), and guide herself with a goal (to reach out to include the parents and guardians of the students because she felt that her success with the students could be extended if the parents and guardians were to support the students in their attempts at using the social problem-solving approaches at home).

She reviewed several alternatives: telephone conversations with each parent to gain involvement; notes home to parents; a homework assignment for students in which they talked with their parents about the social decision making lessons; and a newsletter collaboration. Then she considered the consequences of each: Telephone calls are a good idea but time-consuming to repeat each time a new skill is introduced; notes are not very engaging; homework is an idea worth developing further; a newsletter could provide an ongoing vehicle for communication and be engaging as well. She selected her best solution: a newsletter collaboration.

Her next step was to develop a plan. The teacher personally invited each of the parents to come to the back-to-school open house so she could share her excitement and some information about the social decision making approach. It was decided that the teacher would take the lead at the meeting, and a collaborating staff member would assist by following up the teacher's enthusiastic introduction with a brief newsletter to parents. This also overcame the obstacle of her having to worry about too many new things at once. The teacher shared her own feelings about the program with the parents and guardians when they came to the school: "I'm excited about this new tool I am using with your students; you are important people in their lives, and I want to tell you about what we are trying to accomplish in the classroom." At the end of her presentation about social decision making, she said, "Look for 'Refrigerator Notes'—brief information that will be sent home. You can put them on the refrigerator to encourage conversations in your house about what the students are learning about social decision making and problem solving in school. We will follow up with you to see if you have any questions."

The idea of Refrigerator Notes started with this one special education class and has since expanded to many school sites. It is useful wherever teachers and other school staff members, in both regular and special education, send home brief informational notes to parents to let them know about the social decision making lessons (or other activities, especially those where a home reinforcement or follow-up component can be useful). Ideally, Refrigerator Notes are either preceded by or followed up with direct contacts such as conversations in person or on the telephone. Exhibit 9.1 shows an example of a Refrigerator Note.

COLLABORATING THROUGH SHARED ACTIVITIES FOCUSED ON SOCIAL-EMOTIONAL ISSUES

Parents and middle school educators share an interest in raising emotionally intelligent adolescents who are on a path toward becoming compassionate, committed, creative, and competent adults. This shared interest will lead to students who are more engaged in their academic work than they otherwise would be. At the same

Exhibit 9.1   *Sample Refrigerator Note*

TO: Parents and Guardians

FROM: Mrs. Hett

SUBJECT: Where in Your Body Does Stress Trigger a Signal?

- Head—Pounding headache
- Chest—Rapid breathing
- Stomach—Panicky churning
- Knees—Weak with fright
- Hands—Clenched fists
- Face—Hot cheeks
- Shoulders—Tight with tension

Students are learning to recognize physical signs of stress so they can stop and think about the trigger—the situation that is causing the stress. The social decision making lessons are focusing on helping students to notice physical signs of stress and to pay attention to the Trigger Situations that are causing the stress.

The first step students took was to look for places in the body where one might experience stress and identify the physical sign. For example, if someone who has to speak in front of the class has shaking knees that make it hard to stand up, that is a physical sign of stress.

Physical signs of stress can be located in different parts of the body. Everyone feels stress in a different way. Sometimes the physical sign of stress is obvious and noticeable, and other times it can barely be detected.

Students will be on the lookout for signs of stress that they can notice in themselves and in other people. They are practicing the strategy of noticing stress signals as a clue to stop and pay attention to a Trigger Situation.

Next week we will be diagramming hassles with Trigger Situation Journals. Stay tuned for more information, and write me a note if you have any questions!

time, it recognizes that—especially in middle school—academic success depends on positive social-emotional growth.

Fortunately, there is no mystery about what children need for social, emotional, and academic growth and the development of sound character. Meeting these needs is the crucial area around which schools and parents can collaborate effectively and genuinely (Elias, Bryan, Weissberg, & Patrikakou, 2003). Further, unlike strong academic support for a middle school curriculum, it is within the reach of the vast majority of parents to provide what is needed in the social-emotional arena. The focus of collaboration can be summarized as A, B, and the 3 C's (Elias et al., 2002):

- *Appreciation:* Give clear praise for trying new things, not doing what peers are doing, taking care of even small household or school responsibilities.
- *Belonging:* Help children participate in local teams and extracurricular activities and classes to build hobbies, but avoid overload.
- *Confidence:* Encourage effort and follow-through; celebrate accomplishments.
- *Competencies:* Build study skills and planning skills for projects and assignments. Help children build skills for meeting household and family responsibilities, working in groups and teams, and exercising leadership.
- *Contributions:* Involve children in family charity decisions; encourage giving a percentage of major gifts and holiday presents to those in greater need; model and encourage community service.

Projects and Workshops for Home-School Collaboration

Middle schools can create arenas for true partnerships by assigning projects that will lead youth to work with parents in ways that will build A, B, and the 3 C's in areas of clear relevance and relative comfort. This is important because many curricular and academic areas are arcane, technical, or otherwise inaccessible to parents and do not form the best basis on which to forge lasting partnerships. For example, the mathematics curriculum has changed meaningfully over the past decades, and many of the rules and techniques parents learned are different from those their children are being taught. Working together on math homework can become a difficult task for many parents and the cause of much family friction.

The projects listed here tend to be cross-disciplinary and of obvious importance in everyday life. Parents can and should be systematically involved in each one, at least as interviewees or resources for planning the student's developing involvement in community projects.

Projects Linking Home and School

- Analyzing TV, print, radio, movie theater, billboard, and Internet advertising. Special attention can be given to advertising that is directed at a child's age group and the age groups of others in the family.

- Teaching about the workings of one's community, including the functions of democracy, government, and the media.

- Exploring the importance of the environment (spaceship Earth; Earth as habitat; ecological environment; global interdependence; ecosystems).

- Examining the reasons for and interrelationships of prejudice, terrorism, freedom, citizenship, and liberty.

- Understanding and accepting similarities and differences in such areas as race, ethnicity, religion, and place of origin in the classroom, school, and community.

For such topics as understanding differences in the community, analyzing media, examining terrorism and liberty, and understanding democracy, parents can be asked to play more substantial roles. Indeed, as parents are given the opportunity to engage in dialogue with school staff about projects such as these, excellent ideas emerge for roles they can play. These roles are usually tailored to local context. In one school district in Illinois with a large senior citizen population, for example, the educators and parents worked together to initiate family history projects that included interviewing grandparents or, if grandparents were not available, local residents from the same generation. The project became a living collaboration to help children understand history and the development of democracy. Moreover, many of these projects provide an impetus to get community entities and groups involved in the educational process, thereby adding them to the partnership. An example of one such project follows.

Laws of Life

Plainfield, New Jersey, is an urban school district with a large majority of students who are African American and eligible for the free or reduced-fee lunch program. It has its share of problems and concerns about academics, but it also has a strong sense of hope and a vibrant spirit. The latter fueled the district's involvement in the Laws of Life Essay Contest, a program of the Templeton Foundation. (See www.lawsoflife.org for additional information.)

Students are asked to discuss their "Laws of Life" with their families and to encourage everyone to think about and share their cherished values and life principles. The program is designed to have students in middle school (as well as high school and Grade 5, the year prior to transition to middle school) think about and write an essay about the laws—really, values and guiding moral principles—by which they live their lives. This choice of modalities is something that can be locally determined; in Plainfield's middle school, sixth-grade students are asked to design slogans that reflect their Laws of Life, and older students are asked to write actual essays.

A system of incentives was created so that acknowledgment could be given to every child who wrote an essay or created a slogan, and some students received a little more recognition for the excellence of their work. Each participating school had a team of staff, parents, and students arrange a celebratory banquet for the participants and the authors of the school's best essays. Then a similar team planned a districtwide banquet attended by representatives of the school board, clergy, community and parents' groups, community sponsors, special guests such as the New Jersey commissioner of education and Plainfield's mayor, and, of course, many students and their families. The entire proceedings were broadcast over local cable television and videotaped for school and public libraries and distribution to interested parents. (Top essays, information about the contest, and other parent partnership information can all be found on the district's Web site, www.plainfieldnjk12.org/SEL.html.)

The Laws of Life program has fostered new dialogues among diverse groups of people. Through the collaboration and support of community businesses and leaders, barriers have been broken down and new relationships have been forged. Most promising of all, students and parents have joined in a dialogue about issues related to the central theme of adolescence: Who am I, who am I going to become, and how do I want to live my life?

Workshops for Parents, Staff, and Students

Another aspect of partnership involves schools' (or parent organizations') taking the lead in organizing workshops at the schools in which staff, parents, and students participate. Here are a number of topics for workshops, including both adults and children that have been launched in the past:

- How to organize the family while meeting academic demands with less stress
- How to choose friends thoughtfully, in light of the influence of group norms, popular trends, media, and the importance of belonging
- Ways to develop leadership and initiative-taking skills
- How to deal with conflict among friends and with authority figures

- Finding alternatives to verbal and nonverbal aggression, especially in times of high stress, frustration, exhaustion

- Recognizing likely conflicts and possible points of agreement with regard to parents' and peers' values (for example, clothing, importance of achievement, use of electronic media, curfews, and bedtimes)

- Learning about stages in the lives of teens, adults, and parents

- Pathways for college and careers

- Alcohol, cigarettes, and drugs in the lives of adults and teens

- Understanding the importance of cultural and familial rituals

- Learning about diversity and various handicapping and challenging conditions

Workshops like these nurture the academic, social, and emotional concerns of teens, as well as the A, B, and 3 C's that serve to nourish their spirit and character. By engaging in shared workshops based on these and similar topics, parents and educators, parents and other parents, educators and students, and children and parents engage in new and valuable conversations that continue once the workshops are over. Best results occur when the process of planning workshops and other projects involves collaboration by teams of educators, parents, and students. And some of the workshops lend themselves well to involvement of community agencies and other community resources, further widening the circle of collaboration. Perhaps most important, workshops and projects serve the purpose of encouraging the involvement of families of culturally and linguistically diverse students, students in special education, and students with other special needs.

CONNECTING THROUGH EMOTIONALLY INTELLIGENT PARENTING CIRCLES

Emotionally Intelligent Parenting (EIP) Circles have both an overt and a covert purpose. Besides their stated purpose of supporting and developing emotional intelligence in the parenting process, they create vehicles for parents to network comfortably in a continuous way. EIP Circles are conversation starters for the groups of parents who gather together to read a book or article or to discuss a specific topic. The example here will focus on a book many parents find relevant, *Raising Emotionally Intelligent Teenagers* (Elias et al., 2002). In an EIP Circle, participants have a place to learn together, plan together, test ideas together, and reflect together. The circles work because they allow parents (as well as guardians and grandparents) to think about materials, ideas, and issues; discuss their meaning and importance with others; and then apply what they have learned to their own households on an ongoing basis.

The circles also bring the expertise of many people into the room. Participants find that situations that cause them difficulty are those that others are able to handle, and often vice versa. New ideas from reading materials and discussions combine with support from others in the group to bring ideas into everyday practice.

How to Start and Conduct Emotionally Intelligent Parenting Circles

Educators may initiate EIP Circles in partnership with PTAs and other home-school associations that are already in place. A first step involves discussing the basic idea and setting up a parents' group to take charge of the logistics of making the circles happen. Educators can have an active or supportive role once the process is begun.

EIP Circles can be organized around a topic of interest or set of particular problems parents want to solve, and so this becomes the focus of the first planning meeting. Beyond the logistics of communicating about the program and generating interest and participation, the group needs to decide on a format. The main decision is how often a group will meet. Most groups plan to meet two, three, or four times, especially at first. Sometimes groups are able to meet for a chapter a week or every two weeks, but that may be something to work up to. Don't push it at first.

EIP Circles are sometimes based on written materials. As a sample, Exhibit 9.2 shows various ways to organize the material from *Raising Emotionally Intelligent Teenagers.*

A key part of EIP Circles is to read the material in a way that is most likely to become useful to parents. Worksheet 9.1 provides an outline of how parents can read whatever material is agreed upon. This outline then serves as a framework from which discussions can get started.

Logistical Matters Matter

Holding EIP Circles either just before, just after, or even as the focus of regular meetings makes it more likely that people will attend. The idea of EIP Circles is introduced, and parents are either invited to attend a next meeting at which a book or topic will be decided on or are informed about which book or topic will be the first. Once the circles get going, it is useful to ask the members about what topics to take up, but at first it's usually best to pick a topic—something that covers a range of issues that concern middle school parents—and start.

As people agree to participate, be sure to collect e-mail addresses and phone numbers. In EIP Circles, parents often begin to communicate

RAISING EMOTIONALLY INTELLIGENT TEENAGERS

For a Two-Week Sequence

- Week 1: Chapters 1 and 2
- Week 2: Chapters 3 and 4

For a Three-Week Sequence

- Week 1: Chapters 1 and 2
- Week 2: Chapters 3 and 4
- Week 3: Chapters 5 and 6

For a Four-Week Sequence

- Week 1: Chapters 1 and 2
- Week 2: Chapters 3 and 4
- Week 3: Chapters 5 and 6
- Week 4: Chapters 7, 8, and 9

Alternatively, in the fourth week the group may decide to focus only on Chapter 9 and then subsequently add the other chapters.

Chapters

1. Parenting by Choice and Not by Chance
2. Love, Laughter, and Limits: How to Build a Respectful Relationship with Your Teenager
3. What Our Teenagers Require for Healthy Identity Development
4. Making Your Household an Expanding Oasis of Peace in a Desert of Pressure and Stress
5. Don't Start with Our Teens, Start with Ourselves: The E.Q. Parenting Survey
6. ESP, FLASH, and Other Emotionally Intelligent Parenting Tools in Your Toolbox
7. Stories of Teens, Peers, and Parents
8. Parent-Teen Vignettes and Conversations: Help Your Early Adolescents Deal with Stress, and Help Your Older Teens Deal with Sex, Love, and Relationships
9. The Clinical Corner: How to Spot and Handle Tough Situations
10. Something for Teenagers to Read: Especially with Their Parents

between meetings, as they start to put ideas into action and find they have questions.

Among the things that help EIP Circles work well is that they are realistic in scheduling and that they start and end on time. Leadership is also important. One person should take charge of a particular book and accept the responsibility of getting discussions rolling. Parents also need to be responsible for making sure people know about the next meeting, arranging the logistics, and ensuring that refreshments are available. The optimal group size is between six and ten. When it gets much larger, people cannot participate as much. When interest grows, as it often does, break up into two or more smaller discussion groups, and then come back toward the end of the meeting to share ideas.

Ultimately, how an EIP Circle works depends on the group members. Will people conduct themselves with emotional intelligence? Will they listen as others speak, wait their turns to talk, and avoid giving put-downs? Will they do the reading that everyone agrees to? Bring any problems into the group rather than complain outside it? The interpersonal process is hard to predict and control. Educators can often play an important role working with parent leaders on these issues, as well as encouraging them to hang in there if the first one or two experiences are a bit rough. Like most things worth doing, EIP Circles take practice—and with practice, the process will go more smoothly.

CONCLUDING THOUGHTS

We can offer no shortcuts to involving parents in the education of middle school students. But one thing is certain: Without determined, persistent efforts to encourage that involvement, it is highly unlikely to take place. The problem-solving spirit of FIG TESPN is what has created these varied approaches to engaging parents, and this same spirit sustains groups and guides them around roadblocks when they occur. Keep the goal in mind, bring in collaborators, and problem solve your way to success!

Three Revelations

What are three things you read about that you find interesting, new, thought provoking?

1. _____

2. _____

3. _____

Four Confirmations

What are four things you read that confirm things you are already doing or confirm your intuitions about how to handle a situation?

1. _____

2. _____

3. _____

4. _____

Three Emotional Reactions

What are three things you read that you find trigger a strong emotional reaction, either positive or negative? Your reactions might include surprise, embarrassment, annoyance, pride, or some other feeling.

1. _____

2. _____

3. _____

Four Things That You Will Apply and Where

What are four things from what you read that you feel you can and will apply to your own life? Where and how will you do this? What obstacles or roadblocks can you anticipate? How might you get past them? What other resources might help you?

1. _____

2. _____

3. _____

4. _____

10 Promoting a Multicultural Perspective in Students

Multicultural education needs to be . . . a curricular approach basically oriented toward preparing young people to live with pride and understanding in our multicultural present and increasingly multicultural future.

—Cortés (1990, p. 3)

When we look into the crystal ball of American education, we clearly see a future that is multiethnic. Teachers and students today are at the first steps along the path toward that future; some communities, of course, are further along the path than others. In this chapter, we look at the challenge Carlos Cortés poses: to begin *now* to explicitly prepare children for a multiethnic future. We take the idea of multicultural education and turn it toward a more learner-centered objective: creating *multicultural persons*—that is, people who have enough ingrained awareness of the possibility that others will feel and want different things and the skills and disposition to interact comfortably and confidently with people from a range of different ethnic groups. Multicultural persons require many talents; we provide specific examples of how social decision making skills are basic components of those talents, with the middle school years being an especially formative period of time in which to address these matters systematically with students.

CLASSROOM SNAPSHOTS: A MULTICULTURAL PERSPECTIVE MATTERS

Here is a look at some middle school situations. As you read each one, take a moment to reflect on whether similar incidents might be occurring in your own school among students of varied cultural backgrounds. Ask yourself how a multicultural perspective might make a difference in how each situation is interpreted.

Thanks to Mary Hancock Severtson, Peter J. Gager, and HyunHee Chung for their contributions to this chapter. The authors also wish to thank Carlos Cortés for his inspirational writings and his comments on this chapter.

- Weiping, a nine-year-old Chinese girl, arrived in this country at the end of the school year. She was fascinated by the playground games of her peers and practiced intently over the summer months in order to play with her classmates in the fall. When the school year began, Weiping could be found watching the others play and waiting, at first expectantly, later discouraged, to be asked to join. The playground monitor asked Sarah, Weiping's classmate, why Weiping was not included in the games. "Well, she doesn't want to play with us," Sarah retorted defensively. "She's such a snob. She never talks to anyone."

- "Well, I'll never try that again," grumbled Donna to another seventh-grade teacher. "I tried starting a group discussion on current events related to the Middle East. You know, to get the kids involved, to get them to know each other a little better. I even made some blatant errors and wild conjectures to get the kids riled up. And over half of the eight new kids from Central America just sat there and watched, and so did some others. I don't think they even heard a word I said."

"Don't give it up, Donna," the other teacher replied. "I'll bet those kids were interested, but they were probably overwhelmed. You made two dramatic changes at once—the format went from lecture to open discussion, and you wanted them to question your authority. That probably came as a shock to some of them."

In these situations, nonverbal and interpersonal cues were misread by people from different cultural backgrounds. Just as people speaking different languages need a translator for effective communication, people from different cultures may need help in interpreting behavioral practices, nonverbal communications, and even the values of unfamiliar cultures. No one can be fluent in the practices of all cultures, but a multicultural person can be alert to potential differences and avoid being restricted by an attitude that demands that everyone conform to a familiar way of living. In the first situation, Sarah thought that Weiping was a snob because she did not talk to the other kids or join in their games. Weiping had been taught that it would be rude to barge in without being invited to play. As multicultural persons, each child would be aware that the other is accustomed to doing things differently and would be accepting of these differences. Thus communication between the two girls would be open rather than blocked by misinterpretations.

In the second story, Donna made a similar mistake—reading nonparticipation as a lack of attention or interest. As the second teacher pointed out, the abrupt changes may have bewildered students brought up in cultures where questioning a teacher can be a sign of disrespect. As a multicultural teacher, Donna might explain how the new classroom format will work and help everyone understand that it may take time for all the students to become comfortable with these changes.

Here are some comments overheard in a middle school lunchroom:

He is so aggressive and tough—a typical Italian in this school.

She is smart and stuck-up, like most Japanese.

They are lazy because they are Mexican.

Due to a lack of multicultural awareness, individuals are too likely to be rigidly classified or categorized on the basis of stereotypes about a group of people. These stereotypes are often invalid, create serious distortions in perceptions of ethnic groups, and prevent people from making accurate judgments about individuals who belong to a group. Imagine how students linked with these stereotypes will be treated by their peers. Multicultural awareness helps students understand the dimensions of experience and culture of different ethnic groups, as well as the diversity of the experiences, cultures, and individuals within each ethnic group. Multicultural perspectives thus help students judge on the basis of evidence and not on the basis of stereotypes, and help them develop comprehensive and realistic understandings of the broad range of ethnic group heritages and experiences.

CREATING MULTICULTURAL PERSONS: A NATIONAL EDUCATION OBJECTIVE

It is natural to wonder about the urgency and necessity of addressing multicultural issues in the schools. The reality is that even the smallest and most isolated school settings are affected by the forces of demography, geography, and technology. Population experts predict large increases among African American, Asian, Latino, and Native American groups, increases far greater than those expected among the white American population. As our population increases, the density in our urban and suburban areas also is expected to increase. Any of us is likely to have neighbors—and our children, classmates—who are of a different ethnic, racial, or cultural background from ourselves.

But technology is the most compelling factor of all. As today's schoolchildren enter the adult world, it will be a world of travel and communication. Business, education, and leisure all will occur in a multicultural, global context. It is the job of all teachers and all schools to prepare students for citizenship in a democratic, pluralistic, multiethnic society. Thus it is important to socialize students to be multicultural persons and to reflect the multicultural nature of the world in which they will find themselves as adults and the kind of information and insights they will need for the many social decisions they will face.

Abilities Possessed by Multicultural Persons

It is improper to equate a call for multicultural awareness with a rejection of the so-called traditional, Eurocentric curricular and cultural emphasis. What is required is a more balanced and open perspective, directed toward the common goal of preparing students to make thoughtful, sensitive, sound choices and decisions needed for participation in democratic institutions and for the promotion of fairness and justice in our society (Banks, 1991–1992).

Cortés (1990) suggests that multicultural persons require these abilities:

- Understand the importance and operation of groups.

- Acquire an understanding of various cultures and worldviews.

- Recognize and understand others' perspectives before forming judgments about them.

- Realize the contributions of individuals and diverse groups— *Pluribus* and *Unum*—to our nation's history and future experiences.

- See how shared goals benefit from the contributions of diverse groups, all with their own histories and futures.

- Participate in the mass media as thoughtful, critical consumers and contributors.

- Develop a deep and lasting civic commitment and a concern for others as well as themselves.

Imagine the quality of classrooms populated by educators and students with these abilities. Similarly, envision the quality of school boards, school management teams, corporate boards, city councils, and legislative bodies once they become populated by multicultural persons. And why not extend the vision further and consider the nature of family dinner table conversations, schoolyard interactions, and deliberations at international forums such as the United Nations, once the population of multicultural persons is increased? Taken together, this portends the creation of dynamic, inquisitive, civilizing environments characterized by understanding rather than prejudice, by a spirit of inclusion rather than separation, and by a concern for participation rather than domination.

Watts (1992) outlines a complex set of social, cognitive, and emotional skills that are essential for being a multicultural person. Two of the most prominent are the ability to "code-switch," which involves being able to translate behaviors into their culturally appropriate meaning, and to "blend cultures," which involves incorporating various aspects of different cultures into one's repertoire. It is not until early adolescence that some awareness and internalization of one's own "centralism" begins to influence the sense of self (Keung-Ho, 1992). Further, it is rare for some to code-switch or blend even two cultures. By adolescence, decisions are made related to ethnic and cultural identity and attitudes. Most often, these decisions are made in a way that allows adaptations to one's perceived social circumstances (Heller, 1987; Ogbu, 1985). However, it is clear that occurrences during the middle school years play a pivotal role in the way in which students' multicultural identities are formed.

Approaches to Multicultural Curricula

Banks and McGee (1989) identify four approaches to multicultural curriculum reform. The *contributions* approach is most typical and involves an emphasis on special individuals; holidays; and days, weeks, and months devoted to celebrating certain ethnic groups. The foremost example is Black History Month in February. This approach is limited because it tends to emphasize the separateness of different cultures and to present only an isolated aspect of those cultures. The *ethnic additive* approach includes books, units, or courses in the basic curriculum without restructuring it in any way. While it can be valuable, its main limit is that these special books and units are not woven into the fabric of the curriculum. There is an exposure to some useful examples, but the mainstream cultural perspective prevails as dominant on the students' minds.

The *transformation* approach requires a higher level of change in the curriculum than do the first two. Here, for any subject area, the emphasis is on how that subject emerged from a diverse mix of influences. U.S. history would reflect how our common history emerged out of an interaction of influences from various racial, ethnic, cultural, religious, and national groups. A similar approach can be used in understanding the evolution of science, literature, music, and art. What Banks and McGee (1989) refer to as the *decision-making and social action approach* takes the transformation approach and places it in the context of having students actively explore the background, current status, key decisions, and necessary actions related to social issues such as reducing prejudice and discrimination in their schools, taking positions on community concerns, elections, advances in science and technology (such as in biotechnology, space exploration, consumer electronics, industrial computerization, or robotics), or even international issues. (This approach is highly consistent with the activities in Chapter 4 and Chapter 7.) Such approaches require the convergence of many academic subject areas and cultural perspectives, as well as the interpersonal skills of multicultural persons to allow an exchange of ideas, group participation, and decision making among students.

In the classroom, social decision making skills form an excellent and general basis for the set of skills needed by multicultural persons, regardless of the approach taken for curricular integration. Possession of self-control, social awareness, group participation skills, and the skills and strategies needed for making thoughtful social decisions (particularly under stress) can be seen by middle school students as valuable in their everyday social and academic tasks. These tasks implicitly will involve multicultural situations. The latter can be built into social decision making instruction as examples and then brought in more systematically as a set of application activities.

SOCIAL DECISION MAKING SKILLS AND MULTICULTURAL PERSONS

Social Decision Making/Social Problem Solving includes a variety of skills needed for everyday functioning as a student, citizen, family member, and multicultural person. What follows are specific examples of how the primary social decision making skills can be applied to situations in ways that promote the growth of multicultural persons. In each instance, the ability to exercise a skill with diverse others is related to how well one knows the culture of those persons and the extent to which that knowledge does not take the form of stereotyping (Hayes & Toarmino, 1995).

Skill 1: Listening

Description

A prompt such as "Listening Position" reminds students that it is time to pay attention, not to talk out of turn, and—when the speaker is finished—to ask questions if they want more information about the who, what, where, why, how, or when of what was said.

Link to Multicultural Awareness

The third quality of a multicultural person Cortés describes is the ability to recognize and understand the perspectives of others. The first step in seeing and understanding multiple perspectives must be to listen for them. Social decision making teaches active listening and questioning for clarification. One result of this skill can be a deeper understanding of others. Cortés envisions a multicultural person who neither blindly accepts all points of view nor relies on prejudiced views to understand others. Social decision making listening skills aim to prevent both of these tendencies. As implied in the discussion of the vignettes presented earlier, students will tend to rely less on prejudiced views when they listen actively and fill in missing information, not with stereotypes, but by seeking more information. When a student learns to listen attentively and to question, the result is not blind acceptance, but as Cortés says, "learning to identify, grapple with, and understand multicultural perspectives."

Another quality of a multicultural person derived from listening skills is the capacity to be *media literate:* to use—and not be used by—the media. Social decision making skills help students learn to transfer listening skills developed in the classroom to the "intentional and unintentional multicultural teachings" of the news and entertainment media (Cortés, 1990). Children who listen actively and critically will learn to fill in the gaps in what is presented in the media—often in oversimplified form—through intelligent questioning and not passively soaking in what is offered.

Skill 2: Sharing Ways to Cope with Hassles

Description

Social decision making students share personal experiences and feelings in all phases of curriculum lessons. In later stages, specific interpersonal problems and related solutions and decisions will be shared. In the earlier readiness phase, students can share ways to remain calm, remember things, or make friends. In so doing, they can both give feedback to and receive feedback from the other problem solvers in the class.

Link to Multicultural Awareness

In a multicultural classroom where students share personal aspects of their lives in a safe, trusting environment, they all tend to come to an understanding of the various cultures and differing worldviews of other groups, including ethnic and minority. Students will also develop the ability to see the perspectives of others as revealed through sharing. Both these qualities are goals for multicultural persons. Through discussions of what is shared, students can make connections between the cultures about which they are learning and actions as expressions of those cultures. An example might be a student from an ethnic group who shares that group's characteristic way of keeping calm. Other students, and perhaps the teacher, might find that this behavior had previously been misunderstood as misbehaving or acting out.

As peer feedback can be constructively critical, social decision making does not teach what Cortés and others refer to as the "blind acceptance" of all points of view (Pedersen, 1991). Rather, students are encouraged to understand multiple perspectives, even if this understanding ultimately leads to an informed disagreement.

Skill 3: Group Building

Description

Group cohesiveness and trust is presented to students through a practical rationale: "In class," a teacher might say, "we get to know our classmates in a limited way [in math or reading]. There are many other things that we can learn about our classmates that are interesting to know. We can better act as a team when our classmates see us as more than just people who can add and subtract." Related activities might include learning and practicing ways of meeting new people and getting to know them better. This may involve occasionally or regularly beginning classes with a sharing circle.

Link to Multicultural Awareness

Group building in social decision making relates directly to the first set of abilities Cortés (1990) proposes for multicultural persons—an understanding of "groupness." Social decision making activities enhance children's understanding of the significance of groups and highlight for them what group membership feels like on a personal level (as a member of a class, sharing circle, or smaller activity group). The idea in social decision making is to augment group cohesiveness, not by making students feel as if they are all the same, but by emphasizing both similarities and differences among classmates. In meeting new people and learning what may be different about them, ethnically or otherwise, the students become closer as a group and more aware of the diversity within it.

A social decision making group can become unified, as in the use of the term *Unum* that Cortés cites, with a multiethnic global identity, without displacing the diversity, or *Pluribus,* within the group. Students come to learn interesting things about other students. They also realize all students—including themselves—are members of many groups (classroom, sharing circle, or ethnic group, to mention only a few), often making their definitions of groupness less rigid. Group generalizations will then be less likely to harden into the inflexible distortions of group stereotyping.

Skill 4: Behavioral Rehearsal, Guided Practice, and Perspective Taking

Description

This skill involves a set of behaviors that provide an opportunity to act out interpersonal situations where problem solving might be used. It includes taking the perspectives of others, receiving feedback from others on performances, and heightening social awareness by highlighting awareness of personal feelings and those of others in problematic situations.

Link to Multicultural Awareness

Perspective-taking skills can be effective means of developing the qualities of a multicultural person. The more a child engages in behavioral rehearsal, taking the perspectives of as wide a variety of classmates as possible, the more that child will begin to understand that multiple perspectives exist. And this guided practice makes it necessary to deal with how differing worldviews are expressed in different behaviors. Feedback from classmates makes it more likely that views and actions acted out will be authentic rather than stereotypical.

A student who is successful in this endeavor is moving toward two of the qualities Cortés identifies for multicultural persons: the ability to understand the cultures of others, and the ability to understand their perspectives. Another advantage of perspective taking is that multicultural issues can be dealt with explicitly and acted out in a behavioral rehearsal (such as a racial misunderstanding at recess).

Skill 5: Caring About Classmates

Description

In the social decision making classroom, "Caring" is a cue to look at one's feelings for others and to recognize how others may be showing this concern for you in particular circumstances. Caring skills are strengthened through the sharing of ideas, such as how caring can be shown, and through the reinforcement of caring interactions. Closely related to caring behavior is learning how to give and receive praise and how to give and ask for help in the classroom, as well as outside. Cues and prompts are used in these latter areas to discourage the insulting of others and to encourage students to be helpful to others and to allow others to be helpful to them.

Link to Multicultural Awareness

According to Cortés, a multicultural person must understand the potential contribution that *Pluribus* can make to our society. In a social decision making classroom in which caring and helping behaviors catch on with all students, participants will recognize that positive contributions to the classroom (and eventually to society) can be made by children from diverse ethnic groups. A more direct means of achieving this result would be to set up an activity in which help that only certain minority students can offer is crucial to success. For example, in a classroom with both Spanish- and English-speaking students, classmates could compete in smaller mixed groups in which both English and Spanish are required to complete a task such as a bilingual crossword puzzle.

In a classroom where students help, praise, and show caring for each other, a deeper sense of civic commitment is being developed. Multicultural persons must have a concern for others as well as for themselves (a skill and a value that will come up again later in this chapter in our discussion of the Native American culture in the context of at-risk youth and of "Circles of Courage").

In addition to the abilities just examined, the social decision making strategy consists of an integration of an eight-step thinking process (FIG TESPN). Each skill area within that process has relevance to creating multicultural persons, as does the operation of all the skills in concert.

Skill 6: Identifying Personal Feelings and the Feelings of Others

Description

This skill incorporates the ability to recognize verbal and nonverbal cues that show how people are feeling. It includes the awareness that no matter how adept one becomes at interpreting personal reactions and how considerate one wishes to be of the reactions of others, no one can be certain of knowing how someone else must feel in a particular situation.

Link to Multicultural Awareness

A multicultural person is sensitive to others' feelings and aware that people react differently to the same circumstances (for a variety of reasons, including cultural upbringing) and may want to be treated in ways that would be unwelcome to the individual doing the observation. The multicultural person might ask, "How would I feel if I were in their shoes?" as well as "Why might they feel differently from what I expected?"

A multicultural person may also be aware of personal feelings when interacting with people from other cultural backgrounds. This knowledge could be used to modify or alter behavior and subsequent emotional reactions. For example, if I am consistently becoming frustrated when trying to lead Native American children in a game, I may want to change my goal to be a helpful team member instead of leader—which would make the game a happier, more satisfying experience both for me and for the children.

Skill 7: Identifying Problems in Words

Description

> This skill concerns the ability to develop objective problem statements.

Link to Multicultural Awareness

> Here, the multicultural person recognizes that other children may see problems somewhat differently. The multicultural person will be open to divergent perspectives on the problem definition and will work to incorporate all perspectives into a unified statement. Likewise, the multicultural person will be aware of and acknowledge conflicts arising directly from a clash of cultural values, beliefs, or practices.

Skill 8: Deciding on Goals

Description

> Developing and choosing goals requires the ability to identify and envision the resolution to the problem at hand: What do we want to have happen?

Link to Multicultural Awareness

> Incorporating multicultural perspectives into the problem definition means that the eventual outcome should reflect a comprehensive, equitable view. A multicultural person's goals are designed to take into account the needs and desires of all involved, since multicultural persons are committed to making the best of circumstances for others as well as for themselves.

> In the case of a problem representing disagreement between two or more sets of cultural values, the multicultural person's goal should not be to smooth over the groups' differences superficially. Instead, the challenge for a multicultural person is to respectfully weigh the merits and faults of each cultural perspective and seek enrichment by making use of the positive contributions from every resource.

Skill 9: Thinking of Many Solutions to the Problem

Description

> Students are encouraged to consider a variety of alternative ways to meet their goal.

Link to Multicultural Awareness

Simply by generating different solutions, by stretching their imaginations, students are exercising the kind of flexible thought processes necessary for a multicultural person. During a brainstorming session, students from all backgrounds are asked to share their unique ideas and traditions as contributions to the formulation of the solution. The multicultural person's open-mindedness and celebration of diversity are called upon clearly in this stage of social decision making.

Skill 10: Envisioning Outcomes

Description

Students are asked to picture and anticipate the consequences, both positive and negative, of implementing each solution.

Link to Multicultural Awareness

This skill requires a fundamental ability of the multicultural person—perspective taking: "What will the teacher say if we do . . . ?" "How will Feng, Sara, and Samara feel if I say . . . ?"

Skill 11: Selecting the Best Solution

Description

Students are prompted to make a decision among the available solutions based on their goals and probable consequences and outcomes.

Link to Multicultural Awareness

The best solution from a multicultural person's perspective is the one that comes closest to meeting personal goals without harming or disregarding any of the individuals or groups that may be affected. The goal, as you may recall, has already incorporated a fair consideration of the desires and needs of all parties.

Skill 12: Planning the Procedure, Anticipating Pitfalls, and Practicing

Description

For this stage of social decision making, students must be taught to consider the details necessary for implementing the chosen solution and to anticipate and plan for potential obstacles.

Link to Multicultural Awareness

While these specific skills are not inherently those of a multicultural person, the attention to detail and willingness to reconsider and rework a solution are certainly attributes that would be valued by a multicultural person. Moreover, diverse inputs into plans often increase their effectiveness, particularly if the individuals or settings involved reflect cultural variety.

Skill 13: Noticing What Happens and Remembering It for Next Time

Description

This stage of social decision making promotes taking action, following through on the decisions made, and then reflecting on how the action worked, plunging in again, if necessary, and remembering past learning for future use.

Link to Multicultural Awareness

The multicultural person is not merely sensitive to the differences between cultural groups, but is committed to protecting the freedom that allows these differences to flourish. The assertive implementation of a plan provides students with successful experiences that bolster self-esteem and encourage future participation, not apathy. Finally, the ability to thoughtfully review a course of action and its outcome and make the necessary adjustments to reach a goal reflects the thoroughness, flexibility, and sense of history valued by a multicultural person.

CAVEATS: REFINEMENTS AND LIMITATIONS

In promoting the successful implementation of the various social decision making skills needed by multicultural persons, teachers can benefit from understanding the developmental course of multicultural awareness in their students, as well as in themselves. Teachers gain perspective by considering some factors that may influence students outside the classroom: school environment, family, and community. Finally, it is valuable for teachers to be sensitive to the risk factors related to cultural difference for some students. Here are some refinements and limitations of social decision making that need to be taken into consideration to promote the growth of multicultural persons.

Stages of Multicultural Awareness

A model proposed by Carney and Kahn (1984) provides a helpful framework for understanding different types or degrees of multicultural awareness in a multicultural person. According to the authors' original model, students are believed to pass through five stages of development in multicultural awareness as they acquire multicultural competencies (knowledge, skills, and attitudes).

Although this stage model has not been verified empirically, the descriptions of each stage can help teachers monitor the interaction between each student and the learning environment to ensure that they are appropriately matched to the student's level of multicultural competence. It is crucial that teachers seek out a variety of training resources and become aware of their own ethnic beliefs, attitudes, and values. The resources at www.tolerance.org are excellent for this purpose and are constantly being refined and updated. That Web site is also a valuable source of materials that address students' needs and perspectives as they move through the stages outlined here.

Stage 1

Students at this stage possess little knowledge of other cultural groups. Due to their limited experiences with persons from other cultural groups, students' views of other cultural groups tend to be based on social stereotypes and ethnocentric attitudes rather than on an understanding of particular cultural groups. Here it is appropriate for teachers to encourage the students' attitudinal and behavioral self-awareness through structured values clarification activities.

Stage 2

Students begin to recognize their own ethnocentric beliefs, behaviors, and attitudes. However, to the extent that information about other cultural groups is new to them, they may lack an organized view of cultural differences and deal with such information in a detached manner. Teachers need to continue to provide information about other cultural groups and examine the sources and accuracy of students' ethnocentric views and behaviors by using engaging, interactive procedures to foster exchange of perspectives.

Stage 3

Students who enter this stage may experience feelings of guilt and responsibility. They typically deal with this internal conflict by adopting an attitude of color-blindness that is expressed most often in one of two forms: denial or immersion. However, despite attempts to ignore differences or to take on a new cultural identity, students at this stage soon find that they cannot ignore or bridge the experiential differences that separate cultural groups. Teachers need to encourage

students at this stage to explore the impact of their color-blind attitudes and provide a structured environment in which such exploration
can occur safely.

Stage 4

Students recognize the importance of validating the worldview of
other groups and begin to selectively blend new multicultural knowledge, attitudes, and skills with desirable features of their own reference groups. Teachers at this stage encourage students to clarify and
select their personal directions, but to do so on the basis of accurate
information.

Stage 5

Students finally become self-directed in expanding their multicultural pluralism in society at large. Teachers need to assist in identifying and supplying resources needed for students to accomplish
personal directions.

Pitfalls

Social decision making may fall short in some areas for certain minority
students, regardless of their stage of multicultural development.
Teachers might be more sensitive to these potential shortcomings in
social decision making if they think of *themselves* as multicultural
persons, alert to situations or aspects of the curriculum in which
ethnic students might have special needs. For example, in certain
Native American and Asian American groups, to receive public recognition and to stand out from the group is a potential embarrassment
that may lead to withdrawal from behaviors that would have won
praise (Keung-Ho, 1992). In the giving and receiving praise section of
social decision making curricula, as well as others, a teacher's attitudes
and sensitivity to different perspectives and worldviews will influence
outcomes. Clearly, there is an attitudinal and value base that underlies both becoming and socializing a multicultural person. Where
teachers' values are discrepant, unclear, or ambivalent when compared
to those of a multicultural person, added difficulty in creating multicultural persons can be expected.

Even in classrooms where social decision making is successfully implemented, teachers must be aware that countless outside factors influence
the outcome of attempts to promote multicultural awareness. Cortés
(1979) has labeled these factors as the "societal curriculum." Community, school, family, peer, and media influences are largely beyond the
control of a single teacher. Thus it has been shown that social decision

making is most effective when the entire school, from the principal to the cafeteria aides, becomes involved and consistently uses its prompts (Elias & Tobias, 1996). But, as anyone who has worked in a school system knows, having colleagues agree on a plan of action is no guarantee that they will follow through enthusiastically, if at all, with that plan. There will also be a diversity of views on multicultural education and whether or not it is appropriate to be taught in school.

A significant portion of a child's attitudes toward other groups of people is learned through and shared by family members, peers, and other community members. For children to become multicultural persons, some of their beliefs may have to evolve away from or contradict those learned and reinforced from an early age outside school. This is a difficult and complex task for any child. Even families who share the goals and attitudes of a multicultural society might not support such an undertaking in schools, especially in the context of academic pressures related to No Child Left Behind. However, it is clear that academic success does not ensure students a path to life success; they also need the social decision making and social problem solving skills to get along in the diverse and challenging environments they are likely to encounter.

AT-RISK YOUTH AND MULTICULTURAL AWARENESS

It is important to remember that, for children in schools, traditionally defined cultural differences do not fully account for differences among students. Countless other factors—cognitive, affective, and physical level of development and socioeconomic status, to name just a few—contribute to the development of values and behaviors. One of the most important among these other factors to which a teacher should be alert relates to at-risk youth. Children who are at risk because of emotional or learning disabilities form a subculture that is at risk of being excluded by so-called normal students because of its "differentness." For many students, this question forms another source of social segregation, along with more traditionally defined cultural differences. Therefore, social decision making teachers must work toward developing multicultural awareness in students in a way that is sensitive to all of the risk factors that are operating. For many of these students, being different and often excluded because of it is a curse. Too often, being at educational risk is intertwined with cultural difference and exacerbates the exclusion of these students.

Thus there is clear convergence of concerns related to at-risk youth and the creation of multicultural persons. The central problems of at-risk students are their alienation and detachment from school, seeing what is taught in school as being of too little relevance, and their low motivation and self-esteem. The central skills recommended to assist at-risk children are providing a greater sense of control, critical thinking, goal setting, collaborative problem solving, and social participation. This set of skills is well matched to skills associated with multicultural persons (Mirman, Swartz, & Barell, 1988). Indeed, there are those who feel that the best educational techniques for all students, regardless of level of risk and ability and cultural background, are those recommended for at-risk students (Banks, Cortés, Gay, Garcia, & Ochos, 1976; Presseisen, 1988). Thus, rather than creating yet another set of add-on programs and concerns in the schools, teachers should consider using social decision making and social problem solving to focus on the development of multicultural persons. Doing so can actually enhance and be synergistic with goals related to reducing student risk of failure, dropping out, and self-destructive or antisocial behaviors, and to our national educational agenda of preparing students for excellence in the national and international arena.

The concept of diversity can be extended to understanding the diverse modalities by which information can be presented to children and with which children can express their learning to those around them. Too often, education focuses on lecture and reading as the presentational modalities, and written products as the mode in which children express their learning. By contrast, Native American groups value the storytelling process as a vehicle for both learning and expressing what has been learned. Many of the Asian cultures use drawings as vehicles for both teaching and learning: Indeed, character alphabets such as that of China are themselves drawings. Transition to sound symbols like those of the Roman alphabet can seem limiting to students used to more pictorially based learning processes. Although the learning styles literature and the adequacy of its data base have been the target of much criticism (Curry, 1990), one can still make use of some of the ideas for the purposes of instructional diversity without accepting the linkages of learning style with neurophysiology that have been proposed. One of the best sources of instructional diversity is the 4MAT approach (McCarthy, 1990). It suggests ways to engage learners through various combinations of instructional emphasis on watching, doing, sensing, and reflecting, both on concrete and on abstract levels. Further, it allows students' activities and projects to be derived through combinations of conveying factual information and detail, applying knowledge personally, getting others interested in newly learned subject matter, and practicing new learning to achieve mastery (Blair & Judah, 1990). With 4MAT and related tools at your disposal, it is easier to find ways of teaching that incorporate the diversity of learners in your classroom, including diversity related to culture. Also of obvious relevance is the work of Tomlinson (1999) on differentiated instruction.

PROMOTING A MULTICULTURAL CIRCLE OF COURAGE

Socializing children to become multicultural persons requires both a valuing of a multicultural perspective and the acquisition of a set of skills needed to enact that perspective. The middle school is a critical period for beginning to instill both of these aspects of multicultural awareness. This age marks the convergence of cognitive developmental levels that permit the potential integration and beginning internalization of the values and skills necessary for being a multicultural person. With regard to valuing a multicultural perspective, it is worth noting that traditional Native American approaches espouse an inclusive philosophy that can provide a unifying framework for middle school educators.

Vehicles such as the "Circle of Courage" (Brendtro, Brokenleg, & Van Bockern, 2000) have been used by native North American peoples to emphasize the basic unity of nature, which includes the physical, spiritual, and interpersonal worlds. Implicit in this view is the unity of all persons. The worth of a child is seen as having four basic parts: (a) significance, which is defined in terms of a universal need for, or spirit of, belonging; (b) competence, which is seen in a spirit of mastery of one's environment; (c) power, seen in the spirit of independence and the ability to control one's own behavior and gain the respect of others; and (d) virtue, which is expressed in the spirit of generosity.

Virtue is referred to by Brendtro et al. (2000) as a preeminent, or core, value. Sharing and communal responsibility are seen as vehicles for attaining and expressing the spirits of belonging and competence and as reasons for harnessing the spirits of mastery and independence. An extraordinary anecdote related by Deloria (1943) provides a concrete example of what the Circle of Courage really means. She tells of an incident in which a youth who was known to have committed a murder was brought to the tribal elders for his sentence. The victim's family described the deed and asked for punishment to fit the crime. The elders empathized, but then explained that their philosophy provided for a better way, if the family had the courage to carry it out.

The relatives were asked to bring a valued possession to give to the murderer, to show that the family wanted the murderer to take the place of the loved one who was killed. When this was presented to the murderer at his sentencing, he fell into a stunned, tearful, emotional shock. He became a devoted member of the family. Through appeal to the spirit of belonging and the spirit of generosity, much was accomplished. The murderer served as a living example of the better way, for he had given up some of the independence of his life in the service of other values. Moreover, the paradox of his living his life to make up for the life of the person he killed served as a potent and visible deterrent to other criminals. Much less would have been accomplished by a punishment that removed him from the group and exemplified a violation of the culture's values.

The Circle of Courage shows how multicultural persons are the product of a coming together of both skills and philosophy. The middle school years are a critical time to begin to help students see this connection between behavior and values, whether in classrooms, schools, or communities. To help them become multicultural persons, we must encourage their social decision making skills, their cultural understanding, and their ability to see how these skills and insights are intertwined in their everyday lives and their future adult roles. With this background, they will be more likely to have the courage to carry their perspectives to others who may not be thinking similarly, and to inspire by example.

11 Tools for Monitoring and Evaluating Middle School Programs

Accountability around efforts to promote students' social-emotional growth is no less important, and no less necessary, than accountability around literacy and other traditional content areas. In fact, it can and should be thought of as an ethical responsibility on the part of those in schools entrusted with providing for the growth of students as responsible citizens. The good news is that assessment tools exist to both monitor and evaluate middle school SDM/SPS programs.

The terms *monitoring* and *evaluation* indicate two related but different aspects of accountability that require attention. Monitoring refers to keeping track of the extent to which the program was delivered and received, including how well it was received. Evaluation refers to gains in skills and behavior that result from the program. If a program is not being delivered, or is being delivered but not received well, it is unlikely to have any positive effects—making evaluation a lost cause. That is, if the program itself is too weak to work, efforts to measure its outcomes are misplaced. What's needed is monitoring and corrective action to make sure that the program is delivered with integrity and that both staff and students find it valuable; only then will its outcomes be worth considering.

TOOLS FOR MONITORING SETS OF ACTIVITIES OR PROGRAMS

How Well Is the Program Being Implemented?

Curriculum Feedback from Implementers

The Curriculum Feedback worksheets provide leaders and observers of social decision making activities a place to record immediate feedback about the overall quality of particular activities. Two formats are

Thanks to Maureen Reilly Papke, Judy Lerner, and Lois Brown for their contributions to this chapter.

provided, one more open-ended (Worksheet 11.1), the other including several qualitative rating scales (Worksheet 11.2). Use of these worksheets provides information that allows for ongoing refinement and modification of individual activities or modules being used. (For ease of reading, all the worksheets in this chapter have been collected at the end.)

The worksheets provide documentation of student responsiveness to each activity. They also provide for the recording of the activity's strengths and weaknesses, as well as suggested changes and ideas for activity review. The worksheets are completed by the teacher or group leader, or an aide, an observer, a consultant, or a teaching partner at the end of each session. There is no formal way to evaluate the curriculum feedback worksheets. Typically, the sheets are inserted into the curriculum with each activity so that the recommended changes can be recalled when anyone reviews and carries out the activity in the future or considers modifying it during a program revision period. However, in some schools, principals collect these worksheets from the group leader or teacher, at least, and use them as an indicator of what was provided to students over a particular period of time.

Content Checks

Are children understanding what has just been presented to them? This is not quite the same as asking if they have learned a particular skill. The key question is, by the end of the activity, or at the beginning of the next one, do they still have the basic notions just presented to them? If not, skill gains are unlikely, and moving ahead as if material has been mastered is unwise. The enclosed "SDM/SPS Content Check" (Worksheet 11.3) addresses the key SDM/SPS skills of Keep Calm, BEST, trigger situations, and an understanding of put-downs. In addition, the worksheet has a practice section that helps group leaders see the extent to which students are using skills in different contexts, especially when asked to do so.

Skill Practice Tracker

SDM/SPS activities involve teaching students skills. But even though students may understand skills, they're apt to find it another matter to enact the skills. Skills are best developed through use and practice. "SDM/SPS Skills Practice" (Worksheet 11.4) is completed by students to provide a concrete indication of when they have tried to put into action the skills they have been taught. Group leaders can use the worksheet to focus students' attention on a particular skill, on the cumulative use of skills, or both.

Student and Staff Satisfaction

Student and Teacher Opinion of Social Decision Making Activities

SDM/SPS (and related) activities have two important audiences: the students who receive them and the teachers and other professionals who carry them out. Capturing their views about social decision making activities contributes to the long-term success and acceptance of social decision making programs.

Two measures provide feedback about the consumers' satisfaction with the SDM/SPS program and its implementation. Implementers and those in leadership roles can use this feedback to modify the existing program structure, and the measures also provide leaders with an understanding of the opinions of those engaged in the activities. Over the long term, the measures provide a basis for ongoing classroom, school, and district monitoring, feedback, and modification of the program. The resulting changes often help support and maintain ownership of the skills as well as responsiveness to changing learning environments, shifts in resources, and new mandates.

The sample measures presented here reflect one particular program. Questions can be modified to fit the particular goals and objectives of specific sets of activities or programs. Also, names can be omitted from the forms in the event that total anonymity is desired. Included are two versions of a student opinion survey (Worksheets 11.5 and 11.6) and one version of a teacher/leader opinion survey (Worksheet 11.7). For special education students, veteran educators Lois Brown and Judy Lerner of Highland Park, New Jersey, suggested the adaptation of asking individual students or a group of students these questions in either written or interview format:

1. What are three things that you learned from this set of activities (or from this program)?

2. What skill is the most important to you and why?

3. Where have you used the skills (for example, at home, at school, or on the playground)?

4. Describe one or more times when you used a skill and an occasion when you will try to use the skills in the future.

Students and teachers complete the measures at the end of naturally occurring instructional units, most often at the end of a group or at the end of each school year. The information can be easily summarized for sharing with various school personnel and has been found to be an extremely valuable source of monitoring and feedback. The anecdotal accounts of the students are often especially revealing of a wide range of applications of the skills being learned in the activities.

TOOLS FOR EVALUATING SETS OF ACTIVITIES OR PROGRAMS

Skill Gains

Sample Measures for Assessing Social Decision Making Programs in the Middle School

Unfortunately, the assessment of social decision making and problem solving skills in middle school students has not kept pace with the development of programs. The measures (whether existing or new) are not always well matched to a program's specific goals, content, or outcomes. Consequently, there is considerable emphasis on criterion-referenced or curriculum-linked assessments, as well as on performance indicators such as school behavior and portfolios of work samples. (See Marzano, Pickering, & McTighe, 1993, for guidance on how to create rubrics for performance indicators, as well as Jennings, 1997, and Kimeldorf, 1994, for ideas about portfolios with special and regular education students.)

Getting Along with Others

The evaluation measure titled "Getting Along with Others" (GAWO) (see "Student Evaluation Form for Use in Assessing SDM/SPS Readiness Skills," Worksheet 11.8) assesses a student's acquisition of self-control, group participation, and social awareness skills, especially those taught in the readiness phase of curricula based on the SDM/SPS model. It is a criterion-referenced test. This means those who are implementing SDM/SPS activities at a given grade level or for a given group (such as regular or special education) create the responses they would like to see students have at the end of the instructional period. Assessment is gauged according to the percentage of potentially acquired skills that are actually shown or according to a profile of skill acquisition across different sections of the measure. (Because it lends itself so well to descriptive analysis, the GAWO is particularly useful in middle school special education classes.) The information gathered from the GAWO can be used as baseline data for later assessments, or it can be used as a pretest and posttest to measure skill acquisition over the course of the program and the school year. It can also provide feedback to support teachers' efforts to adapt the program to become most beneficial to their classes.

The questionnaire is completed by the students involved in the program; the time needed for administration is approximately thirty minutes. The measure should be completed at the beginning or at the end of the school year (or both) and can be group-administered in a regular classroom setting. Individualized administration, or as close to it as possible, is recommended for special education students.

Group Social Problem Solving Assessment

The "Group Social Problem Solving Assessment" (GSPSA) (see "Student Evaluation Form for Use in Assessing SDM/SPS Skills," Worksheet 11.9) screens a student's knowledge of the eight social decision making steps taught in the instructional phase of the SDM/SPS curriculum. As with Getting Along with Others, which measures readiness skills, the GSPSA information can be used as baseline data for later assessments or as a pretest and posttest to measure skill acquisition over the course of the school year. Again, it can also provide feedback that allows the teacher to adapt the instructional phase lessons to make them more beneficial to the class.

The measure is completed by the students and should require less than thirty minutes. It should be administered at the beginning or at the end of the school year (or both) and can also be done in a regular classroom setting. This measure can identify deficits in any of the three main social decision making areas: interpersonal sensitivity, problem analysis and action, and specificity of planning. Children's scores are compiled to indicate "at-risk," "average," or "highly skilled" in those three main social decision making areas. At the middle school level, the GSPSA is especially valuable as a screening tool for students with highly deficient skills; that is, a ceiling effect exists and "at-risk" scores tend to be strongly indicative of maladaptive behaviors (Elias et al., 1986). The scoring manual is presented following Worksheet 11.9.

Profile of Social Decision Making Strengths

The evaluation tool titled "Profile of Social Decision Making Strengths" (PSDM) (see "Adult Assessment of Student SDM/SPS Skills," Worksheet 11.10) helps assess a student's acquisition of the self-control, group participation, social awareness, and social decision making and social problem solving skills as taught in the readiness and instructional phases of the elementary and middle school SDM/SPS and related curricula. The information gathered from this rating scale can be used as baseline data, or it can be used by a teacher to gain an initial understanding of a student's or class's strengths and weaknesses in a variety of SDM/SPS skill areas. This measure can also contribute to a teacher's or group leader's planning and implementation of activities for skill building, and it provides immediate feedback regarding SDM/SPS skill acquisition.

The format is a rating scale completed by teachers and various support staff who interact with activity or program recipients on a regular basis. The questionnaire can be filled out for each student at the beginning of intervention and periodically during the course of the activities to provide ongoing feedback. The measure can also be completed at the end of individual units or used as a pretest and posttest. The measure requires approximately ten minutes per student to complete.

Observations of each student are recorded by using a simple mastery rating, adjusted to appropriate age, grade, and ability expectations. These combined observations provide an overall profile of students' or classes' decision-making and problem-solving strengths.

Variations in the use of the PSDM have included administering it to only a sample of participating students or having it completed on intact groups, such as gym classes, where only some students are receiving intervention activities and the teachers doing the ratings do not know who the SDM/SPS participants are. Also, the form can be completed based on overall class or group performance, rather than completing it for individual students and then making inferences about the group by aggregating the individuals' scores. Finally, skills may be added, deleted, or redefined, as appropriate to the content of a particular program or set of activities.

Behavioral Gains

Assessing Behavior or Adjustment Change

Administrators and district evaluators alike express an interest in assessing behavior or adjustment change. Information such as this can be gleaned from the report cards completed by teachers on a quarterly basis. Report cards provide an objective measure of a child's academic and behavioral progress while participating in the program. Other school behavior indicators include mid–marking period warning notices and detention records. These items can be used in assessing individual students' change over time or as part of a statistical analysis of detention patterns of students receiving the program compared to students not receiving it. If a more standardized behavior index is desired, the Teacher-Child Rating Scale (Hightower et al., 1986), which is completed individually for each student, can be valuable. It consists of twenty-eight items in two broad categories: social competence behaviors and problem behaviors. The items are clear, easy to rate, and have two advantages: They include norms for boys and girls and urban and nonurban samples, and they come with a companion rating scale that can be completed by parents or other home caretakers. Additional well-validated rating scales such as the Social Skills Rating System, are also constantly under development and can be used to the extent to which they seem well matched to the goals of your activities or program.

BRINGING MONITORING AND EVALUATION ACTIVITIES TOGETHER: END-OF-YEAR PLANNING

SDM/SPS Trainers' Program Planning Guide

A worksheet for planning activities involving social decision making is a useful tool for administrators and program planners at the beginning of program implementation and at the end of each consecutive year of implementation as plans are being formulated for the following school year. Worksheet 11.11 outlines the various aspects that must be considered when planning a new program or the expansion of an existing program during the upcoming school year. The form is completed by one or more persons involved in leadership aspects of program implementation, such as principals, guidance counselors, student assistance personnel, and child study team members. The key leadership person of the SDM/SPS program should complete and compile the forms prior to final planning meetings.

SDM/SPS Evaluation Planner

Monitoring and evaluation should be thought of as part of a program and built in from the beginning. To aid in making these decisions and in formulating an evaluation plan, we have created the "SDM/SPS Evaluation Planner" (Worksheet 11.12). This worksheet includes the pertinent questions that should be answered prior to beginning any evaluation study, however minimal it may be.

As noted on the worksheet, begin with a basic description of the activities or module to be studied. The brief narrative should include information concerning what and how many schools, teachers, and students are involved in carrying it out. An outline of the program goals, as well as whatever will occur as part of the program, should also be included. Define who will do the actual work with students and describe the time line of the program that year. Any other pertinent details may be added as well.

The first decision that must be made concerns the nature of the monitoring and evaluation activities that will take place. Administering pretests and posttests is common; however, one must consider the goal of the evaluation. For example, during the first year of a program, when teachers are newly trained and unfamiliar with the curriculum, students' skill gains may not appear significant and administrators may want to consider measuring consumer satisfaction (teacher and student) and gathering baseline data for use the following year. The goal of the first year of program implementation is usually to have teachers and group leaders reach a degree of ease and comfort in leading the activities and decide on any modifications to fit differences in populations or teaching styles. This goal should be considered when evaluating any new program.

Another decision must be made as to what research questions the evaluation will address, if any. In formulating the research questions, it is important to take the goals of various members of the implementing team into consideration. For example, those financing the program may be interested in overall skill gains or behavior changes or both. Building administrators may be interested in evaluating the impact of activities on their staff and on school climate. Teachers might be interested in how students reacted to a module and may want to use feedback to modify activities. A comprehensive evaluation will take these various components into consideration when determining which measures to use to evaluate the program. The evaluation design could contain several measures that would address these various questions. Obviously, answering all possible relevant questions is likely to require assessment tools beyond those included here. Useful sources of information for finding specific tools for monitoring and evaluating social-emotional learning activities, including SDM/SPS, are the Web sites of the Character Education Partnership (www.character.org) and the Collaborative for Academic, Social, and Emotional Learning (www.CASEL.org).

Many of the questions contained in the Evaluation Planner concern details of evaluation implementation. These questions were included to encourage those planning SDM/SPS activities to identify and address as many logistical problems as possible before implementing the monitoring and evaluation plan. The same questions are repeated, differentiating pretesting and posttesting, thereby enabling an evaluator to thoroughly plan both components and determine the cost of the overall evaluation.

The last four questions on the worksheet are directed to the final report. Information from any kind of evaluation study usually has several audiences or constituencies besides the classroom teacher. The components of the report may be determined by requirements of funding sources or district administrators. A thorough final report should begin with a brief general explanation of social decision making and social problem solving and the goals of the program as it is being applied in the particular circumstances. A summary of the intervention, training, and, if relevant, consultation, coaching, or other support provided to teachers or other group leaders, and a description of the children receiving lessons (for example, grade level, special education classification, or any unusual circumstances that would affect the outcome study) are essential. Baseline data may also be included when relevant. Findings should be put in prose and graph form, and copies of all measures used and their scoring manuals may also be included.

The Evaluation Planner should be reviewed and approved by the appropriate people. For example, in larger districts, this would include a staff member designated as the evaluation coordinator for one or several programs, the district administrators, and key program implementers.

A SAMPLE EVALUATION PLAN: ANYTOWN MIDDLE SCHOOL

Anytown is a small middle-class suburb of a major metropolitan city. The Anytown School District contains three elementary schools (kindergarten through fifth grade) and one middle school (sixth through eighth grades); high school students are sent to a regional high school in a nearby town. The middle school has a population of approximately 445 students, which includes two classes of special education students.

In Anytown Middle School, social studies teachers worked with the guidance counselors and the school psychologist to carry out the social studies modules during social studies class time. The evaluation component of this program follows the steps outlined in the SDM/SPS Evaluation Planner (Worksheet 11.12). In response to Question 1, it has been decided that the evaluation will include a pretest and posttest component. The next important step is to formulate the questions that this evaluation should answer. For example, several questions relate to the program in this district:

1. How well do these activities fit the particular teachers and their classes?

2. What were the SDM/SPS skill gains and applications?

3. How satisfied were the teachers with the lessons and their implementation?

4. How satisfied were the counselor and school psychologist with the lessons and implementation?

5. How satisfied were the students with the lessons?

The measures chosen for each particular grade level or group should provide answers to these five questions.

The program has been in place in Anytown Middle School for less than one year at the time of pretesting. All teachers, as well as the counselor and school psychologist, received training during the preceding school year and had begun implementing the program immediately following the end of the training workshop series. The guidance counselor served as an in-class co-leader with the teachers; the school psychologist, who attended leadership training, acted as a consultant to teachers.

The social studies module lessons are taught once per week, with each teacher following the basic outline in this volume. Special education teachers implement the lessons on consecutive days, rather than once per week; they also take longer than the regular education classes to complete each topic. The implementing team, along with district administrators, decided to evaluate the program during its first full year of implementation, allowing for those involved to gain some experience with the curriculum during the preceding school year.

A sampling of students will be included in the evaluation. The samples will include thirty sixth- and seventh-grade regular education students and ten special education students, five from each class. The regular education students will complete the Group Social Problem Solving Assessment (Worksheet 11.9) while the special education classes complete the Getting Along with Others measure (Worksheet 11.8). The Profile of SDM/SPS Strengths (PSDM; Worksheet 11.10) will be completed by teachers and the guidance counselor for all special education students and for a random sample of regular education students (eight girls and eight boys from each grade of the middle school). All three of these worksheets are discussed in the "Skill Gains" section of "Tools for Evaluating Sets of Activities or Programs," earlier in this chapter.

Work samples in the social studies area from each of the students being evaluated will also be included as a component of the evaluation. This is consistent with the growing movement toward the use of portfolios for assessment purposes (National Education Association, 1993; Paulson, Paulson, & Meyer, 1991). The purpose of the work samples is to supplement information gleaned from an analysis of more structured measures of social decision making and social problem solving. Work samples provide diverse ways to see students' ability to apply their knowledge of the skills. The work samples can be obtained from the class during which the lessons are taught, but samples from other classes can provide interesting indicators of transfer of learning. For example, if students receive their SDM/SPS lessons during social studies class, then work samples will be obtained from the social studies curriculum (current events writing samples, for example). However, themes from language arts and art projects also could be examined. Part of a work sample could include any improvement in overall behavior, as recorded in report cards, which provide important data regarding academic gains and behavior change over the course of a school year. Meanwhile, much value can be gained from involving students in the process of defining and creating their samples. Work sample or portfolio fairs, expositions, and conventions have been found to be rewarding ways to get comprehensive overviews of learning while also promoting a spirit of exchange and sharing among learners and instructors (Barone, 1991).

In addition, the SDM/SPS Curriculum Feedback worksheets (Worksheets 11.1 and 11.2) are very helpful to those who are implementing SDM/SPS activities.

Questions 4 through 7 of the SDM/SPS Evaluation Planner (Worksheet 11.12) address the logistics of administering the pretest instruments. In this case, the pretest is being administered by the teachers and guidance counselor, with the assistance of the school psychologist (the appointed evaluation coordinator) in September, before the lessons start. As requested in Questions 8 through 11, it is noted that the school psychologist will score and analyze the data according to the scoring manual or guidelines explained in the narratives accompanying each measure.

The posttest procedures are similar to those used for the pretest. The Group Social Problem Solving Assessment and Getting Along with Others (Worksheets 11.9 and 11.8) will be administered to the same students. The teachers and guidance counselor will fill out the PSDM rating scale (Worksheet 11.10) for these students, and work samples will be obtained from them as well. Report cards, completed each marking period, will be analyzed for any changes noted in the area of behavior and adjustment. Also, each teacher and student, as well as the guidance counselor, will complete a consumer satisfaction or opinion survey that will help those working with SDM/SPS to modify or expand the program for the following year. Finally, the school psychologist will coordinate the completion the SDM/SPS Trainers' Program Planning Guide (Worksheet 11.11) while considering details and proposals for program expansion during the upcoming school year.

The posttest measures will be administered and completed in May and June, just after the end of the SDM/SPS module (perhaps earlier for the special education classes). Again, the school psychologist will be responsible for scoring and analyzing the posttest data. The final report will be completed by the guidance counselor and will include the data analysis, recommendations, and anecdotes gleaned from the consumer satisfaction measure. The report will be distributed to the middle school principal, chief school administrator, and the board of education, which will ultimately decide if the program is to be funded and possibly expanded the following year.

Teachers/leaders _____ **Date** _____

Class period and group worked with _____

1. General outline of lesson or class activities:

   _____

   _____

2. Student reactions to this session (for whom was it most or least effective):

   _____

   _____

3. Most effective or favorable aspects of this session:

   _____

   _____

4. Least effective or favorable aspects of this session:

   _____

   _____

5. Points to follow up in the next meeting:

   _____

   _____

6. Points to follow up in the following weeks outside group meetings (that is, in other class periods, other school settings, outside of school):

   _____

   _____

7. Suggested changes in this activity for the future:

   _____

   _____

Teachers/leaders _____ Date _____

Class period and group worked with _____

Topic or activity _____

Student Involvement Feedback	Low		*(Circle one.)*		High
Engagement	1	2	3	4	5
Demonstration of skill in practice	1	2	3	4	5
Instructional Feedback					
Impact on students	1	2	3	4	5
Potential for follow-up and continuity	1	2	3	4	5
Need for additional practice and supplements	1	2	3	4	5

1. For which students was this most effective?

   _____

   _____

2. For which students was this least effective?

   _____

   _____

3. What changes or supplements will you use to help reach students for whom it was least effective?

   _____

   _____

4. What prompts, cues, and follow-up will you use to continue to reach students for whom it was most effective?

   _____

   _____

   _____

Student _____ Date _____

1. Skill: Recognizing types of put-downs

We know that put-downs are words or actions that are intended to deliberately hurt someone's body or feelings. Name the four major categories of put-downs that we have been studying in class.

_____   _____

_____   _____

2. Skill: Understanding what trigger situations are and their impact on our bodies

a. Name at least five ways in which your body reacts when it experiences a surge of adrenaline.

_____   _____

_____   _____

_____   _____

b. From our readings in English and language arts, name two characters and a trigger situation for each of them.

Character _____ Trigger situation _____

Character _____ Trigger situation _____

c. The body has a three-stage reaction to stress. List the terms next to the appropriate definition:

The body mobilizes for action: _____

The body takes action: _____

The resistance wears down: _____

3. Skill: Keep Calm

List the steps of Keep Calm:

_____   _____

_____   _____

4. **Skill: What does "BEST" stand for?**

   B _____

   E _____

   S _____

   T _____

5. **Practice**

   I use ideas that I learned in our social decision making meetings *(Circle Yes or No.)*

On my walk or bus ride to school	Yes	No
In home room or advisory	Yes	No
During change of classes	Yes	No
In my language arts or English class	Yes	No
In my math and science classes	Yes	No
In physical education class	Yes	No
During lunch	Yes	No
On my walk or bus ride home	Yes	No
With my friends outside school	Yes	No
With the other kids at home	Yes	No
With the adults at home	Yes	No

Please describe a time when you used one or more of our social decision making ideas to help you with a problem in school.

_____

_____

_____

_____

_____

_____

_____

_____

_____

Student _____ **Date** _____

Skill practiced _____

1. When did you do this?

   _____

2. Where were you?

   _____

3. Who else was there?

   _____

4. What did you do?

   _____

5. What did you observe?

   _____

6. How did the others react?

   _____

7. What else happened?

   _____

8. How would you rate yourself on your use of this skill? *(Circle one.)*

              Poor   Fair   OK   Good   Excellent

9. What would you do differently next time?

   _____

10. What other skill would you like to work on?

    _____

Student _____ Date _____

Teacher/leader _____

1. I thought the SDM/SPS activities were *(circle one)*:

   a. Lots of fun

   b. Pretty good

   c. OK

   d. No fun at all

2. I would like to have activities like this *(circle one)*:

   a. More often

   b. Just as we had them

   c. Once in a while

   d. Never again

3. What were the best things about the activities?

   _____

   _____

4. What would make the activities better?

   _____

   _____

For the following questions, circle Yes or No.

5. The activities have helped me to:

a. Get to know my classmates better	Yes	No
b. Handle my problems better	Yes	No
c. Do better in math	Yes	No
d. Feel happier	Yes	No
e. Like my teacher more	Yes	No
f. Stay calmer	Yes	No
g. Better understand things I read	Yes	No

6. I use the things I learned in the SDM/SPS activities when I am:

   a. In class   Yes   No

   b. At lunch   Yes   No

   c. At gym   Yes   No

   d. In the hallway (between classes)   Yes   No

   e. At home, with my parents   Yes   No

   f. At home, with other kids in the family   Yes   No

   g. With my friends   Yes   No

7. Please write about one or two times you used what you learned in SDM/SPS activities to help you with a problem at school or at home. Tell how you solved the problem and what was most helpful to you.

_____

_____

_____

_____

_____

_____

_____

_____

_____

_____

_____

_____

_____

_____

_____

Your homeroom or advisory teacher _____ Your grade _____

Please answer these questions as carefully and honestly as you can.

1. What are some things you remember learning in the SDM/SPS activities?

_____

_____

Please circle the best answer to the following two questions.

2. How often do you use social decision making/social problem solving skills at school or at home?

Not at all	Once or twice	Sometimes	Many times	All the time
1	2	3	4	5

3. How useful are the skills you learned in social decision making activities?

Not at all	Used them, but they were not very useful	Useful	Very useful	Extremely useful
1	2	3	4	5

4. Please describe a time when you used what you learned in the program (for example, if you stopped to use Keep Calm when you were nervous or upset or used FIG TESPN to think about how to handle a problem). Use the back of this page if you need to.

_____

_____

_____

_____

_____

5. What goals have you set for yourself for using social decision making/social problem solving skills through the rest of the year or in the summer?

_____

_____

_____

_____

_____

Teacher/leader _____ Date _____

School/grade level or group _____

Activities used _____

_____

1. I thought the activities were *(circle one)*:
   a. Highly valuable
   b. Moderately valuable
   c. Of some value
   d. Of little value

2. I would like to continue using the activities next year *(circle one)*:

   Yes   No   Unsure

3. What were the most valuable aspects of the activities you used?

4. What difficulties were there in implementing the program?

5. I used the SDM/SPS concepts or prompts at times other than during the formal lesson *(circle one)*:
   a. Often
   b. Sometimes
   c. Rarely
   d. Never

6. The SDM/SPS activities have helped me to *(circle Yes or No for each answer)*:

a. Get to know the students better	Yes	No
b. Manage classroom problems better	Yes	No
c. Maintain a positive classroom atmosphere	Yes	No
d. Other _____		

7. The SDM/SPS activities helped the students in my class to *(circle Yes or No for each answer)*:

   a. Get to know each other better   Yes   No

   b. Handle their problems better   Yes   No

   c. Stay calmer   Yes   No

   d. Focus better on their academic work   Yes   No

8. Did your students use the skills covered in the SDM/SPS activities *(circle Yes or No)*:

   a. In other classroom situations   Yes   No

   b. At lunch, gym, and in the hallway   Yes   No

   c. At other times *(give examples)*:

   _____

   _____

9. Please write about one or two times you or your students were able to use SDM/SPS skills to help with a problem. Tell how the problem was solved and how the skills covered in the lessons were helpful. (Use the back of this page if you need to.)

10. I found the ongoing discussions with my consultant coach to be *(check appropriate boxes)*.

	Very	Somewhat	Not particularly
a. Helpful for preparation	❐	❐	❐
b. Helpful for discussing how activities went	❐	❐	❐
c. Helpful for discussing problems that occurred	❐	❐	❐
d. Supportive	❐	❐	❐
e. Helpful in generating ways to reach more students	❐	❐	❐
f. Useful in integrating SDM/SPS with academics	❐	❐	❐

   g. Other *(specify)* _____

11. Please describe any suggestions you may have concerning improvement in the areas of consultation, coaching, or program implementation. (*Use the back of this page if you need to.*)

Worksheet 11.8
Student Evaluation Form for Use in Assessing SDM/SPS Readiness Skills

Getting Along with Others

1. Sometimes it is hard to listen and pay attention to what the teacher is saying in class. Sometimes you need to pay attention, but you have a hard time because it is noisy or maybe because you are tired.

   a. Name three things that you do to help yourself listen and pay attention.

   (1) _____

   (2) _____

   (3) _____

   b. When the teacher gives you directions, how do you remember them?

   _____

2. Almost everybody gets angry or upset at someone in their class at one time or another.

   a. Name three ways you can tell when you are upset.

   (1) _____

   (2) _____

   (3) _____

   b. What do you do to help yourself become less upset?

   _____

   c. Name three things you do when someone is bothering you.

   (1) _____

   (2) _____

   (3) _____

3. What does the word *help* mean?

   _____

4. It's bad to ask others for help. *(Circle one.)*   True   False

5. Name two times when you might give help to someone else.

   a. _____

   b. _____

(page 1 of 2)

6. Let's say that you want to go over to talk to someone who is upset or having a tough time with something. Write how you would do it.

   _____

   _____

   _____

7. Name four things that you look for in a friend.

   a. _____

   b. _____

   c. _____

   d. _____

8. It's more important to show that you can work on your own than it is to show that you can work as part of a team. *(Circle one.)*   True   False

Worksheet 11.9
Student Evaluation Form for Use in Assessing SDM/SPS Skills

Group Social Problem Solving Assessment (GSPSA)

I. Feelings

1. Who has feelings? _____

_____

2. Where are feelings? _____

_____

3. How can we tell how a person is feeling? _____

_____

4. Everyone feels the same about the things that they do or that happen to them. *(Circle one.)*
   True   False

5. What kind of feelings are there? _____

_____

6. Feelings always stay the same. *(Circle one.)*   True   False

7. Name a good feeling: _____

8. Name a not-so-good feeling: _____

II. Problems and Goals

1. What is a problem? _____

_____

2. What must we do with problems? _____

_____

3. Name a problem: _____

_____

4. What is a goal? _____

_____

5. Why is it important to stop and think before you act? _____

_____

6. Name a problem and its goal: _____

_____

7. How can we tell when we're having a problem? _____

_____

III. Solutions

1. How many different ways are there to solve a problem? _____

_____

2. How many solutions should we try to think up? _____

_____

3. Name a problem and two solutions: _____

_____

IV. Consequences

1. What is a consequence? _____

_____

2. How can you tell if a solution is a good one? _____

_____

3. When you think you have a good solution, what should you do next? _____

_____

4. There is only one good way to solve a problem. *(Circle one.)*   True   False

V. Making Solutions Work

1. Does thinking of good solutions always solve your problem? _____

_____

2. Name some reasons why good solutions might not solve your problems: ___

_____

3. What should you do if your first solution to a problem does not work? ____

_____

4. Do you think that you can usually solve your own problems if you try? ____

_____

Scoring Manual for the Group Social Problem Solving Assessment (GSPSA)

GSPSA Student Data Form

Student _____ Date _____

Class _____ School _____

Scoring

I. Feelings	II. Problems and Goals	IV. Consequences
1. _____	1. _____	1. _____
2. _____	2. _____	2. _____
3. _____	3. _____	3. _____
4. _____	4. _____	4. _____
5. _____	5. _____	**V. Making Solutions Work**
6. _____	6. _____	1. _____
7. _____	7. _____	2. _____
8. _____	**III. Solutions**	3. _____
	1. _____	4. _____
	2. _____	
	3. _____	

Summary Scores

Interpersonal sensitivity = Feelings 1 + 2 + 3 + 4 + 5 + 6 + 8

TOTAL _____

Problem analysis and action = (Problems and Goals 1 + 2 + 3 + 4 + 5 + 6 + 7) + (Solutions 1 + 2 + 3)

TOTAL _____

Specificity of planning = (Consequences 1 + 3 + 4) + (Making Solutions Work 1 + 3 + 4)

TOTAL _____

Comparison Scores

	At Risk	Average	Highly Skilled
Interpersonal sensitivity	≤ 8	9–10	≥ 11
Problem analysis and action	≤ 8	9–13	≥ 14
Specificity of planning	≤ 4	5–6	≥ 7

(page 1 of 4)

GSPSA Item Scoring Guide

I. Feelings   Points

Item 1
3 = Concept of *all* or *everybody*
2 = Several specifically named persons (me and Mrs. Brown and my mom)
1 = One particular person
0 = Other responses

Item 2
1 = Inside, in you, in your heart or mind, and the like
0 = Other

Item 3
1   *Each* for different ways of representing asking, looking, and listening

Item 4
1 = False
0 = True

Item 5
2 = Examples of *both* "good" and "bad" feelings
1 = Examples of *either* "good" or "bad" feelings
0 = Other

Item 6
1 = False
0 = True

Items 7 and 8
3 = *General,* clearly positive (negative) feeling (happy, glad, sad)
2 = Positive (negative) more *specific* feeling or event (a new bicycle, getting yelled at, not getting what you want, going to your room with no TV, being smart, being stupid or ugly)
1 = Questionably positive (negative) feeling or event (silly, being on an airplane)
0 = Inappropriate answer

II. Problems and Goals   Points

Item 1
3 = Response includes both an *event* and a *feeling* (something that happens between people that gives you a bad feeling)
2 = Response emphasizes a *bad feeling* (when I don't feel so good)
1 = Response describes *something bad* that happens (when you lose your keys, when you hit someone)
0 = Other

Item 2
1 = Solve them
0 = Other

Item 3   2 = Child describes some *interpersonal* situation or event
1 = Child mentions a *specific* person or object that causes him or her difficulty
0 = Other

Item 4   3 = Abstract definition, generally positive or neutral in tone (how we want things to end up, what we want to happen)
2 = Specific interpersonal outcome (make friends, be happy)
1 = Specific material outcome (a new bike)
0 = A negative goal or other response

Item 5   1 = For *each* of the following mentioned:
     (a) need time to think of solutions
     (b) if you act too quickly, the problem might get worse
     (c) so you can figure out what's going on
     (d) so you can see how you're feeling
     (e) so you can decide on your goal

Item 6   3 = Problem and goal clearly given
2 = Problem only clearly given
1 = Goal only clearly given
0 = Other

Item 7   2 = General answers (upset feelings)
1 = Specific answers (when I get sent to my room)
0 = Other

III. Solutions   **Points**

Item 1   2 = An "infinite" number (lots)
1 = Multiple but finite (2, 4, 19, 376)
0 = 1 or other

Item 2   2 = As many as we can (lots)
1 = Specific number greater than 1
0 = 1 or other

Item 3   2 = Accurate presentation of problem and two solutions
1 = Not clear if all is presented accurately
0 = Definitely not accurate

IV. Consequences   Points

Item 1

3 = Concepts of "after" or "next" and an action that the child committed (something that might happen after you try something)
2 = An event (you get punished, you can't watch TV, you get rewarded)
1 = A feeling (you feel sad, you feel proud)
0 = Other

Item 2

3 = Thinking ahead
2 = Thinking about it or asking someone else
1 = Trying it and seeing what happens
0 = Other, some specific action

Item 3

1 = Try it
0 = Other

Item 4

1 = False
0 = True

V. Making Solutions Work   Points

Item 1

2 = No, but usually
1 = No
0 = Yes

Item 2

1   For *each* clear reason:
(a) other person in a bad mood
(b) other person busy
(c) might work with one person but not another

Item 3

3 = Think about others and try another
2 = Think about others
1 = Try another
0 = Other

Item 4

2 = Yes
0 = No

Profile of Social Decision Making/Social Problem Solving Strengths

Student _____ Date _____

Observer _____ Title/position _____

Record your observation for each student by using this simple mastery rating, adjusted to appropriate age, grade, and ability expectations.

1 = Clearly does not demonstrate a satisfactory level

2 = Level in this area is uncertain

3 = Clearly demonstrates a satisfactory level

	To what extent can this child:		**Observation** *(circle one)*		
A. Readiness Area					
1. Self-control	1a.	Listen carefully and accurately	1	2	3
	1b.	Remember and follow directions	1	2	3
	1c.	Concentrate and follow through on tasks	1	2	3
	1d.	Calm himself or herself down	1	2	3
	1e.	Carry on a conversation without upsetting or provoking others	1	2	3
2. Social Awareness	2a.	Accept praise or approval	1	2	3
	2b.	Choose praiseworthy and caring friends	1	2	3
	2c.	Know when help is needed	1	2	3
	2d.	Ask for help when needed	1	2	3
	2e.	Work as part of a problem-solving team	1	2	3
B. Social Decision Making/Social Problem Solving Area					
1. Feelings	1a.	Recognize signs of personal feelings	1	2	3
	1b.	Recognize signs of feelings in others	1	2	3
	1c.	Accurately describe a range of feelings	1	2	3
2. Problems	2a.	Clearly put problems into words	1	2	3
3. Goals	3a.	State realistic interpersonal goals	1	2	3
4. Alternatives	4a.	Think of several ways to solve a problem or reach a goal	1	2	3
	4b.	Think of different types of solutions	1	2	3
	4c.	Do (a) and (b) for different types of problems	1	2	3

(page 1 of 2)

	To what extent can this child:	Observation *(circle one)*		
5. *Consequences*	5a. Differentiate short- *and* long-term consequences	1	2	3
	5b. Look at effects on self *and* others	1	2	3
	5c. Keep positive *and* negative possibilities in mind	1	2	3
6. *Choose*	6a. Select solutions that can reach goals	1	2	3
	6b. Make choices that do not harm self or others	1	2	3
7. *Plan and Check*	7a. Consider details before carrying out a solution (who, when, where, with whom, and so on)	1	2	3
	7b. Anticipate obstacles	1	2	3
	7c. Respond appropriately when plans are thwarted	1	2	3
8. *Learn for Next Time*	8a. Try out ideas	1	2	3
	8b. Learn from experience or from seeking input from adults and friends	1	2	3
	8c. Use previous experience to help next time	1	2	3

Use the back of this page or extra pages if necessary.

Questions to consider when planning to implement or expand social decision making/social problem solving activities

1. Briefly list your goals in developing a program (for example, changes in teaching practices, curriculum change, student acquisition of problem-solving or other specific skills, parent follow-through).

2. In your setting, which schools, grades, or other areas would you target? Why?

3. How would you obtain support for implementing a program? Who would you approach to work with you? What are some incentives for collaborating in developing this program? Who would be your contacts in the school? Other key groups?

4. Briefly outline how you would structure the training for the program (for example, conduct inservice with staff in your setting; send staff for training; purchase materials and use with teachers; connect teachers with outside consultants; contact local university or mental health center for assistance).

Additional questions for program development

5. In your community, what advice would you give to someone building a new program to keep the effort running smoothly?

    a. What existing strengths and resources can be used to support and promote the program?

    b. What existing constraints must be taken into account?

6. How would you evaluate the impact of the program?

7. Please list the specific steps you will take over the next six months to begin to carry out your plans. Begin by listing what you will do in the next two weeks, then each month for the following six months.

Name of district _____ **Date form completed** _____

Person responsible for evaluating program _____

Use the back of these pages or extra pages if necessary.

Briefly describe program and activities being evaluated:

_____

_____

_____

_____

1. Nature of evaluation: Will your evaluation involve *(circle those that apply)*:

   a. Pretest/posttest

   b. Only a follow-up of work done during preceding school year

   c. Gathering of baseline data

   d. Other *(please explain)*: _____

2. What are the questions you want to answer? These questions should reflect your goals (that is, process and implementation; skill gains and changes; relative changes; long-term outcomes).

   _____

   _____

   _____

3. What pretest instruments do you want to use?

   _____

   _____

4. When will the pretest instruments be administered?

   _____

5. Who will complete the pretest instruments? *(Please specify the number of students.)*

   _____

6. Who will administer the pretest instruments?

   _____

7. What procedures will be followed for administration of the pretest instruments?

_____

_____

_____

8. Who is going to score the pretest instruments?

_____

9. When will the pretest instruments need to be scored?

_____

10. Will a computer be needed to analyze the pretest data? If yes, who will enter the data?

_____

11. How will the pretest data be analyzed or summarized?

_____

_____

_____

12. What posttest instruments do you want to use?

_____

_____

13. When will the posttest instruments be administered?

_____

14. Who will complete the posttest instruments? *(Please specify the number of students.)*

_____

15. Who will administer the posttest instruments?

_____

16. What procedures will be followed for administration of the posttest instruments?

_____

_____

_____

17. Who is going to score the posttest instruments?

_____

18. When will the posttest instruments be scored?

_____

19. Will a computer be needed to analyze the posttest data? If yes, who will enter the data?

_____

20. How will the posttest data be analyzed or summarized?

_____

_____

_____

21. When is the final report due?

_____

22. For whom is the report intended (that is, district, county, state, federal, funders)?

_____

23. Who is going to be responsible for the write-up of the final report, to provide the feedback regarding the questions and instruments?

_____

Reviewed by the evaluation coordinator _____ _____

                                                            (signature)   *(date)*

Comments:

_____

_____

Reviewed by principal or administrator _____ _____

                                                            (signature)   *(date)*

Comments:

_____

_____

Reviewed by SDM/SPS committee or liaison _____ _____

                                                            (signature)   *(date)*

Comments:

_____

_____

References

Abell, S. K. (1990). The problem-solving muse. *Science and Children, 28*(2), 27–29.

Abrams, F. (1991). Pupils "starved" of lessons on planet. *Times Educational Supplement* (No. 3912).

Adler, A. (1927). *Understanding human nature.* New York: Greenburg.

Banks, J. A. (1991–92). Multicultural education: For freedom's sake. *Educational Leadership, 49*(4), 32–37.

Banks, J. A., Cortés, C., Gay, G., Garcia, R., & Ochos, A. (1976). *Curriculum guidelines for multicultural education.* Washington, DC: National Council for the Social Studies.

Banks, J. A., & McGee, C. (Eds.). (1989). *Multicultural education: Issues and perspectives.* Boston: Allyn & Bacon.

Barone, T. (1991). Assessment as theater: Staging an exposition. *Educational Leadership, 48*(5), 57–59.

Barton, D. E., & Washburn, J. L. (1991). Environmental education— An exemplary program. *Science and Children, 23*(8), 20–21.

Battistich, V., Elias, M. J., & Branden-Muller, L. (1992). Two school-based approaches to promoting students' social competence. In G. Albee, L. Bond, & T. Monsey (Eds.), *Improving students' lives: Global approaches to prevention,* pp. 212–234. Newbury Park, CA: Sage.

Blair, D., & Judah, S. (1990). Need a strong foundation for an inter-disciplinary program? Try 4MAT! *Educational Leadership, 48*(2), 37–38.

Blyth, D., Simmons, R., & Carlton-Ford, S. (1983). The adjustment of early adolescents to school transitions. *Journal of Early Adolescence, 3*(1 & 2), 105–120.

Blythe, T., & Gardner, H. (1990). A school for all intelligences. *Educational Leadership, 47*(7), 33–37.

Boyer, E. L. (1990). Civic education for responsible citizens. *Educational Leadership, 47*(3), 4–7.

Brandwein, P. E., & Glass, L. W. (1991). A permanent agenda for science teachers. Part II: What is good science teaching? *Science Teacher, 58*(4), 36–39.

Brendtro, L., Brokenleg, M., & Van Bockern, S. (2000). *Reclaiming youth at risk: Our hope for the future* (Rev. ed.). Bloomington, IN: National Educational Service.

Bruene Butler, L., Hampson, J., Elias, M. J., Clabby, J., & Schuyler, T. (1997). The Improving Social Awareness-Social Problem Solving Project. In G. Albee & T. Gullotta (Eds.), *Primary prevention works* (pp. 239–267). Thousand Oaks, CA: Sage.

Calcaterra, S., & Rippas, J. (1981). *Basic skills at work.* Unpublished manuscript. Woodbridge, NJ: Woodbridge School District.

Carney, C. G., & Kahn, K. B. (1984). Building competencies for effective cross-cultural counseling: A developmental view. *Counseling Psychologist, 12,* 111–119.

Carnegie Council on Adolescent Development. (1989). *Turning points: Preparing American youth for the 21st century.* Washington, DC: Carnegie Corporation of New York.

Centers for Disease Control and Prevention (CDC). (2000, October 13). CDC Surveillance Summaries. *Morbidity and Mortality Weekly Report, 49,* p. SS-10.

Cole, C. G. (1979). A group guidance approach to improving students' study skills. *School Counselor, 27,* 29–33.

Consortium on the School-Based Promotion of Social Competence. (1991). Preparing students for the twenty-first century: Contributions of the prevention and social competence promotion fields. *Teachers College Record, 93,* 297–305.

Cortés, C. (1979). The societal curriculum and the school curriculum: Allies or antagonists? *Educational Leadership, 36*(7), 475–480.

Cortés, C. (1990, March). A curricular basis for multicultural education. *Doubts and Uncertainties,* pp. 1–5.

Crabbe, A. (1989). The future problem solving program. *Educational Leadership, 46*(1), 27–29.

Curry, L. (1990). A critique of research on learning styles. *Educational Leadership, 48*(2), 50–56.

Damon, W. (1988). *The moral child: Nurturing students' natural moral growth.* New York: Free Press.

Deloria, E. (1943). *Speaking of Indians.* New York: Friendship Press.

Deshler, D. D., & Schumaker, J. B. (1986). Learning strategies: An instructional alternative for low-achieving adolescents. *Exceptional Children, 52*(6), 583–590.

Dewey, J. (1933). *How we think.* Boston: Heath.

Dodge, K., Pettit, G., McClaskey, C., & Brown, M. (1986). Social competence in students. *Monographs of the Society for Research in Child Development, 51.*

Dorman, G. (Ed.). (1984). *Middle grades assessment program.* Carrboro, NC: Center for Early Adolescence.

Dorman, G., & Lipsitz, J. (1984). Early adolescent development. In G. Dorman (Ed.), *Middle grades assessment program.* Carrboro, NC: Center for Early Adolescence.

Dryfoos, J. (1998). *Safe passage: Making it through adolescence in a risky society.* New York: Oxford University Press.

Eisner, E. (2002). The kind of schools we need. *Phi Delta Kappan, 83*(8), 576–583.

Elias, M. J. (1983). Improving coping skills of emotionally disturbed boys through television-based social problem solving. *American Journal of Orthopsychiatry, 53*(1), 61–72.

Elias, M. J. (1987, March 10). Parents' guidelines get children organized. *Home News,* pp. 1–2.

Elias, M. J. (2003). *Academic and social-emotional learning: Educational Practices Booklet No. 11.* (Available at www.ibe.unesco.org/International/Publications/EducationalPracticesSeriesPdf/prac11e.pdf)

Elias, M. J., Bryan, K., Weissberg, R., & Patrikakou, E. (2003). Reconceptualizing home-school partnerships. *School Community Journal, 13*(1), 133–153.

Elias, M. J., & Clabby, J. (1989). *Social decision making skills: A curriculum guide for the elementary grades.* Gaithersburg, MD: Aspen.

Elias, M. J., Gara, M., Schuyler, T., Branden-Muller, L., & Sayette, M. (1991). The promotion of social competence: Longitudinal study of a preventive school-based program. *American Journal of Orthopsychiatry, 61,* 409–417.

Elias, M. J., & Maher, C. A. (1983). Social and affective development of children: A programmatic perspective. *Exceptional Children, 49*(4), 339–346.

Elias, M. J., Rothbaum, P., & Gara, M. (1986). Social-cognitive problem solving in children: Assessing the knowledge and application of skills. *Journal of Applied Developmental Psychology, 7,* 77–94.

Elias, M. J., & Tobias, S. E. (1996). *Social problem solving interventions in the schools.* New York: Guilford Press. (Available from www.nprinc.com)

Elias, M. J., Tobias, S. E., & Friedlander, B. S. (2002). *Raising emotionally intelligent teenagers: Guiding the way for compassionate, committed, courageous adults.* New York: Random House.

Elias, M. J., Zins, J. E., Weissberg, R. P., Frey, K. S., Greenberg, M. T., Haynes, N. M., Kessler, R., Schwab-Stone, M. E., & Shriver, T. P. (1997). *Promoting social and emotional learning: Guidelines for educators.* Alexandria, VA: Association for Supervision and Curriculum Development.

Engle, S. H. (1990). The commission report and citizenship education. *Social Education, 81,* 431–433.

Erikson, E. H. (1954). *Childhood and society.* New York: Norton.

Fay, G. M. (1991). The project plan: Encouraging individual growth with group projects. *Science Teacher, 58*(2), 40–42.

Fine, M. (1986). Dropout prevention. *Teachers College Record, 87,* 164–170.

Fowler, D. (1990). Democracy's next generation. *Educational Leadership, 47*(3), 10–15.

Fredericks, L. (2003). *Social and emotional learning, service-learning, and educational leadership.* Chicago: Collaborative for Academic, Social, and Emotional Learning.

Gerzon, M. (1997). Teaching democracy by doing it! *Educational Leadership, 54*(5), 6–11.

Gilligan, C. (1987). Adolescent development reconsidered. In C. E. Irwin, Jr. (Ed.), Adolescent social behavior and health. *New Directions for Child Development,* No. 37, pp. 63–92. San Francisco: Jossey-Bass.

Gullotta, T., Adams, G., & Montemayor, R. (Eds.). (1990). *Developing social competency in adolescence.* Newbury Park, CA: Sage.

Haboush, K. (1989). An evaluation of student learning outcomes under a critical thinking–social studies program. Psy.D. dissertation. Rutgers University, New Brunswick, NJ.

Haggerty, R. J., Sherrod, L. R., Garmezy, N., & Rutter, M. (Eds.). (1994). *Stress, risk, and resilience in children and adolescents: Processes, mechanisms, and interventions.* New York: Cambridge University Press.

Hamburg, B. (1990). *Life skills training: Preventive interventions for young adolescents.* New York: Carnegie Council on Adolescent Development.

Hayes, S., & Toarmino, D. (1995). If behavioral principles are generally applicable, why is it necessary to understand cultural diversity? *Behavior Therapist, 18*(2), 21–23.

Heller, M. (1987). The role of language in the formation of ethnic identity. In M. Rotheram and J. Phinney (Eds.), *Children's ethnic socialization: Pluralism and development,* pp. 180–200. Newbury Park, CA: Sage.

Hergert, L. F. (2002). A vital link. *American School Boards Journal, 189*(11), 45–47.

Hightower, A. D., Work, W. C., Cowen, E. L., Lotyczewski, B. S., Spinell, A. P., Guare, J. C., & Rohrbeck, C. A. (1986). The teacher-child rating scale: A brief objective measure of elementary children's school problem behaviors and competencies. *School Psychology Review, 15,* 393–409.

Irwin, C. E., Jr. (Ed.). (1987). Adolescent social behavior and health. *New Directions for Child Development,* No. 37. San Francisco: Jossey-Bass.

Jennings, M. (1997). Kids + portfolios = responsible, reflective learners. *New Jersey Federation of the Council for Exceptional Children Special Edition Newsletter, 1*(1), 3–4.

Kahn, L., Kinchen, S. A., Williams, B. I., Ross, J. G., Lowry, R., Grunbaum, J., & Kolbe, L. J. (2000). Youth risk behavior surveillance: United States 1999. *Morbidity and Mortality Weekly Report, 49,* SS5.

Kessler, R. (2000). *The soul of education: Helping students find connection, compassion, and character at school.* Alexandria, VA: Association for Supervision and Curriculum Development.

Keung-Ho, M. (1992). *Minority children and adolescents in therapy.* Newbury Park, CA: Sage.

Kimeldorf, M. (1994). *Creating portfolios for success in school, work, and life.* Minneapolis: Free Spirit.

Klopfer, L. E. (1991). A summary of research in science education. *Science Education, 75*(3), 284–322.

Kolbe, L. (1985). Why school health education? An empirical point of view. *Health Education, 16,* 116–120.

Kubey, R., & Csikszentmihalyi, M. (1990). *Television and the quality of life: How viewing shapes everyday experience.* Hillsdale, NJ: Erlbaum.

Lipsitz, J. (1980). The age group. In M. Johnson (Ed.), *Toward adolescence: The middle school years. Seventy-ninth yearbook of the National Society for the Study of Education.* University of Chicago Press.

London, P. (1987). Character education and clinical intervention: A paradigm shift for U.S. schools. *Phi Delta Kappan, 68,* 667–673.

Marzano, R., Pickering, D., & McTighe, J. (1993). *Assessing student outcomes.* Alexandria, VA: Association for Supervision and Curriculum Development.

Massialas, B. G. (1990). Educating students for conflict resolution and democratic decision making. *Social Studies, 54,* 282–285.

Masten, A. S., Best, K., & Garmezy, N. (1990). Resilience and development: Contributions from the study of students who overcome adversity. *Development and Psychopathology, 2,* 425–444.

McCarthy, B. (1990). Using the 4MAT system to bring learning styles to schools. *Educational Leadership, 48*(2), 31–36.

Mirman, J., Swartz, R., & Barell, J. (1988). Strategies to help teachers empower at-risk students. In B. Z. Presseisen (Ed.), *At-risk students and thinking: Perspectives from research* (pp. 138–156). Washington, DC: National Education Association/Research for Better Schools.

Moulds, (2004). Rich tastes. *Educational Leadership, 61*(4), 75–78.

National Center for Innovation and Education. (1999). *Lessons for life: How smart schools prepare students for success in school and life. A video training kit for educators.* Bloomington, IN: HOPE Foundation (www.communitiesofhope.org).

National Education Association. (1993). *Student portfolios.* Washington, DC: NEA Professional Library.

National Mental Health Association. (1986). *The prevention of mental-emotional disabilities: Report of the National Mental Health Association Commission on the Prevention of Mental-Emotional Disabilities.* Alexandria, VA: National Mental Health Association.

Natoli, S. (1989). Editor's notebook. *Social Education, 80,* 336.

Novaco, R. (1975). *Anger control.* Lexington, MA: Lexington Books.

Ogbu, J. (1985). A cultural ecology of competence among inner-city Blacks. In M. Spencer, O. Brookins, and W. Allen (Eds.), *Beginnings: The social and affective development of Black children,* pp. 45–66. Hillsdale, NJ: Erlbaum.

Otto, P. B. (1991). Finding an answer in questioning strategies. *Science and Children, 28*(7), 44–47.

Otto, P. B., & Schuck, R. F. (1983). The effects of a teacher questioning strategy training program on teaching behavior, student achievement and retention. *Journal of Research in Science Teaching, 20*(6), 521–528.

Paulson, F., Paulson, P., & Meyer, C. (1991). What makes a portfolio a portfolio? *Educational Leadership, 48*(5), 60–64.

Pedersen, P. (1991). Multiculturalism as a generic approach to counseling. *Journal of Counseling and Development, 70,* 6–12.

Perkins, D. N. (1986). Thinking frames. *Educational Leadership, 43*(8), 4–11.

Piaget, J. (1984). *Intelligence and affectivity.* Palo Alto, CA: Annual Reviews Press.

Presseisen, B. Z. (Ed.). (1988). *At-risk students and thinking: Perspectives from research.* Washington, DC: National Education Association/Research for Better Schools.

Rutter, M. (1987). Psychosocial resilience and protective mechanisms. *American Journal of Orthopsychiatry, 57,* 316–331.

Salomon, G. (1979). *The interaction of media, cognition, and learning.* San Francisco: Jossey-Bass.

Schneider, M., & Robin, A. (1975). *The turtle technique: A method for the self-control of impulse behavior.* Stony Brook: State University of New York.

Seif, E. (2004). Social studies revived. *Educational Leadership, 61*(4), 57–59.

Selye, H. (1956). *The stress of life.* New York: McGraw-Hill.

Snyder, H. N., & Sickmund, M. (1999). *Juvenile offenders and victims: 1999 national report.* Washington, DC: Office of Juvenile Justice and Delinquency Prevention.

Spivack, G., & Shure, M. (1974). *Social adjustment of young students.* San Francisco: Jossey-Bass.

Tomlinson, C. (1999). *The differentiated classroom.* Alexandria, VA: Association for Supervision and Curriculum Development.

Watts, R. J. (1992). Elements of a psychology of human diversity. *Journal of Community Psychology, 20,* 116–131.

Wilkinson, B. (1987). *Not separate, not equal.* New York: HarperCollins.

Wise, K. C., & Okey, J. R. (1983). A meta-analysis of the effects of various science teaching strategies on achievement. *Journal of Research in Science Teaching, 20*(5), 419–435.

Wynne, E., &., & Walberg, H. (1986). The complementary goals of character development and academic excellence. *Educational Leadership, 43*(4), 15–18.

About the Authors

MAURICE J. ELIAS, Ph.D., is professor, Department of Psychology, Rutgers University, and directs the Rutgers Social-Emotional Learning Lab. He is vice chair of the Leadership Team of the Collaborative for Academic, Social, and Emotional Learning (www.CASEL.org) and senior advisor for Research, Policy, and Practice to the New Jersey Center for Character Education. He devotes his research and writing to the area of emotional intelligence in children, schools, and families. His books for parents include *Emotionally Intelligent Parenting: How to Raise a Self-Disciplined, Responsible and Socially Skilled Child* (Three Rivers Press, 2000) and *Raising Emotionally Intelligent Teenagers: Guiding the Way for Compassionate, Committed, Courageous Adults* (Three Rivers Press, 2002), both published in several languages. His recent releases are *Engaging the Resistant Child Through Computers: A Manual for Social-Emotional Learning* (available through www.nprinc.com), *Building Learning Communities with Character: How to Integrate Academic, Social, and Emotional Learning* (Association for Supervision and Curriculum Development, 2003), and *EQ + IQ = Best Leadership Practices for Caring and Successful Schools* (Corwin Press, 2003), as well as *Bullying, Peer Harassment, and Victimization in the Schools: The Next Generation of Prevention* (Haworth, 2004). Dr. Elias is married and the father of two children.

LINDA BRUENE BUTLER, M.Ed., has worked on the development of school-based programs in social and emotional learning for over two decades. Currently, she is director of the Social Decision Making/Social Problem Solving (SDM/SPS) Program at the Behavioral Research and Training Institute of the University of Medicine and Dentistry of New Jersey, University Behavioral HealthCare's Behavioral Research and Training Institute. She has also served as adjunct faculty for courses in the area of social-emotional learning at the Department of Psychology, Rutgers University; Teachers College, Columbia University; and Department of Psychology, University of Illinois. Ms. Bruene Butler has published and lectured extensively in the area of social-emotional learning and has trained many others to become SDM/SPS consultants and trainers. Her current area of interest is exploring ways that distance learning methods can be used to share and evaluate innovative methods for promoting social-emotional learning.